With gratitude.

12/10/2014

A NEW NAPA CUISINE

A NEW NAPA CUISINE

Christopher Kostow

PHOTOGRAPHS BY

Peden+Munk

TEN SPEED PRESS
BERKELEY

CONTENTS

A JOURNEY TO NAPA

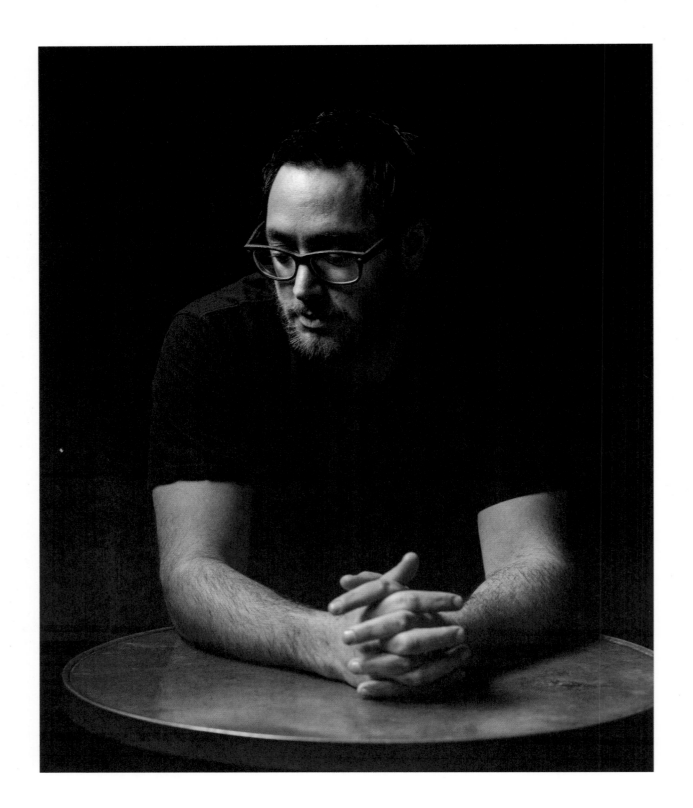

With consistency a great soul has simply nothing to do. He may as well concern himself with his shadow on the wall. Speak what you think now in hard words, and to-morrow speak what to-morrow thinks in hard words again, though it contradict every thing you said to-day. . . .

—RALPH WALDO EMERSON

The prospect of writing a book terrifies me. My DNA screams against the idea of creating something permanent. To take a snapshot of my work now, to record something that is physically temporary (food meant to be eaten) and philosophically incomplete (ideas not yet there) seems foreign to me. I have never for a moment believed that I have arrived. Perhaps the only thing that I hope for is to be better tomorrow than I am today. My approach to the processes of cooking has evolved over time and will continue to change. It's comforting to know that my mistakes, foibles, and all things not quite perfect are being hammered out by the passing of time and gaining of wisdom. Like a river rock whose sharp sides have been smoothed by water, my thoughts and ideas about food lose their jagged edges and grow ever more succinct. I am nothing if not relentless, and I'm not sure what I would do without the comfort of knowing that I have another year to perfect an idea or follow an inspiration. That's probably why I'll do this forever.

As time goes by, I meet more people who contribute to what we do at The Restaurant at Meadowood: purveyors who raise a tastier squab or age a better beef, artisans who collaborate on a new plate, growers who successfully raise forgotten heirloom vegetables. New cooks and sous chefs bring the knowledge of their experiences; fresh activities are explored (frogging!). I read more books and meditate a bit more on the place I am in. These efforts are not Sisyphean. We are not pushing the same rock up the same hill each year. I think (hope) that we are getting smarter and better. We need to, for as the hill becomes taller, our climb gets steeper.

I have long favored the idea of wizened chefs writing books and sharing recipes in the twilight of their careers. I imagine these tomes—the accumulated knowledge and perspective of that chef—filling the sagging shelves of a great library. When taken together, these retrospectives would make up the whole of culinary history. But that's not how it works. Food is fluid, and our ideas as chefs are like those rocks in the river. What I have come to realize in thinking about this book is that those rocks are beautiful well before they become smooth, and that the smoothness is less interesting when not seen against the jaggedness that preceded it. The journey has its own value. The river's story ought to be told as well.

So I'm writing this book not as prematurely released greatest hits but rather as a celebration of where I am now. I don't want to cement my place in one locale or style or perspective. I just want to explore where I have been and share where I am today. When I lived and worked in Provence early in my career, I came across an old edition of Ralph Waldo Emerson's writings. I carried that little, bright blue book with me for many years, memorizing the passages that I should have learned in college. If I disappoint anyone by departing from things that I have said or done in the past, I point to the quote that opens this introduction. While not a "great mind," I fear that if I create a consistent definition of who I am as a chef, I will cease to be able to absorb new thoughts and ideas. In saying "this is who I am," I don't want to unwittingly ensure that I can never be anything else.

BACKGROUND

I grew up in Highland Park, Illinois, a suburb about a half hour north of Chicago and a million miles from Napa Valley. Dining out was de rigueur at our house (my father had a penchant for ethnic holes-in-the-wall), and my youth was filled with Italian dishes eaten off red-checkered tablecloths and barely passable Mexican food. We would often journey to the hinterlands of Milwaukee, Wisconsin, for the city's German fare and the fair food served at the annual Summerfest. I'm not sure why my food memories are sharper than the circumstances during which they were experienced. Perhaps it's because those memories are simpler, don't require a filter, and can be seen unencumbered by the weight of hindsight or commentary.

When I was fourteen, I got a job at Ravinia, an annual summer music festival in Chicago. Outfitted with a green apron and matching visor, I worked as a cashier at one of several small restaurants circling the concert venue. I quickly noticed that the guys in the kitchen—who got to wear T-shirts and baseball caps—seemed to be having all the fun. The head guy, nicknamed Shaky the Clown, made the female employees search for the walk-in keys in his pocket. And there was Ozzie, who wore a plastic batting helmet instead of a toque. They were fun camp-counselor types, and at the time it seemed like the place for me. So I engineered a transfer to the kitchen and spent the next several summers elbow deep in seasoned flour and raw chicken. I relished the environment—the fast pace and loud music along with the order and control. Although I would not return to cooking for many years, my love of restaurants was born during those summers slaving over a deep fryer and a griddle.

While attending Hamilton College in upstate New York, I discovered a passion for philosophy, which I eventually chose as my concentration. As it turns out, I am a more successful raconteur than philosopher. In fact, I am better at most things than I am at philosophy. That includes, apparently, cooking. Studying philosophy did teach me to absorb a lot of information with a critical eye and then use that information in a singular and personal manner. Cooking is similar. I am confronted with different flavor memories and techniques—some created, most borrowed—and whether or not I am successful is driven by my ability to retain this information, distill it through my lens, and create (on my best days) something that is uniquely my own.

With cooking, as with philosophy, most of the credit is owed to those who came before. Chefs don't rise out of the ashes fully formed. Our entire métier is based on skill sets that were first developed and perfected by other people. I cannot simply stand on a corner and proclaim myself a chef (although television shows and marketers certainly try). I am a student of a craft that requires more time spent in pursuit of competence than is possible between commercial breaks. I knew early on that I would not excel at my craft solely through an intellectual understanding of it. I also needed to love the series of actions that make up restaurant cooking—the pace and pressure, the camaraderie and repetition. And then I had to take every opportunity given to me through grace, generosity, and a restaurant's needs to embrace the process and invest the time.

Every chef needs a first chance, and I got mine when I moved to California after college. At the time, I had a kernel of an idea that I wanted to be a chef, that there was a creative and entrepreneurial side to the profession that I would find appealing.

On arriving in the coastal town of La Jolla, I sent my first résumé to Trey Foshee, the new award-winning chef at a restaurant called George's at the Cove. In the months that followed, I sent several more résumés to Trey. I camped at the hostess stand. I called and called. And then finally, Trey called me back, and I found myself being led into my first professional kitchen. It was hot, small, and cramped, full of hulking cooks and cast-iron pans. To a philosophy student and dilettante, it looked like a blacksmith's foundry.

I was eager for knowledge, propelled by the uncertainty of having an expensive liberal arts education and no real career prospects. I was fanatical about learning as much as I could about cooking and sought out every avenue toward that end. I didn't have much money to buy cookbooks, so I bought one, *Chez Panisse Café Cookbook* by Alice Waters, photocopied the content, then exchanged the book for another and another and another. (Belated apologies to Warwick's bookstore in La Jolla.) I spent the rest of my free time at the public library reading the works of Jacques Pépin and Julia Child.

After a few months of plating desserts and shucking oysters (which still strikes me as an odd combination of tasks), I was given the chance to pick up the restaurant's produce from the legendary Chino Farms, about a half hour north of La Jolla in Rancho Santa Fe. I'm sure Trey assigned me this task so he would have an extra hour with his kids in the morning, but walking to the back of the farm stand to pick up that day's produce made me feel like I had been knighted.

I spent three years in Trey's kitchen, working my way through the various stations, before I headed to France for the first of two stints. In addition to spending time in Montpellier, Salon-de-Provence, and Paris, I worked under Christian Morisset at La Terrasse in Juan-les-Pins. Chef Morisset is one of the fiercest and most driven people I have ever encountered, ruling over his kitchen with a handlebar mustache and frightening intensity. Our daily schedule was more or less from nine o'clock in the morning to midnight, with a break of only a couple hours in between—a schedule that I still follow. I'll never forget one particular encounter at the tail end of the very long summer season. After a Saturday night service we began immediately working on dishes for Noël. Every hour we were kept in the kitchen was one less hour of sleep before the morning's reveille. Despite the late hour and the staff's exhaustion, Morisset began discussing new dishes and playing with different ideas. One of the *chefs de partie*, a seasoned Grenoblois named Chou-Chou, stood up and said tearfully, "I can't, Chef, I can't. You, Chef, are a warrior. *Vous êtes un guerrier.* I cannot be a warrior." Then he left. I remember realizing at that moment that chef Morisset had lost the thing that binds a kitchen together. Without people following you, you cannot lead. Morisset fumed and then dismissed us, and in that moment, I felt a chapter in French cooking closing. In years past, hoards of young *commis* lined the steps to Morisset's kitchen, waiting to be called in when another cook failed. But now, when Chou-Chou and the rest of us left, the stairs were empty and Morisset was alone in his kitchen. I think about this almost every day as I deal with my staff—people who love what they do are a far more powerful force than people who fear what happens if they don't do it well.

Belief is everything when it comes to being a chef. When you are shucking oysters and plating desserts, it is *unreasonable* to believe that you are going to be a chef one day. It is a long road that presents multiple opportunities to quit, settle, or do something else entirely. And although success in the form of financial recompense and notoriety is far more possible these days than it used to be, it nevertheless requires a steadfastness and resolve that borders on the delusional. I reached a point before traveling to France for the second time when I was ready to leave the kitchen behind. I was working in an environment that I loathed, and wasn't sure if I believed in the path enough to justify the expenditure of time and economic hardships any longer. I took some time away from the kitchen. But after a few months of contemplation, I realized that I was closer to my goal of being a chef than I was to the beginning of my now several-years-old journey. I also came to believe in those months of repose that I possessed the requisite drive and ability to become a decent chef. If given the right opportunity, I thought I could get there.

Being hired as a sous chef at Campton Place in San Francisco was that opportunity. I worked under Daniel Humm, then an unknown, young, Swiss-born chef mastering American sensibilities and (which we laugh about now) the English language. Daniel and I shared an almost old-world perspective on many things. He gave me the same creative freedom to make mistakes that I give my sous chefs today. I was offered a chance to be as much a chef as is possible in a great chef's kitchen, creating dishes, training young cooks, and sourcing ingredients. When Daniel left for New York, I moved on as well, to a small restaurant in Silicon Valley named Chez TJ, where I would become the chef.

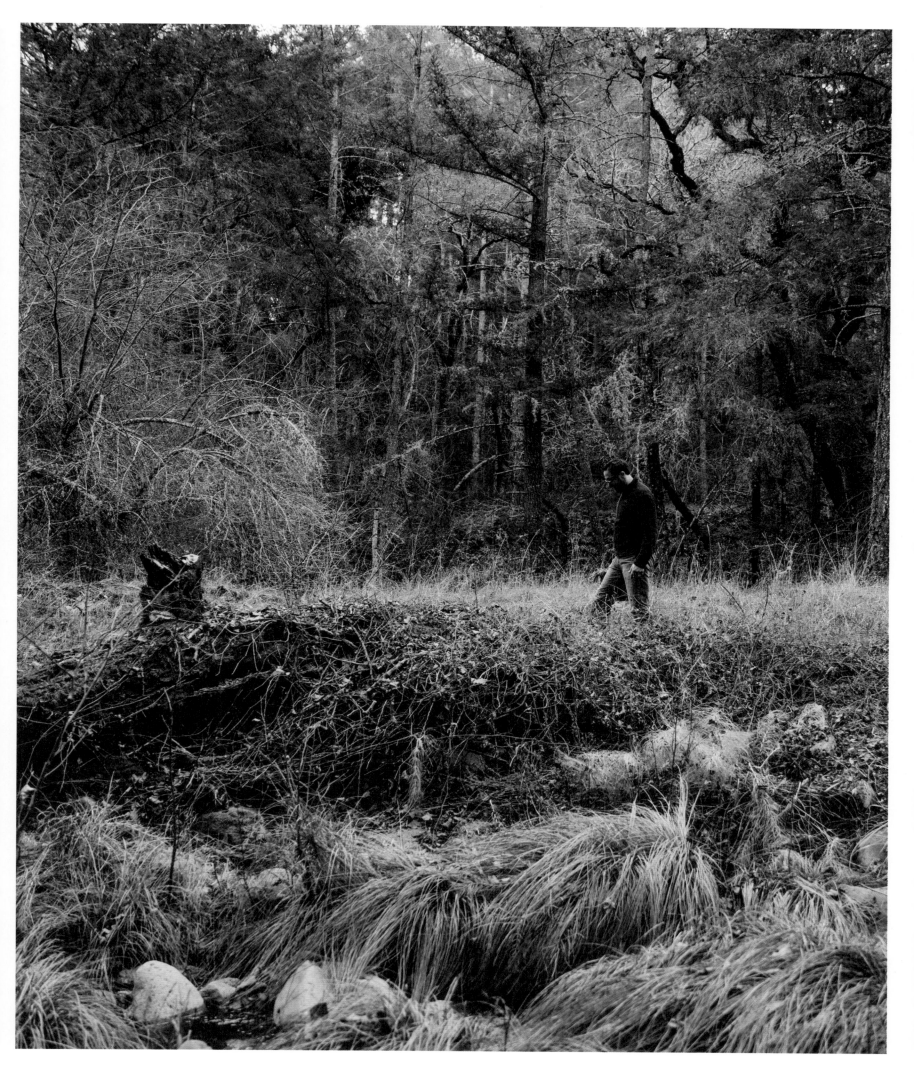

Every young chef deserves a Chez TJ experience. The restaurant, housed in a four-room Victorian, was situated far enough away from the limelight to allow me to make mistakes, yet close enough to people who care about food to win attention if deserved. It was open five days a week, had a simple menu, and provided me with a double-wide trailer behind the building to call home. I tended a small garden next door and dreamed of the masses of people who would drive from all over the Bay Area to see the work we were doing in Mountain View, California.

Although that didn't necessarily happen, I loved that little restaurant. With a ragtag kitchen, a terribly dated dining room, a tiny staff of misanthropes, and one great sous chef (who somehow managed to convince his wife that they needed to move to Mountain View), we did work that I am still proud of. We cultivated the garden, smoked meats in an old Weber out back, and stored things in my home freezer whenever the restaurant's old freezer broke down. I drove to all of the purveyors to handpick the product myself because, without an established reputation, I wanted to make sure we were getting the best. In my time there, I learned that if I didn't push for greatness, no one else would. That is what it means to be a chef: to drive in the direction at the speed that you deem correct while trying as best you can to keep everyone around you holding on.

My first year at Chez TJ coincided with the introduction of the Michelin restaurant guides in the San Francisco Bay Area. Amazingly, our tiny Victorian, with its sagging floors and fake Tiffany lamps, earned itself a shiny star. We were on the map, though I still had to explain to people where Mountain View was. The owner of the restaurant, George Aviet, was a wonderful supporter, and I am eternally grateful to him. He has helped launch the career of many a chef, all while fixing every leaky pipe and broken stove. Without George and that tiny restaurant, I would not be writing this book today.

In my second year at Chez TJ, I recall being convinced that we were going to lose that star, that the previous year was a fluke. Before the release of that year's guide, I went so far as to call David Kinch of the famed Manresa restaurant to seek his counsel. He told me not to worry, that he hadn't heard from them either (he was awarded two stars that first year). A couple days later, we were awarded our second Michelin star. And Kinch was the first to text me . . . to call me an asshole.

After a couple years at Chez TJ, I began looking for a larger stage in a more beautiful setting. During my time in Mountain View, I had become enamored with the idea of creating a destination restaurant, like Michel Bras in Laguiole, Maison Troisgros in Roanne, or, closest to mind, Thomas Keller's French Laundry in Yountville, California. I thought there was something beautiful in this idea of standing somewhere and drawing people to you through the quality of the work alone. I still love the antiquated *aubergiste* ideal of sweeping the steps of your own small-town restaurant while saying hello to fellow *commerçants* and guests alike. When I was offered the position of chef at The Restaurant at Meadowood in Napa Valley, I took it. I didn't realize at the time how fortunate an opportunity it would be.

Looking back, I still wonder what led me to pursue this profession. I guess I enjoyed, and still enjoy, the feel of a kitchen. These days, many kitchens are more akin to laboratories than pirate ships. There are poets everywhere and not a Shaky the Clown in sight. I love the sound of a knife on a cutting board and the aggressive music blasting through the sound system—just as I did when frying chicken and drinking Franzia during my summers at Ravinia. Call it arrested development, or a heightened degree of self-awareness, but then—as now—there is nothing on earth that I would rather do. Although I wasn't aware of it at the time, when I entered that first kitchen, I would never really leave.

THE BOOK

This book is about what has happened to me since coming to Napa Valley. It details the transformative process of putting down roots, and the incredible relationships and inspirations that resulted when I did. Whatever life holds for me in the future, the people here and this place have forever changed the way that I look at food and the world that surrounds it. I couldn't be more thankful.

The stories I describe take place both in and around Napa Valley. I have not spent much time thinking about county lines and political boundaries, so I hope no one begrudges me this liberty. Instead, the *place* of these tales encompasses the areas within a short distance of my home and kitchen. The farthest point to which it extends is the Pacific coast, an hour's drive from Saint Helena. Richard Carter's homestead (see page 105) lies on the slope leading into Pope Valley. Phillip Paine's squabs (see page 203) are raised in Carneros at the southern tip of the Napa Valley. We go frogging (see page 199) just past the Napa County line to the north, above the old trout farm near the peak of Mount Saint Helena. And Lynn Mahon's studio (see page 102) sits atop Mount Veeder, where it straddles the counties of Sonoma and Napa. Apologies to any geographic purists.

The recipes in these pages, which were culled and finalized by sous chef Poncho Vasquez, are presented as we write them for use at The Restaurant at Meadowood, which means that some require professional-level tools and at times cannot be made to yield a standard number of servings without additional waste. That said, all of these dishes can be prepared in a home kitchen provided you have the requisite equipment. Use these recipes as inspiration and starting points for your own ideas about food and cooking. Try not to fixate on the specific ratios (although we have provided both U.S. and metric measurements in each recipe), but do pay attention to the techniques and their results. We cook potatoes in beeswax (see page 235), but why not turnips or rutabagas or carrots? We cook sturgeon in coals (see page 249), but another type of fish or vegetable or meat would be great, too. I view these recipes as part of the larger narrative of the book, in much the same way that I view technique to be the syntax by which a sentence (or theme) is conveyed. I hope that you cook and eat these dishes, and are inspired in your own cooking as a result. More importantly, I hope that you see these words and dishes and recipes as detailing one larger thing that makes up the whole of my thinking and the work of my partners and friends.

These recipes are studies in the four main influences on the food served at The Restaurant and in the very specific and personal cuisine we are creating: the gardening operations (see The Growers, page 31), our artisan collaborators (see The Artisans,

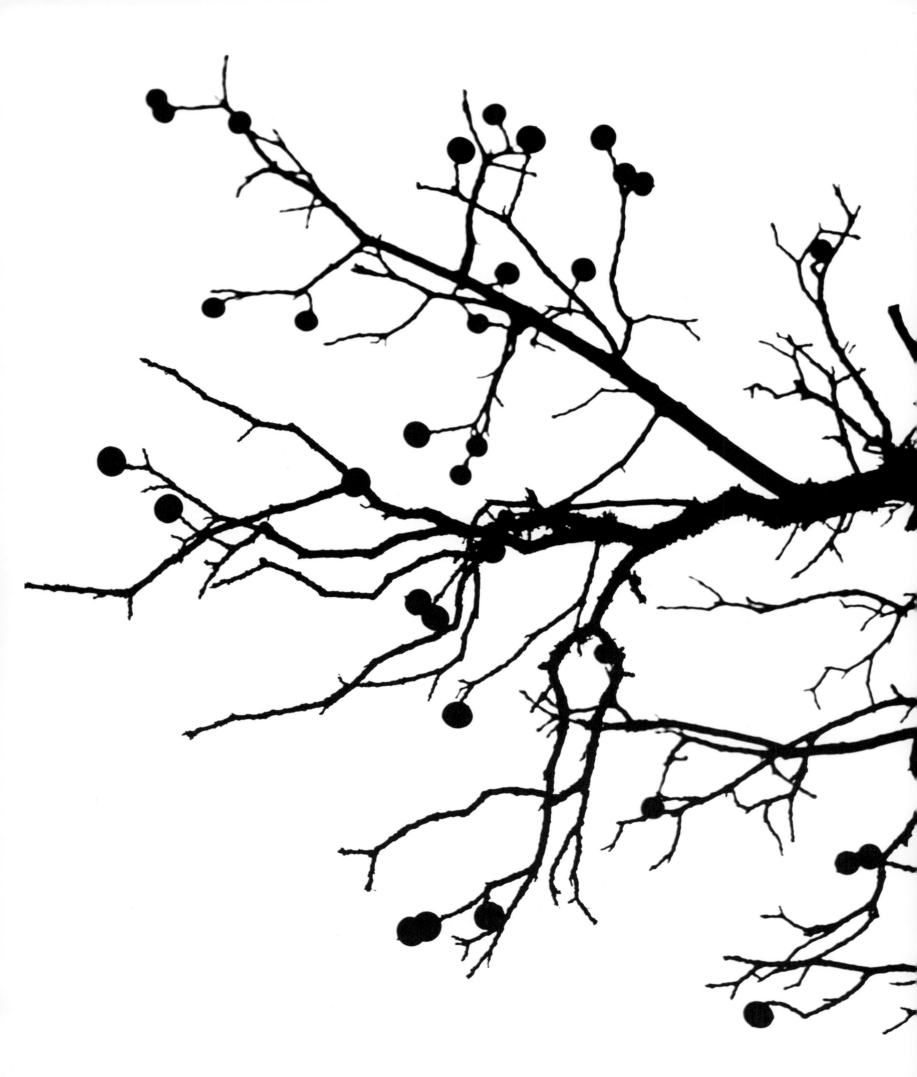

page 95), our foraging endeavors (see The Wilds, page 161), and the bounty of Napa Valley (see Materia Prima, page 217). Most of the dishes contain more than one of these elements, but for each recipe, I have chosen to focus on what was for me, and for the people with whom I collaborate, the jumping-off point for the dish.

I chose to write this book myself because I didn't want someone else to tell my story. I've always been jealous of writers. I imagine them retiring to quiet surroundings and clacking away the hours (on a typewriter, of course) in the throes of a meditation or a confession. The self-restraint, focus, acumen, and craftsmanship that define true writers amaze me. I am no such writer, but in the hours available to me, I have tried my best to record a sensible and organized account of my time and experiences. I woke up at the crack of dawn, made many pots of coffee, and labored over these words. If this is the only way I'll see my name on the spine of a book, I'll take it.

I hope that the writing adequately demonstrates that this story is not mine alone. I am merely holding the thread that binds together the wonderful people discussed here— connecting generations and trades, mediums and passions. I hope that my stewardship of their perspectives and work will continue.

IMAGES

I met Taylor Peden and Jen Munkvold in 2012 at a restaurant in downtown Los Angeles. I had flown there to woo them into photographing this book. I was fortunate that a number of amazing photographers had generously offered their services, but I only wanted to work with Peden + Munk. I love their photography. Their images have a heightened sense of reality, with an undercurrent of viscera and unblinking honesty. After viewing their textured images of pit masters and rustic farmland, I felt both engaged and informed. Their photographs reveal without telling and are dramatic without being melodramatic. I hoped that by turning their rustic lens on my very composed food, Taylor and Jen would help strip away any visual preciousness and artifice.

I explained to them as best I could who I was and what I wanted this book to be, describing the valley, the people, the collaborations. Thankfully, they bought it. When I began introducing Taylor and Jen to the people and places that would make up the soul of this work, we made a decision that ended up shaping the book's character.

In a historic homestead in Pope Valley, my friend the famed ceramist Richard Carter operates his wood-fired kilns, which are fueled by felled oak and charged with salt and soda. The removable shelves of these kilns, glazed with the accumulation of numerous firings, are full of texture and character. As we walked the kilns, Jen spotted a shelf and recommended using it as a backdrop for one of the food shots. We took the shelf with us and tried it out the next day. After seeing the arresting image of plated food on that ceramic slab, we decided that we should shoot all of the recipes at Richard's. Beyond the kiln shelves, the homestead is replete with textures and hues: old wood and aged glass, decaying barn doors, a collection of deer antlers. Like a band holing up in a specific studio to record an album, we hoped this magical place would impart its singular feel to the images we shot there.

Richard's place has a spirit that is beyond my words, a timelessness that inspires the art created there and that I try to reflect in my cooking. There's the long, curvy drive from the floor of the valley up and through the redwoods—a route that seems to transport the traveler to another world. As we walk the property with Richard, he tells tales of the generations of a family that once lived there. I cannot help but feel as though we are also somehow telling their story through our photographs: the glass and wood and bone of their lives, the ceramic shelves of Richard's life's work, my food, the photographers' images. We gathered there, in an old barn structure, shooting food and spanning a century, for a few hours at a time.

In many ways, this book mirrors the cooking process that drove it. It is a distillation of the challenges, triumphs, and discoveries that keep me running up the steps to the kitchen every day. I'm still trying to find my place among the ghosts of Richard's ranch and among the tales of Napa Valley. The daily struggle between my own limited knowledge and the limitless beauty that surrounds me continues to drive me forward.

I imagined that the making of this book would be a form of documentation, recording the work done to this point. I was thrilled to learn that, in fact, this process was an educational one, that clarified the way I think about my daily work. Adhering to the organizing principle of these four chapters has helped me better determine whether or not a new idea for a dish makes sense and is relevant to what we are trying to create. The themes of this book have become the tenets around which we are creating a specific Napa cuisine. I know that I am a better chef and that we are closer to that goal because of this book.

charlie

There are, and always have been, a multitude of stories that spring from the small valley of Napa. This one is mine.

I used to say that I would cook anywhere if the opportunity was right. The work itself was of the greatest consequence; the life that surrounded it, I thought, was secondary. And so I followed the work—from a tiny abbey in Provence to a double-wide trailer in Silicon Valley—while attempting to find my identity and forge a career in cooking. What I didn't realize at the time is that without the *where*, the work has less meaning. Moving to Napa Valley taught me that where I live is not just a place to sleep between shifts in the kitchen. It can also be a prism through which my work can be seen. But I'm getting ahead of myself.

I knew little of Napa Valley before I moved here at age thirty-one. Although I had lived in the Bay Area for several years, I had done only a small amount of wine tasting and had catered a couple wine-country dinners. I had never been on the wine train. Like most everyone in this part of the state, I was vaguely familiar with the legendary families in Napa—Mondavi and Heitz and Davies—wine personalities that hung over the place like oil paintings of the founding fathers. I had heard about the chefs who turned backwater hamlets into dining destinations, and I dreamed vaguely of building something special myself. So when I saw a job opening at The Restaurant at Meadowood—a bigger stage in a hidden corner of the valley—I believed with the arrogance of a young chef that it would provide me with the opportunities my food deserved. I came to Napa Valley believing that I was looking for a place to grow. But what I found over time were the roots necessary to do so.

People think the valley is one thing, and it *is* that thing. At a certain point, people came here to grow grapes and make wines of a certain style. Big wineries were built, many beautiful, some not. Napa became a temple for devotees of leisure. People come here seeking a lifestyle, a *façon de vivre* that is celebrated in furniture catalogs and on supermarket labels. In the summer months, cars line Highway 29 as visitors clamor for the chance to swirl Cabernet and breathe in the fragrance of old stone walls. It seems silly to pretend that Napa is not, in some part, what people assume it to be. However, what I came to find by living here is that Napa is also something else entirely. Beyond the vineyards, past the artifice, through the meandering creeks and overhanging oaks, and up the mountain roads exists another place entirely—a place at once wild, complex, and beautiful.

My discovery of this other Napa began with a dog named Charlie, a spastic mix of shepherd and ridgeback (and dingo?) that I had adopted with my then girlfriend (and now wife), Martina. At the time we lived in a rental house in Saint Helena that backed up to an estuary, which ended at the Napa River about a half mile on. Charlie would zip into that field, his head popping up now and then as he made his way through the chest-high, muddy grasses like a crazed jackrabbit. I'd call his name, and he'd stop as if to tell me that he'd heard and then continue on his way. Morning after morning, I'd find myself alone in that field with leash in hand as Charlie bounded toward the river.

On those wet, hazy mornings, away from the kitchen and the distractions of life, I began to notice my surroundings. The ground was covered in miner's lettuce and chickweed! Those tiny flowers were wild radish! The creek where I would eventually find Charlie was full of watercress and wild rhubarb! And it had an untouched, primordial look dramatically different from the quadrants of planted land visible elsewhere in the valley. Day after day, the land began to reveal itself to me. It was Willy Wonka–like in its plenitude: wild plums hung heavy on the trees and purple amaranth grew wild in all directions. The trees that we passed under were walnut, the remnants of a long-forgotten orchard. The trail was bordered by wild blackberry bushes. The wood peeking up from the grasses was an old barn structure, an artifact from another time. On those morning walks, Charlie and I were discoverers of a lost world, both ancient and new.

As the fog clung stubbornly to the Mayacamas Mountains, I was struck as never before by the beauty of the place. Maybe walking in the country, with mud clinging to my boots and a dog at my side, made me more contemplative. Or maybe I was noticing how the global influencers of food were beginning to embrace the importance of locality far more than in the past. Or maybe, with my future wife at home and buoyed by the confidence that success can bring, I was truly happy and prepared to look down as opposed to just looking forward. Whatever the reason, those mornings with Charlie initiated a new way of thinking about my work and my life.

Napa has long been the provenance of chefs. Big names abound, and I'm sure all have been inspired by this place in some fashion. But I wondered if it would be possible to harness the physical, emotional, and historical power of this place in a new and persuasive way to create a cuisine that is *rooted* here rather than just *happening* here. Could I not endeavor to understand this place, its past and its present, and in doing so help write its future? There were no immediate changes to the work we were doing at The Restaurant. Things evolved slowly, and continue to do so. To be sure, we made directional changes in those early days. Connecting to a sense of place is one way of describing it now, though I'm not sure that I had those words then. All I knew at the time was that I had found a vein of authenticity and history and gravitas and beauty, and I needed to tap it.

We began to use a less rigid approach to presenting our food, which felt disconnected from the fine white china we were using, so I sought out local artists and artisans to design new plates and serving pieces. In keeping with the agricultural legacy of the valley, we expanded our gardening operations. I found a craftswoman who pressed local olives into oils that surpassed the elegance of any I had ever tasted. We began to harness wild edibles like those I found on my walks with Charlie. Everywhere we looked were elements that could contribute to a beautiful local cuisine, and we pursued those elements with the fervor and single-mindedness that only true believers possess.

At every turn, I met people whose skills and vibrancy were remarkable in the eyes of this child of a Midwestern suburb. The gardeners and plate makers, foragers and olive oil producers—while their skills were foreign to me, they were similarly drawn to the valley because of the wealth and tourists and lifestyle. I found a community: young, dynamic, and bright. I came to realize that these talented people were not in this place alone, disconnected. Rather, they are the collective spirit of Old Man Niebaum, of the Chinese laborers whose hands dug the tunnels that still lie beneath Meadowood, and of the people who flocked here during the first chapters of our nation, their dreams far outweighing their means. We are the spirit of a place that is far greater than the sum of its parts—and far more than the wealth and the wine. With all of these great people helping, I began to consider that perhaps I might one day fashion my own story in this valley of big people and large tales.

Years onward, Charlie is grown, Martina and I are married, and our daughter, Daisy, is beginning her own explorations. We own a home near that early rental, and sometimes Charlie and I walk the train tracks to the old property so Charlie can relive his youth. This is now home. We are embedded in this community and enjoy nothing more than walking down Main Street in Saint Helena as a family, greeting our neighbors along the way. I have come to helm a restaurant that is known well beyond the valley's borders, and in so doing have been blessed to work with many talented people who have helped me grow into the person I am today.

I believe that somewhere in the field, looking for that dog, I found a place that my cooking could give voice to, a thread that connected me to the people of its past and present and to the land and its history. In those moments, I became a chef.

THE GROWERS

Farming [is] that vocation which conduces most directly and palpably to a reverence for Honesty and Truth.

—HORACE GREELEY

My wife doesn't know this, but I snuck out on the day of our wedding to water the garden. I escaped my future in-laws and the visitors who had gathered at our house and stood alone in the field trying not to get dirt on my suit pants as I watered the first plantings of what would become The Restaurant's Montessori Project. Although now, in its grand scope, the Montessori garden represents the successful culmination of a long-sought agricultural effort, its beginnings were much more humble.

EFFORTS

When I first started working at The Restaurant, we had a small and underutilized garden at the Napa Valley Reserve, a sister property to Meadowood. The reserve is a genteel social and wine making club and counts among its members many Hollywood and Silicon Valley elites. Like most of Napa, the land on which the reserve sits is rich in agricultural history. For over a century, it was the homestead and farm of the Kelperis family, who grew grapes and prunes and raised livestock. In those early days, my sous chef and I would "borrow" golf carts from Meadowood and speed down the hill to pick over the remains of the previous year's plantings—a carrot here, a cilantro flower there. One of the first efforts I encouraged at The Restaurant was to overhaul that garden.

I would stop by every day and walk the rows, touching the leaves and rubbing the dirt in my hands. The garden was inspiring in its foreignness. I knew a little about growing vegetables, having planted a small garden at Chez TJ, but this process—seed to plant to fruit—was magic. The cow horns we buried in the corner of the garden in keeping with the tenets of biodynamic farming reinforced the point.

As we remade this garden along with The Restaurant, I met people who possessed incredible amounts of knowledge on topics I knew little about: the gardener cum artist cum balloonist who led the way in the early years, and the vineyard manager cum beer maker cum beekeeper who oversaw it all. Over the years, and with much help, we were able to transform that garden into a source of immense productivity and beauty.

Today, the garden is still flourishing, bordered by a creek that meanders through a vineyard and past a long line of stone fruit trees just beyond the entrance to the property. The rows are impossibly manicured and are shaded in spots by the overhang of figs, apples, and pears. You enter under a trellis covered by pea flowers in spring and by a verdant web of Cascade hops in autumn. At various points of the day, the sun, which filters through the fruit tree branches, seems to glide in over the vineyard and gently touch the inner circle of the diminutive garden.

ROOTS

In 2011, I had the good fortune to forge a partnership with the Saint Helena Montessori School, a relationship that has given me far more than just a quiet place of repose on my wedding day. The school had previously been located in town and was beginning construction of a ten-acre farm campus on the Silverado Trail opposite Meadowood. Because agriculture is a central part of the school's curriculum, school heads Elena Heil and Alex Heil wanted to provide the students with a professional example of the lessons they were learning in the classroom. So they offered us some acreage of the former vineyard to use as a restaurant garden.

Working with then-gardener Gretchen Kimball, my cooks and I trenched the earliest rows and created a rudimentary infrastructure: a hose, an extension cord to bring power from the nearby barn, and a stolen banquet table on which to work. As we tilled the dirt, there was a palpable sense of giddiness: our pastry chef struggled to plant in a straight line, and my mother-in-law, who is an avid gardener, lent a hand.

Years onward, my cooks spend their days off working among the rows, seeding trays of microgreens and helping the gardeners harvest and plant. They come into the kitchen, sunburned and happy, to drop off that day's produce. Every few months, the kids, aided by my cooks, prepare lunch for the Montessori parents and community members at The Restaurant.

I have never wanted to create one of those restaurants to which young cooks flock for a short time and then quickly move on, their résumés burnished. Instead, I want to build a culture that is lasting, a family of people whose work and lives intertwine with that of a place and a community. Some restaurants tend to be skilled at teaching technique but totally inept at creating the context that gives the techniques and tasks real value: an understanding of the ideals of service, community, and hospitality. Perhaps I am overly optimistic to believe that the young cooks who walk through our kitchen doors will understand the principles that we try to espouse, but we'll continue to try. I don't want to own it all. I just want to be one of many creators. This is how we'll achieve the level of dynamism necessary to create something lasting.

To watch our cooks, veterans of the finest restaurants of the world, work with the kids is a revelation. Like growing vegetables, teaching children requires the rarest of kitchen commodities: patience. We actually learn more about the depths of our knowledge by attempting to distill it into simple lessons for the students. The kids teach us humility. They don't care how many stars we have.

These relationships and this work act as buffers between us and the machinations of a restaurant industry that is enjoying its moment in the sun. It is easy in the modern food world to get caught up in the awards, lists, trends, and personalities. We have created this theater of the absurd where every idea that is posted online on Monday shows up on other chefs' menus by Friday. The insecurity, frenetic competition, and mind-blowing hubris that infects our business is put into proper perspective while you're harvesting a vegetable or teaching young kids how to cook it. This process of growing food is without limit or end: it embodies what we are trying to be and offers us a chance to be a different kind of restaurant and better people.

The Montessori garden land is not my own. In legal terms, I am simply a tenant of the school. But I am out there most mornings, having moved Charlie's stomping ground to the adjacent field, where he can chase cranes and rabbits. I will always remember the first time I took my daughter, Daisy, to the garden, carrying her through the elevated beds, bending down so she could see the flowering vegetables of her first winter. I love that piece of dirt. I appreciate that it was transformed from a dormant vineyard into a successful social experiment. And I'm proud that on any given Sunday there are kids and dogs and gardeners and random community members who stumble on that patch of land and allow me to give them an enthusiastic tour of our efforts.

The garden is a living thing; it grows and changes over time under the same Napa sky. One constant is the presence of our head gardener, Christine Kim. Christine, who came aboard one year into the life of the Montessori garden, is the heart and soul and muscle of our agricultural endeavors. She helped us turn this into a place where ideas can take shape. She's an artist and a taskmaster, enlisting the cooks to smash cucumber beetles for pest management, employing sous chef Poncho to oversee snail farming, and forcing Zach the baker to cobble together a shade structure.

We began our gardening efforts thinking that our creativity would drive the workings of the garden; that we would say, "I want to do a carrot dish, so let's plant some carrots." This has proven to be only partially true. A garden is part of nature, and nature is imperfect. Despite our spreadsheets and best-laid plans, the garden doesn't always give us what we were expecting. Sometimes it provides more than we thought we needed. And other times (read "often"), Christine plants things on the sly and brings them to us without warning. In all cases, the garden informs us more than we inform the garden.

Although I'm by no means a farmer myself, and our agricultural efforts are limited to growing produce for a high-end kitchen, working with our growers helps me bind together the various elements that influence my cooking. When I develop a dish based on an old food memory, the fact that we have harvested the vegetables ourselves gives what could otherwise be a conceptual or overly precious dish a sense of gravitas.

Similarly, a very cerebral or esoteric dish meant to interpret the nature around us is made complete when we plant the seeds for the food ourselves.

At times I've struggled to reconcile my desire to showcase the natural surroundings of Napa with a lifetime of food experiences. How do I combine the call of a bubbling wine country stream with my memories of a Chinese diner in suburban Chicago without being derivative? How can I bind together the whole of my cooking life to create something that is my own? Before he found his calling cooking his ancestral Italian food, a chef friend of mine used to say that he was "cooking with one foot off the ground." I would be cooking with one foot off the ground if I ignored those eating experiences that have formed how I think about food. I'm a product of the American Midwest, and my food memories are based on the ethnic foods—Thai, Chinese, Mexican, German— found there. They also draw on simple meals like a just-caught river fish cooked in a campfire skillet and served with white bread and lemon. Such experiences are incredibly powerful tools. I have to cook from what I know. As a result, food memories are my greatest single source of inspiration when creating a new dish, and more often than not, they serve as my starting point. But how do I reflect my own experiences without the end result being merely an interpretation or reevaluation of something I've eaten the past?

Trends will always sweep through the food world. The best of them can lay waste to those elements of cooking whose time has passed. The worst of them, and the blind adoption of any of them, creates homogeneity in food that is only aggravated by the rise of online photo sharing and food blogs—where all food begins to look alike. I am always open to new ideas. The struggle is to stay connected to the part of me that someone else cannot emulate by looking at an amateur photo posted online. The key to creating a unique style is to find a kernel of something that is wholly mine, that can become my legacy if allowed to flourish and mature. I am an American chef. I am a product of this country's suburbs and of all the experiences that have followed. Working with our growers has enabled me to reflect my own identity in the cooking we do at the restaurant and to immunize myself a bit to the popular trends and ideas of others. Without necessarily looking to Scandinavia or Spain or France or Peru, and without having to disregard my personal experiences, I endeavor to cook food that is mine.

Even the best restaurants are transient places. Staff come and go, some carrying with them the seed of an idea begun here. People who work with us arrive here from all over, having moved to the valley to cook like I did. They are often far from home and live like visitors in this place. We were all outsiders in the valley—my sous chefs, cooks, Christine, and myself. But there is something about our collaboration with the Montessori school that makes us feel less so. That piece of dirt, which others cultivated before us and which others will likely tend after us, creates a continuum that brings permanence to our efforts. By working with the community and within the community, we are becoming part of it. By opening our doors and offering our labor, The Restaurant has become more than simply a place where food is served. All by planting seeds.

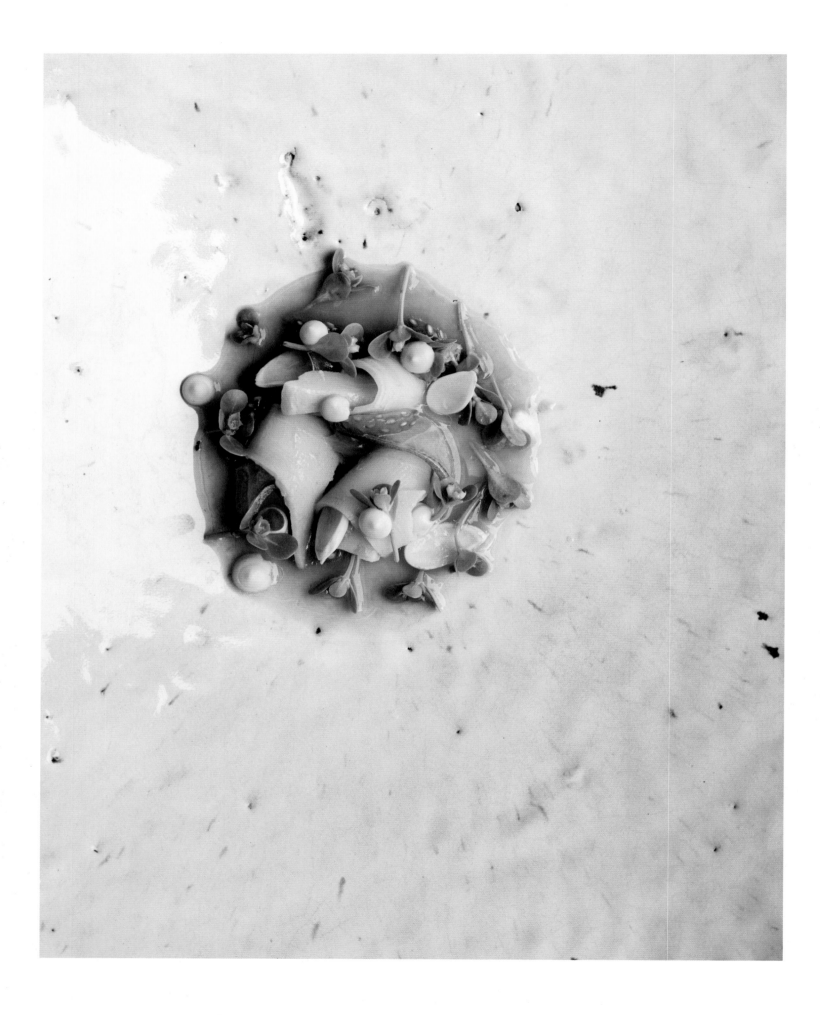

artichoke aji green tomato

A snapshot of a moment in the garden: raw fish lightly cured in the acidic juice of tomatoes not yet ripe. Almonds, also green and early, and artichokes arrive right on time to complete the picture.

SERVES 4

CURED SHIMA AJI

140 grams | 5 ounces shima aji fillet
    (striped jack)
1.5 kilograms | about 12 green tomatoes,
    quartered
20 grams | $^1/_3$ cup flat-leaf parsley leaves
40 grams | 1.3 ounces green garlic
120 grams | $^1/_3$ cup sel gris
60 grams | 2 cups New Zealand spinach

BRAISED ARTICHOKES

20 grams | 1 $^1/_2$ tablespoons ascorbic acid
4.5 kilograms | about 5 quarts water
4 | large artichokes
40 grams | $^1/_3$ cup diced carrot
40 grams | $^1/_3$ cup diced celery
60 grams | $^1/_3$ cup diced yellow onion
20 grams | 1 $^1/_2$ tablespoons extra virgin
    olive oil
kosher salt
750 grams | 3 cups dry white wine
500 grams | 2 cups freshly squeezed
    lemon juice

HUMMUS

100 grams | $^2/_3$ cup blanched almonds
480 grams | 2 cups water
300 grams | 10.5 ounces reserved braised
    artichoke trim (recipe above)
80 grams | $^1/_3$ cup Twin Sisters olive oil
6 grams | 1 teaspoon kosher salt
freshly squeezed lemon juice

FOR THE CURED SHIMA AJI:

To remove the skin of the shima aji, trace the perimeter of the fillet with the tip of a boning knife. Insert the knife in one corner of the fillet, just under the skin, and gently peel the skin away. It is important to keep the silver skin just under the outer skin intact. Discard the outer skin and place the fillet in a metal tray on ice in the refrigerator.

In a blender, combine the tomatoes, parsley, green garlic, sel gris, and spinach and mix on high speed until smooth, about 30 seconds. Pour the marinade into a vacuum seal bag and add the fillets to the bag. Seal with full pressure, return the bag to the metal tray on ice in the refrigerator, and marinate for 5 hours.

Remove the fillet from the bag and discard the marinade. Thinly slice the fillet against the grain into at least 12 slices. To maintain color and freshness, store the slices between parchment paper on the metal tray on ice in the refrigerator until needed.

FOR THE BRAISED ARTICHOKES:

In a large bowl, dissolve the ascorbic acid in 3.8 kilograms (4 quarts) of the water. Working with 1 artichoke at a time, use a paring knife to remove and discard the leaves by cutting straight across the outer ridge of the artichoke, exposing the thistles underneath. Remove the thistles with a spoon and, using a vegetable peeler, peel the green skin from the stem. Submerge the artichokes in the acidulated water to ensure they don't oxidize.

In a small rondeau, combine the carrot, celery, onion, and oil over low heat and sweat for about 5 minutes, or until translucent. As the vegetables cook, season them with kosher salt. Do not let the vegetables caramelize. Add the wine and increase the heat to high. Bring to a boil and cook for 3 minutes. Drain the artichokes and add them along with the lemon juice and the remaining 900 grams (4 cups) of water to the rondeau. When the liquid reaches a simmer, reduce the heat to low and cook the artichokes for about 40 minutes, until tender, checking them periodically with the tip of a knife for tenderness. Remove from the heat and let the artichokes cool, submerged in the cooking liquid, in the refrigerator.

Slice two of the artichokes lengthwise into 12 ribbons about $^1/_{16}$ inch (2 millimeters) thick. Cut the remaining two artichokes lengthwise into wedges $^1/_4$ inch (6 millimeters) wide. Weigh the leftover artichoke trim and reserve 300 grams (10.5 ounces) for the hummus recipe. Divide the cooking liquid into three batches and hold the artichoke slices, dice, and trim each in its own batch to avoid oxidation.

FOR THE HUMMUS:

Combine the almonds and water in a pressure cooker and cook on high pressure for 30 minutes. Drain the almonds and transfer them to a blender. Drain the artichoke trim and add to the blender along with the oil. Mix on high speed for 3 minutes, until a smooth puree forms. Season with kosher salt and with lemon juice to taste, then strain through a chinois. Transfer to a squeeze bottle and reserve in the refrigerator.

continued

artichoke aji green tomato *continued*

FOR THE GREEN TOMATO VINAIGRETTE:

Strain the green tomato juice through a very fine cloth filter and season with the oil and Maldon salt. Cover and store in the refrigerator.

FOR THE GREEN TOMATOES AND GREEN ALMONDS:

Following the natural sections between the seeds, cut the tomatoes into segments. Remove the outer flesh and reserve the seed portions. Combine the milk and ascorbic acid in a container. Slice each green almond in half lengthwise and submerge the almonds in the acidulated milk.

TO SERVE:

In a small bowl, season the tomato seed segments and artichoke wedges with oil and Maldon salt. Spoon the salad into 4 narrow bowls. Shape the artichoke slices and shima aji slices into loose curls, and arrange 3 pieces of each in each bowl. Place the halved green almonds on top. Finish with a few dots of the hummus and 10 purslane leaves, then spoon some vinaigrette into each bowl.

GREEN TOMATO VINAIGRETTE

400 grams | 1 $^2/_3$ cups green tomato juice
50 grams | 3 $^1/_2$ tablespoons Twin Sisters olive oil
Maldon sea salt

GREEN TOMATOES AND GREEN ALMONDS

4 | green tomatoes
16 | green almonds, shelled
300 grams | 1 $^1/_4$ cups whole milk
2 grams | $^1/_2$ teaspoon ascorbic acid

Twin Sisters olive oil
Maldon sea salt
40 | garden purslane leaves

charred bavette onions

This is a play on my grandmother's brisket. She would cover the brisket with Lipton onion soup mix, onions, and mustard, and then braise it in water for about three hours too long. Her method has been updated here, with the brisket traded for bavette and the soup mix replaced with a dusting of a "char" made from dried mushrooms, onion, and sugar. The variety of onions from the garden is impressive enough to brag about: ramps cultivated on the hill above The Restaurant, tiny pearl onions, and creamed onion thickened with kuzu root starch.

SERVES 4

BAVETTE PREPARATION

510 grams | 18 ounces bavette (skirt steak)

3 grams | 1 ¹/₂ teaspoons transglutaminase

40 grams | 1.5 ounces Périgord truffles

kosher salt

100 grams | ¹/₂ cup rendered beef fat
    (page 286), plus more for finishing

300 grams | 1 ¹/₄ cups veal jus
    (page 289), warmed

charred onion crust (recipe below)

24 grams | 2 tablespoons Twin Sisters
    olive oil

Maldon sea salt

ONION JAM

400 grams | 2 ²/₃ cups sliced yellow onions

200 grams | ³/₄ cup heavy cream

800 grams | 3 ¹/₄ cups whole milk

44 grams | ¹/₃ cup kuzu root starch

kosher salt

ONION CONFIT

100 grams | ¹/₂ cup rendered beef fat
    (page 286)

100 grams | ¹/₂ cup unsalted butter

4 | pearl onions

kosher salt

4 | spring onions, white part only (2 inches/
    5 centimeters long, from root end)

4 | tiny ramps with roots intact

FOR THE BAVETTE:

Trim the bavette of any fat and sinew and place between 2 sheets of plastic wrap. Using a butchery mallet, flatten the bavette to a uniform ¹/₂ inch (12 millimeters) thick. Fill a small strainer with half of the transglutaminese. Tap the side of the strainer with a spoon to dust the transglutaminese thinly and evenly over the bavette. Using a fine-tooth grater, grate the truffles evenly over the bavette. Then dust the bavette with the remaining transglutaminese. Cut the bavette in half with the grain. Lay one half of the bavette, prepared side down, on top of its corresponding half so they match up perfectly. Wrap the stacked halves tightly in plastic wrap, place in a shallow dish, and top with a 4.5-kilogram (10-pound) weight. Refrigerate for 6 hours.

Unwrap the bavette and cut into four (80-gram/2.8-ounce) rectangles each about 1 by 4 inches (2.5 by 10 centimeters). Season the rectangles with kosher salt, and put each portion into a vacuum bag. Add 25 grams (2 tablespoons) of beef fat to each bag and seal each bag on high. Cook the beef in a hot-water bath set at 138°F (59°C) for 1 ¹/₂ hours. Remove the bags from the bath and immerse them in a large bowl of room-temperature water. After 15 minutes, add ice cubes to the bowl and let cool for 2 hours. Store in the refrigerator.

FOR THE ONION JAM:

Combine the onions, cream, and 300 grams (1 ¹/₄ cups) of the milk in a rondeau. Cover the surface with a piece of parchment paper and heat slowly to a low simmer. Cook for 35 minutes, until the liquid has reduced by half. Transfer the contents of the pan to a blender and mix on high speed for 4 minutes, until a smooth puree (soubise) forms. Strain the puree through a chinois into a heatproof bowl.

Have ready an ice bath. Combine the remaining 500 grams (2 cups) of milk and the kuzu root starch in a saucepan and bring to a boil over high heat while whisking continuously. When the milk has thickened, cook for an additional 30 seconds, then strain through the chinois into the bowl holding the onion puree. Fold the two mixtures together and season with kosher salt. Nest the bowl in the ice bath and let the jam cool completely. Transfer the jam to an airtight container and refrigerate until serving.

FOR THE ONION CONFIT:

Combine the beef fat and butter in a small saucepan and melt over low heat to combine. Lightly coat the pearl onions with the melted fat and season with kosher salt. Transfer the pearl onions to a vacuum bag and seal on high. Repeat with the spring onions, then reserve any remaining fat for serving. Cook the pearl and spring onions in a steam oven set at 200°F (95°C); the spring onions are ready in 15 minutes and the pearl onions are ready in 20 minutes. Remove from the oven and let cool to room temperature, then remove from the bags and pat dry with paper towels. Store the onions in an airtight container in the refrigerator until serving.

continued

FOR THE CHARRED ONION CRUST:

Put the dried onions and morels in a blender and mix on high speed for 2 minutes, until a fine powder forms. Add the panko, sugar, and Maldon salt and mix on high speed for 2 minutes longer. Transfer the powder to a bowl, add the flour and vegetable ash, and stir to mix. Reserve in a cool, dry area.

FOR THE GLAZED SALSIFY:

In a large bowl or other container, dissolve the ascorbic acid in the water. Peel each salsify evenly on all sides to create a perfect cylinder, then immerse in the acidulated water to prevent oxidation. When all of the salsifies are peeled, drain, pat dry on paper towels, and season lightly with oil and kosher salt. Arrange the salsify cylinders neatly in a vacuum bag and seal on high. Cook in a steam oven set at 200°F (95°C) for 20 minutes. Remove the bag from the oven and cool in an ice bath for 5 minutes. Remove the cylinders from the bag and cut crosswise into pieces 1 inch (2.5 centimeters) long.

Put a little water (about 30 grams/2 tablespoons) in a small sauté pan over medium heat. When the water begins to boil, whisk in a little of the butter alternately with a little of the beef fat until all of the butter and beef fat are in the pan. As soon as the mixture begins to emulsify, turn down the heat and continue to whisk until emulsified. Add the salsify pieces and heat slowly. When the salsify is well coated with the fat, season with kosher salt. Remove from the pan and keep warm until needed.

FOR THE BEEF JUS:

Place a sauté pan over low heat. Add the extra virgin olive oil and then the shallots and stir continuously so the shallots do not caramelize. When the shallots are translucent, add the Madeira and reduce until the pan is dry.

Meanwhile, heat the beef jus in a small saucepan over low heat. When the shallots are ready, add them to the jus along with the truffles, Twin Sisters oil, and vinegar. Taste and season with Maldon salt, if needed; keep warm until ready to serve.

TO SERVE:

To finish the bavette preparation, reheat the bags holding the bavette portions in a hot-water bath set at 138°F (59°C) for 15 minutes. Remove from the bags and pat dry on paper towels. Season each portion lightly on all sides with kosher salt one more time. Using a pastry brush, lightly coat each portion on all sides with the veal jus, then dredge in the charred onion crust and tap off any excess.

Spray a sheet of parchment paper with nonstick cooking spray and place near the stove top. Heat a cast-iron skillet over high heat and add 20 grams (1 1/2 tablespoons) of beef fat. When the fat is hot, add the bavette portions and lightly crisp on all sides (about 15 seconds per side). Use a slotted flat spatula to turn the bavette portions, being careful to maintain an even layer of crust. When the bavette portions are ready, transfer them to the prepared parchment to rest in a warm place for at least 4 minutes and no more than 8 minutes.

To reheat the onions, place the reserved beef fat in a sauté pan and melt over medium heat. Add the pearl and spring onions and warm through, being careful to not caramelize the onions. Add the ramps during the last second or two just to wilt slightly. Season with kosher salt.

After resting, cut a very thin slice against the grain off of one side of each meat portion to show the interior. Brush the cut side of each meat portion with olive oil and season with Maldon salt. Place the beef in the center of a plate and garnish with the onion jam; the confit of spring onions, pearl onions, and ramps; and the salsify. Finish the plate with the beef jus, truffle slices, and watercress.

CHARRED ONION CRUST

85 grams | 1 cup dried onions
32.5 grams | 1 cup dried morels
50 grams | 1/2 cup panko bread crumbs
85 grams | 1/3 cup raw cane sugar
12.5 grams | 2 teaspoons Maldon sea salt
100 grams | 3/4 cup instant flour
12.5 grams | 2 teaspoons vegetable ash
  (page 289)

GLAZED SALSIFY

8.5 grams | 2 teaspoons ascorbic acid
1.8 kilograms | 2 quarts water
120 grams | 4.2 ounces salsify
extra virgin olive oil
kosher salt
25 grams | 2 tablespoons unsalted butter,
  cut into cubes
25 grams | 2 tablespoons rendered
  beef fat (page 286)

BEEF JUS

12 grams | 1 tablespoon extra virgin olive oil
35 grams | 1/4 cup shallots, in brunoise
30 grams | 2 tablespoons Madeira
60 grams | 1/4 cup veal jus (page 289)
15 grams | 1 tablespoon Périgord truffles,
  in brunoise
10 grams | 2 teaspoons Twin Sisters olive oil
5 grams | 1 teaspoon sherry vinegar
Maldon sea salt

Périgord truffles, sliced
wild watercress

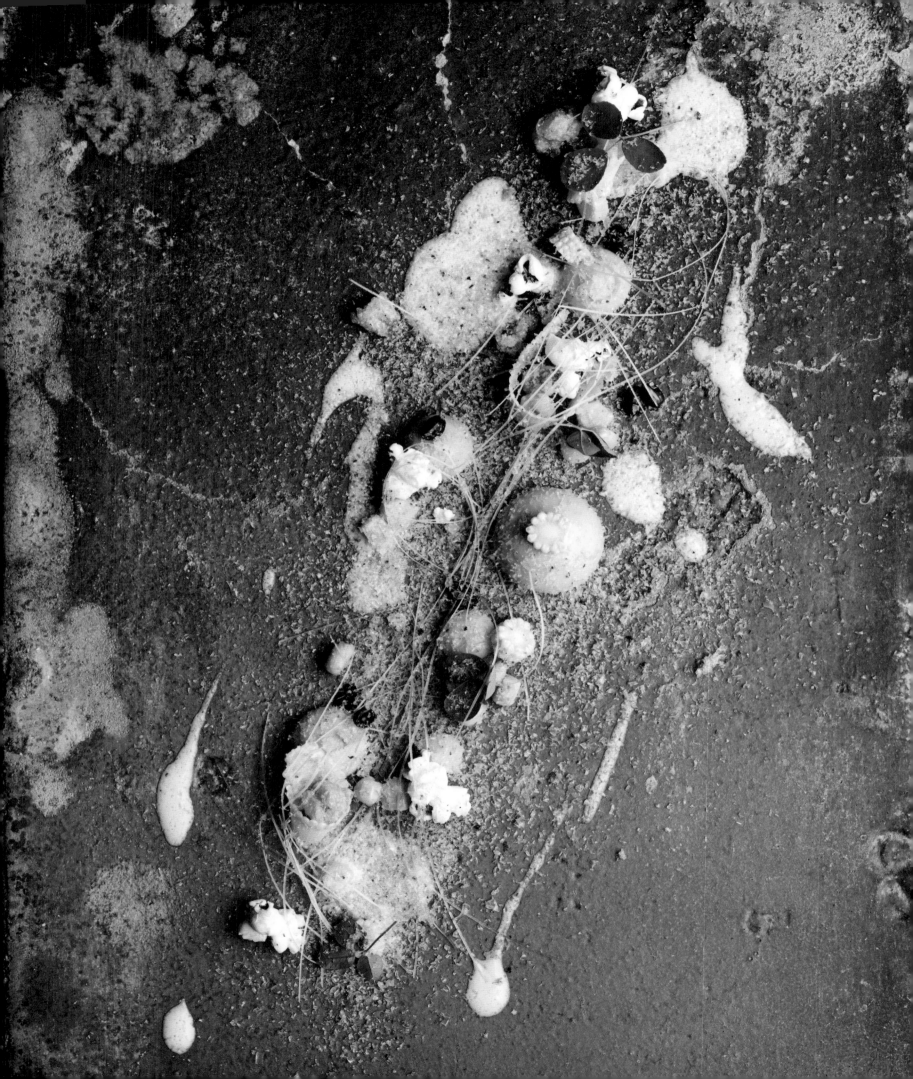

corn huitlacoche brown butter

For me, all corn dishes start with memories of Midwestern nights, of Summerfest in Milwaukee: grilled ears of corn, with the husk pulled down as a handle, dipped in coffee cans of melted butter. Here the textures are paramount, with the corn from the garden accented by a trio of other corn-centric elements: hominy, heirloom popcorn, and corn smut.

SERVES 4

CORN NUTS

100 grams | $^2/_3$ cup dried nixtamalized corn kernels

700 grams | about 3 cups water

grapeseed oil, for deep-frying

kosher salt

CORN MILK

400 grams | 1 $^2/_3$ cups whole milk

200 grams | 1 $^1/_4$ cups yellow corn kernels

xanthan gum

Maldon sea salt

PUMPKIN SEED BROWN BUTTER

225 grams | 1 cup unsalted butter

75 grams | $^1/_2$ cup raw pumpkin seeds

100 grams | 3.5 ounces sourdough baguette, cut into 1-inch (2.5-centimeter) slices

12 grams | 2 teaspoons Maldon sea salt

liquid nitrogen

FOR THE CORN NUTS:

Combine the corn and water in a pressure cooker and cook on high pressure for 45 minutes. Drain the corn and spread the kernels in a single layer on silicone baking mats. Place the mats in an area with a steady temperature of 100°F to 130°F (38°C to 54°C) for at least 18 hours, until the kernels are completely dry and slightly translucent. (Placing the trays in an oven set to the lowest temperature with the door left open works.)

Pour the oil to a depth of 4 inches (10 centimeters) into a deep fryer or deep, heavy pot and heat to 375°F (190°C). Add the corn to the hot oil and fry for about 30 seconds, until crispy. Transfer to paper towels to drain and season with kosher salt. Let cool, then store in an airtight container with silica gel packets at room temperature.

FOR THE CORN MILK:

Combine the milk and corn in a vacuum bag and seal on high. Using a butchery mallet, pound the kernels until they break apart slightly and begin to release their juice. Refrigerate the bag for 12 hours to infuse the milk.

Strain the milk through a very fine cloth filter into a container, then weigh the milk. Multiply the weight of the milk by 1 percent, then weigh out that amount of xanthan gum. Transfer the milk to a blender, turn on the blender to the lowest speed, and slowly add the xanthan gum. Continue to blend for 10 seconds more, until the milk thickens. Season the corn milk with Maldon salt, then store in an airtight container in the refrigerator.

FOR THE PUMPKIN SEED BROWN BUTTER:

Melt the butter in a small saucepan over medium heat. Whisk occasionally to redistribute the butter solids. Turn down the heat slightly and add the pumpkin seeds, baguette slices, and Maldon salt. Once the butter and the seeds have turned a rich brown, pour the mixture into a few shallow containers, about 1 inch (2.5 centimeters) in depth, distributing the bread and seeds evenly between the containers. Freeze the butter for at least 3 hours, until completely solid.

Carefully put the liquid nitrogen into a deep metal container (excessive changes in temperature or agitation of the liquid nitrogen may cause it to become volatile). Using a fine-tooth grater, shave the brown butter into the liquid nitrogen. Pour the liquid nitrogen through a small strainer to remove the shavings and store the shavings in a dry plastic container in the freezer until needed. (To discard the liquid nitrogen, carefully pour it back into its original container.)

continued

FOR THE ROASTED CORN PUDDING:

Preheat the oven to 450°F (230°C). Roast the corn for about 25 minutes, until the husks are dark brown. Let cool slightly, then remove the husks. Using a sharp knife, remove the kernels from 7 ears and set the kernels aside. Remove the kernels from the remaining 3 ears; you should have 370 grams (2 $^1/_4$ cups) of kernels. Juice these kernels and measure 250 grams (1 cup) of juice.

Prepare an ice bath. Add the reserved kernels (from the 7 ears), the corn juice, and the gellan base to a blender and mix on high speed for about 3 minutes, until a smooth puree forms. With the blender on medium speed, slowly add the butter, 1 cube at a time, until all of the butter is incorporated. Strain the puree through a chinois into a bowl, then nest the bowl in the ice bath to cool the puree. Season the cooled puree with vinegar and kosher salt. Transfer to a large squeeze bottle and reserve in the refrigerator until needed.

FOR THE HUITLACOCHE PUREE:

Prepare an ice bath. Combine the huitlacoche and water in a saucepan over low heat, bring to a simmer, and cook for about 20 minutes, until soft. Drain the huitlacoche, transfer to a blender, and mix on high speed for 3 minutes, until a smooth, thick puree forms. Strain the puree through a chinois into a bowl, then nest the bowl in the ice bath to cool the puree. Season the cooled puree with vinegar and kosher salt. Transfer to a squeeze bottle and reserve in the refrigerator until needed.

FOR THE ROASTED BABY CORN:

Prepare a fire in a wood-burning oven. When the fire is at about 600°F (315°C), place the baby corn on the oven grate and roast for 2 minutes on each side. Remove from the oven and rest for 5 minutes. Remove and discard the charred husks and reserve the silks. Slice 3 ears of the corn into thin lengthwise strips. Cut the remaining ears into coins about $^1/_4$ inch (6 millimeters) thick.

FOR THE POPPED CRIMSON POPCORN:

Heat a small, shallow rondeau with a lid over high heat. Add half of the oil and immediately follow with half of the corn kernels. Season with a little kosher salt, cover the pan, and then agitate the pan. When the kernels begin to pop, turn down the heat slightly. After 30 seconds have elapsed, transfer the popped corn to paper towels to drain. Repeat with the remaining corn kernels and oil. Let cool, then store in an airtight container with silica gel packets at room temperature.

TO SERVE:

Place a few dollops of the corn pudding and huitlacoche puree on each of 4 long plates. In a small bowl, season the raw corn kernels and the baby corn strips and coins with vinegar, olive oil, and Maldon salt, then arrange them on the plates on and around the pudding and the puree. Scatter the reserved baby corn silks, corn nuts, popcorn, and sweet clover around each plate. Lastly, spoon a small amount of the corn milk on the plates, and scatter the brown butter over the surface.

ROASTED CORN PUDDING

10 | ears yellow corn with husks intact
250 grams | 8.8 ounces gellan base (page 285)
150 grams | $^2/_3$ cup unsalted butter, cut into small cubes
sherry vinegar
kosher salt

HUITLACOCHE PUREE

300 grams | 10.5 ounces fresh huitlacoche
500 grams | 2 cups water
sherry vinegar
kosher salt

ROASTED BABY CORN

6 | ears baby corn with husks intact

POPPED CRIMSON POPCORN

25 grams | 2 tablespoons extra virgin olive oil
75 grams | $^1/_2$ cup crimson red popcorn kernels
kosher salt

100 grams | $^2/_3$ cup corn kernels, from fresh corn
sherry vinegar
Twin Sisters olive oil
Maldon sea salt
16 | sweet clover pluches

duck heart chrysanthemum

Gamey duck hearts are treated to a marinade of green flavors—chrysanthemum, dill, parsley—and then roasted over a fire. They are joined by cooling fresh ricotta, the first fava beans of the season, and a touch of acid in the form of pickled green garlic and spring onions—all primal flavors at the emergence of spring.

SERVES 4

DUCK JUS

480 grams | about 2 duck frames,
    fat removed

25 grams | 2 tablespoons rendered duck fat

320 grams | about 2 carrots, peeled
    and diced

120 grams | about 2 celery stalks, diced

200 grams | about 2 white spring
    onions, diced

20 grams | 2 tablespoons allspice berries

6 grams | 1 $^1/_2$ teaspoons fenugreek seeds

475 grams | 2 cups dry red wine

980 grams | 4 cups veal stock (page 288)

2.8 kilograms | 3 quarts chicken stock
    (page 283)

8 grams | 1 $^1/_2$ teaspoons unsalted butter

7 grams | 1 $^1/_2$ teaspoons freshly squeezed
    lemon juice

Maldon sea salt

FRESH RICOTTA

1.9 kilograms | 8 cups whole milk

475 grams | 2 cups heavy cream

230 grams | 1 cup buttermilk (page 284)

22 grams | 1 $^1/_2$ tablespoons freshly squeezed
    lemon juice

kosher salt

GREEN CHICKPEA HUMMUS

3.9 kilograms | 4 quarts water, at room
    temperature

240 grams | $^3/_4$ cup kosher salt

500 grams | 3 $^1/_2$ cups fresh green
    chickpeas, shucked

80 grams | 1 cup chopped green garlic tops

80 grams | 1 cup chopped spring onion tops

120 grams | about $^1/_2$ cup ice-cold water

40 grams | 3 tablespoons Twin Sisters
    olive oil

Maldon sea salt

FOR THE DUCK JUS:

Preheat the oven to 500°F (260°C). Arrange the duck frames in a roasting pan and roast for 25 minutes, until golden brown.

Heat the duck fat in a large rondeau over medium-high heat. Add the carrots, celery, and onions and cook, stirring occasionally, for about 10 minutes, until the vegetables begin to caramelize. Add the allspice and fenugreek and continue to cook for 2 minutes. Pour in the wine and cook for about 5 minutes, until reduced by half. Add the roasted duck frames and veal and chicken stocks and bring to a boil. Turn down the heat to low and simmer uncovered for 14 hours.

Strain through a very fine cloth filter into a saucepan. Place over medium-high heat and cook until reduced to a light jus (about 80 percent reduced). This should take no longer than 3 hours. Strain once more through a very fine cloth filter. Keep the jus in an airtight container in the refrigerator until needed.

FOR THE FRESH RICOTTA:

In a container, stir together the milk, cream, buttermilk, and lemon juice, then season with kosher salt. Pour into a vacuum bag and seal the bag on high. Cook in a hot-water bath set at 190°F (88°C) for 2 hours. Remove the bag from the bath and immerse in an ice bath for 1 hour.

To set up a resting tray for the curds, place a colander above a container. Line the colander with a piece of cheesecloth and pour the curds into the colander. Wrap the entire setup in plastic wrap and store in the refrigerator for at least 6 hours or up to 24 hours. Transfer the strained curds to a container with a lid, then discard the whey. Taste for seasoning and adjust with kosher salt if necessary. Cover and refrigerate.

FOR THE GREEN CHICKPEA HUMMUS:

Prepare an ice bath. Pour the room-temperature water into a large pot, add the kosher salt, and bring to a boil over high heat. Add the chickpeas and blanch for 4 minutes. Scoop out the chickpeas, transfer them to the ice bath, and let cool for 2 minutes, then pat dry on paper towels. Add the green garlic and spring onion tops to the boiling water and blanch for 2 minutes. Drain and transfer to the ice bath for 1 minute, then pat dry on paper towels.

Prepare a fresh ice bath. In a blender, combine the garlic and spring onion tops and ice-cold water and mix on high speed for 2 minutes, until smooth. Strain through a chinois into a bowl, then nest the bowl in the ice bath to cool the puree.

Put the chickpeas in a food processor and turn it on. Slowly add the garlic-onion puree and then the oil. Stop the processor before the mixture is smooth, as some texture from the chickpeas is desirable. Transfer the hummus to a container with a lid and season with Maldon salt. Cover and refrigerate.

continued

duck heart chrysanthemum *continued*

FOR THE RELISH:

Combine the vinegar, 120 grams (about ¹/₂ cup) of water, and sugar in a small saucepan and bring to a boil over high heat. Add the green garlic, turn down the heat to medium, and simmer for 10 minutes. Season to taste with kosher salt and transfer to a container. Let cool in the refrigerator.

Prepare an ice bath. Combine the 2 kilograms (about 8 ¹/₂ cups) of water and the 120 grams (¹/₃ cup) of kosher salt in a large pot and bring a boil over high heat, stirring to dissolve the salt. Add the chickpeas and blanch for 4 minutes. Scoop out the chickpeas, transfer them to the ice bath, and let cool for 1 minute, then pat dry on paper towels. Add the fava beans to the boiling water and blanch for 5 minutes. Drain and transfer to the ice bath for 1 minute, then pat dry on paper towels.

Using a slotted spoon, transfer the pickled green garlic to a small bowl. Add the chickpeas, fava beans, and a small amount of the pickling liquid, then season with Maldon salt. Set aside.

FOR THE CHRYSANTHEMUM-MARINATED DUCK HEARTS:

To make the marinade, combine the shallots, garlic, chrysanthemum leaves, dill, parsley, and cilantro in a blender and mix on medium speed for 30 seconds while slowly adding the oil. Increase the speed to high and mix for 1 minute, until smooth. Pour into a bowl and reserve at room temperature.

Trim the excess fat and sinew from the duck hearts. Add the hearts to the marinade and mix thoroughly. Remove the hearts from the marinade and place them in a vacuum bag. Add about 20 grams (1 ¹/₂ tablespoons) of the marinade to the bag and seal the bag on high. Refrigerate the bag for 3 hours.

Prepare a fire in a wood-burning oven. When the fire is at about 600°F (315°C), remove the hearts from the bag, wipe off any excess marinade, and season with kosher salt. Place the hearts on the oven grate and char for 30 seconds on each side. Remove from the oven and let rest for 1 minute. Slice each heart in half lengthwise. Season with Maldon salt.

TO SERVE:

Measure 200 grams (about ²/₃ cup) of the duck jus into a small saucepan over low heat. Whisk the butter and lemon juice into the jus until emulsified, then season with Maldon salt. Remove the saucepan from the heat and keep in a warm place while plating the rest of the dish. Arrange 2 quenelles of the hummus in each of 4 shallow bowls. Place 5 duck heart halves in each bowl, arranging them next to the quenelles. Scatter a few piles of the relish and fresh ricotta in each bowl. Finish each bowl with 3 fava flowers, 4 fava leaves, and 10 chrysanthemum leaves. Spoon the seasoned jus into the empty spaces in each bowl.

RELISH

118 grams | ¹/₂ cup white wine vinegar

120 grams | about ¹/₂ cup water

25 grams | 2 tablespoons sugar

50 grams | ¹/₃ cup green garlic, in rounds ¹/₈ inch (3 millimeters) thick

120 grams | ¹/₃ cup kosher salt, plus more for seasoning

2 kilograms | about 8 ¹/₂ cups water

112 grams | ³/₄ cup fresh green chickpeas, shucked

112 grams | ³/₄ cup fresh fava beans, shucked

Maldon sea salt

CHRYSANTHEMUM-MARINATED DUCK HEARTS

40 grams | ¹/₄ cup diced shallots

7 grams | 2 ¹/₂ teaspoons minced garlic

60 grams | 2 ounces chrysanthemum leaves and stems

6 grams | 0.2 ounce dill fronds and stems

15 grams | 0.5 ounce flat-leaf parsley leaves and stems

20 grams | 0.6 ounce cilantro leaves and stems

120 grams | ¹/₂ cup Twin Sisters olive oil

10 | duck hearts

kosher salt

Maldon sea salt

12 | pink fava flowers

16 | tiny fava leaves

40 | tiny chrysanthemum leaves

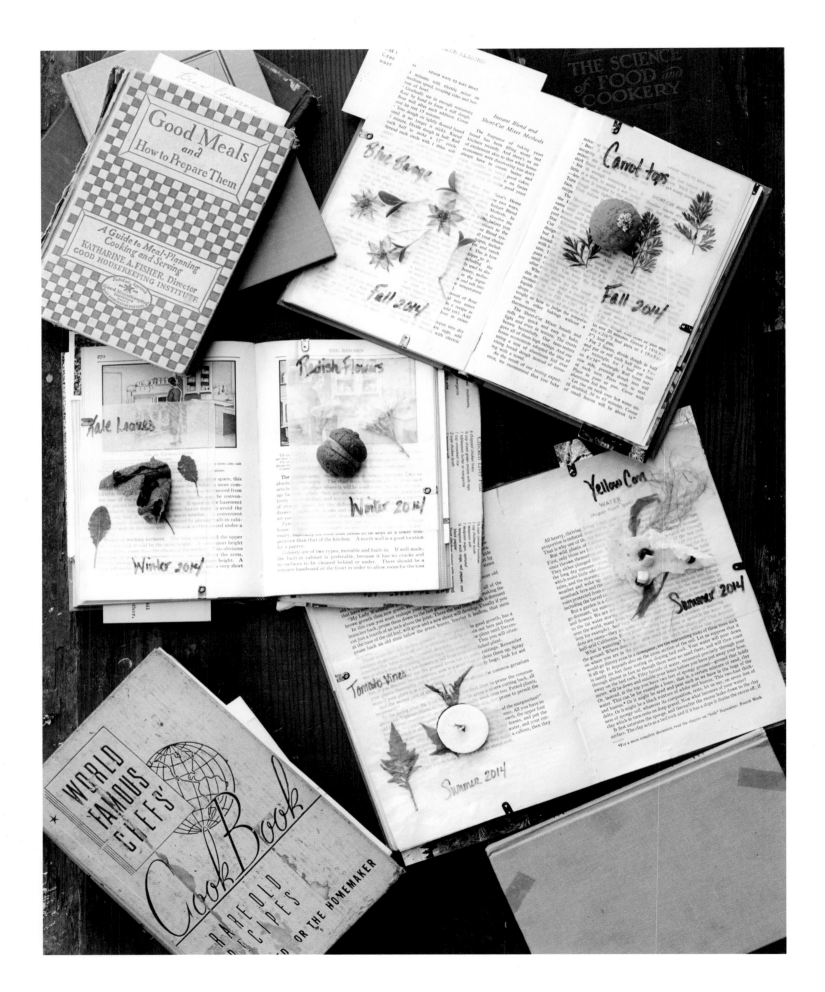

garden scrapbook

Depending on the season, I will serve as a canapé one of these "scrapbooks," old worn copies of food-related books filled with photos of Charlie and of the garden. The small canapés themselves sit atop pressed waxed paper with the small leaves specific to that dish and an inscription with the date they were picked—an ever-changing testament to the daily life of the garden.

SERVES 8 TO 10

MAKES ABOUT 24 CHIPS

GRIT CHIP

20 grams | 1 1/2 tablespoons extra virgin
 olive oil
20 grams | 2 tablespoons finely diced
 yellow onion
150 grams | 1 cup Geechie Boy Mill white grits
75 grams | 1/3 cup dry white wine
kosher salt
rice bran oil, for deep-frying

PILONCILLO PUREE

200 grams | 1 cup granulated piloncillo
500 grams | 2 cups water
8 grams | 1 3/4 teaspoons low acyl
 gellan gum
2 grams | 1/2 teaspoon calcium
 lactate gluconate

100 grams | 2/3 cup raw yellow corn kernels
sherry vinegar
Twin Sisters olive oil
Maldon sea salt

grit chip piloncillo puree

FOR THE GRIT CHIP:

Combine the oil and onion in a pot over medium heat and sweat the onion for about 3 minutes, until translucent. Add the grits and continue to sweat until grits have completely absorbed the oil. Add the wine and deglaze the pan, then cook until the wine is absorbed. Add just enough water to cover the grits and stir with a wooden spoon until the grits have absorbed the liquid. Repeat with fresh water until the grits have softened. Remove from the heat, season lightly with salt, and pour into a metal tray to cool slightly.

Transfer three-fourths of the grits to a food processor and mix until smooth. Transfer to a bowl, add the remaining grits, and stir to mix well. Transfer the grit mixture to silicone baking mats and spread about 1/8 inch (2 millimeters) thick. Let dry at room temperature for 24 hours.

Pour the oil to a depth of 4 inches (10 centimeters) into a deep fryer or deep, heavy pot and heat to 375°F (190°C). Break the grit chip into roughly 2-inch (5-centimeter) pieces. Working in batches, drop the chip pieces into the hot oil and fry for 10 seconds, until doubled in size. Transfer to paper towels to drain, then season with kosher salt.

FOR THE PILONCILLO PUREE:

Put the piloncillo in a heavy saucepan over low heat. Using a wooden spoon, stir constantly until the sugar melts and becomes very fragrant, about 2 minutes. Add the water and whisk to dissolve the caramelized sugar. Continuing to whisk, add the gellan gum and bring to a boil. Boil for 10 seconds, then remove the pan from the heat and whisk in the calcium until dissolved. Pour the mixture into a heatproof container, and let it cool and set in the refrigerator for about 1 hour. Transfer to a blender and mix until smooth. Strain through a chinois.

TO SERVE:

Dress the corn kernels with vinegar, olive oil, and Maldon salt. Place a few kernels on each chip along with a few dots of piloncillo puree.

continued

radish macaroon

FOR THE PUMPERNICKEL MACAROONS:

Preheat the oven to 280°F (140°C). Place the aged egg whites in the bowl of a stand mixer fitted with the whip attachment and begin whipping on medium speed. Meanwhile, place the water and granulated sugar in a small saucepan and stir to combine. Place the saucepan over medium-high heat and, without stirring, heat to 248°F (120°C). At this point, the egg whites in the mixer should be at medium peaks (4 to 6 minutes). Remove the sugar syrup from the heat and slowly stream it into the whipping egg whites. While the egg whites are continuing to whip, sift together the confectioners' sugar and bread crumbs through a tamis into a large bowl. Once the meringue in the mixer has reached full peaks (another 3 to 4 minutes), add the second measurement of egg whites to the sifted bread crumbs and quickly follow with the meringue, caraway seeds, and kosher salt. Using a rubber spatula, fold everything together as quickly as possible.

Line a full sheet pan with a silicone baking mat. Spoon the egg white mixture into a piping bag fitted with a size 12 round tip. Pipe quarter-size rounds onto the baking mat, spacing them about 2 inches (5 centimeters) apart. Bake for 6 minutes, until the surface is dry and the macaroons have risen in the center. Let cool on the pan to room temperature, then carefully peel the macaroons from the baking mat. Store in an airtight container with silica gel packets at room temperature.

FOR THE RADISHES:

Place the radish slices in a vacuum bag and seal on high to compress. Place in the refrigerator for 20 minutes, then remove the radish slices from the bag and season with Maldon salt.

TO SERVE:

To make each macaroon sandwich, smear a little butter on the flat side of 2 macaroons, then sandwich a radish slice between them.

PUMPERNICKEL MACAROONS

90 grams | about 3 egg whites (aged in the refrigerator for 1 week)

150 grams | ²/₃ cup water

235 grams | 1 cup plus 3 tablespoons granulated sugar

100 grams | scant 1 cup confectioners' sugar

320 grams | 11.3 ounces pumpernickel rye bread (page 289), dehydrated at 125°F (52°C) for 24 hours and finely ground (1 ¹/₂ cups)

90 grams | about 3 egg whites

3 grams | about 2 teaspoons toasted and ground caraway seeds

3 grams | ¹/₂ teaspoon kosher salt

RADISHES

6 | radishes, sliced into rounds about ¹/₈ inch (3 millimeters) thick

Maldon sea salt

cultured butter (page 284), tempered

borage sprouts horseradish vinegar

FOR THE HORSERADISH VINEGAR:

Combine the horseradish and vinegar in a vacuum bag and seal the bag on high. Refrigerate the bag for at least 1 week or for up to 1 month. Open the bag, strain the vinegar through a chinois and discard the horseradish.

TO SERVE:

Dress the borage sprouts with vinegar, oil, and salt.

HORSERADISH VINEGAR

30 grams | 2 tablespoons peeled and grated fresh horseradish

300 grams | 1 ¹/₄ cups white wine vinegar

48 | young borage sprouts

Twin Sisters olive oil

Maldon sea salt

KALE CHIP

27 grams | 2 tablespoons extra virgin olive oil

25 grams | 2 $^1/_2$ tablespoons sliced shallot

450 grams | 1 pound kale, stems removed

950 grams | 4 cups water

75 grams | $^1/_3$ cup tapioca starch

rice bran oil, for deep-frying

kosher salt

CHORIZO PUREE

27 grams | 2 tablespoons extra virgin olive oil

15 grams | 2 $^1/_2$ tablespoons cumin seeds

10 grams | 1 $^1/_2$ tablespoons coriander seeds

20 grams | 3 tablespoons ground hot
    Spanish paprika

75 grams | 2.8 ounces shallots, sliced

30 grams | $^1/_4$ cup garlic cloves

550 grams | 1.3 pounds kale,
    roughly chopped

900 grams | 3 $^3/_4$ cups water

kosher salt

27 grams | 2 tablespoons Twin Sisters
    olive oil

SMOKED ESPELETTE THREADS

2 | fresh Espelette peppers

200 grams | $^3/_4$ cup water

kale flavors of chorizo

FOR THE KALE CHIP:

Combine the olive oil and shallot in a large rondeau over medium heat and sweat the shallot for about 3 minutes, until translucent. Add the kale and heat just to wilt. Add the water and simmer for 35 minutes. Drain the kale, reserving 450 grams (2 cups) of the liquid. Transfer the kale to a blender and mix on high speed until smooth. Pass through a chinois into a bowl and keep warm.

In a saucepan, combine the tapioca starch and the reserved cooking liquid and place over medium-high heat. Whisking constantly, bring to a boil for 1 minute to hydrate the starch properly. Transfer to a food processor, add the kale puree, and mix for 5 minutes, until smooth, stopping to scrape down the sides of the processor bowl as needed. Measure 250 grams (1 cup). Transfer the kale puree to a large silicone baking mat and spread evenly about $^1/_{16}$ inch (1 millimeter) thick. Transfer the mat to a dehydrator tray and dehydrate the kale at 115°F (46°C) for 12 hours, until the chip has reduced in size by one-third and releases itself from the tray.

Portion the kale sheet into chips roughly 2 inches (5 centimeters) square. Pour the rice bran oil to a depth of 4 inches (10 centimeters) into a deep fryer or deep, heavy pot and heat to 375°F (190°C). Working in batches, fry the kale chips in the hot oil for about 6 seconds, until they release steam and have a variegated exterior. Remove the chips from the oil and mold into wrinkled shapes while still hot. Let the chips rest on paper towels and season with kosher salt.

FOR THE CHORIZO PUREE:

Place a saucepan over medium heat and add the extra virgin olive oil. Add the cumin, coriander, and paprika and toast for 20 seconds. Add the shallots, garlic, and kale and sweat for about 10 minutes, until the vegetables are fragrant and the kale has wilted. Add the water and simmer for 15 minutes, until the kale is very tender but still vibrant green.

Prepare an ice bath. Transfer the kale mixture to a blender and mix on high speed for 3 minutes, until smooth. Pass through a chinois into a bowl, then nest the bowl in the ice bath to cool the puree. Season with salt and Twin Sisters olive oil and reserve.

FOR THE SMOKED ESPELETTE THREADS:

Using a wooden skewer, pierce about 20 small holes in the peppers to allow for optimum smoke absorption. Using the cold-smoking technique on page 287, smoke the peppers for 30 minutes. Transfer the peppers to a dehydrator tray and dehydrate at 100°F (38°C) for 36 hours.

Combine the peppers and water in a small saucepan over low heat and rehydrate the peppers at about 120°F (49°C) for 20 minutes. Remove the peppers from the liquid, reserving the liquid, and place on a cutting board. Slice into threads 1 inch (2.5 centimeters) long, then put the threads in the reserved liquid. Let cool.

TO SERVE:

Place 4 dots of the chorizo puree on each chip, and put 2 Espelette threads on top of each dot of puree.

continued

steamed carrot cake

FOR THE CARROT CAKE:

Grind the isomalt to a powder in a blender or spice grinder. Combine the whole eggs, egg whites, and isomalt in the bowl of a stand mixer fitted with the whip attachment. Whip on medium speed for 7 minutes, until the eggs fall in a ribbon when the whip is lifted. Meanwhile, put the carrot puree in a large bowl.

When the whipped eggs are ready, slowly add them to the carrot puree, folding the two mixtures together carefully. Sift the flour, salt, and baking powder directly into the batter and fold in gently.

Spray 2 half sheet pans with nonstick cooking spray. Pour 700 grams (2 $3/_4$ cups) of the batter into each pan. Wrap tightly with plastic wrap and put into a steam oven set at 200°F (95°C) for 34 minutes. Remove the plastic wrap and let cool at room temperature for 1 hour.

Cut the cakes into 35-gram (1 $1/_4$-ounce) cubes, then, using scissors, shape each cube into a sphere.

FOR THE CARROT TOP MOUSSE:

Prepare an ice bath. Bring a large pot of water to a boil and season with kosher salt. Add the carrot tops and blanch for 2 minutes, then drain and transfer to the ice bath for 1 minute. Scoop the carrots from the ice bath, put into a blender, add the ice water, and mix on high speed for 3 minutes, until smooth. With the blender running on medium speed, slowly add the Ultra-Tex 3 and continue blending for 15 seconds. Pass the puree through a chinois into a bowl, then nest the bowl in the ice bath to cool the puree.

In a stand mixer fitted with the whip attachment, whip the mascarpone on medium speed until stiff. Using a spatula, fold the carrot top puree into the mascarpone until evenly combined. Season with salt and transfer to a squeeze bottle.

TO SERVE:

Pierce the bottom of the carrot cake with the tip of the squeeze bottle holding the carrot top mousse and squeeze a small amount of mousse into the cake. Garnish the top with a carrot flower.

CARROT CAKE

130 grams | $2/_3$ cup isomalt

188 grams | 4 whole eggs

60 grams | 2 egg whites

200 grams | $2/_3$ cup carrot puree (page 283)

160 grams | 1 $1/_4$ cups cake flour

4 grams | $3/_4$ teaspoon kosher salt

3 grams | $3/_4$ teaspoon baking powder

CARROT TOP MOUSSE

kosher salt

200 grams | 7 ounces carrot tops, stems removed

150 grams | $2/_3$ cup ice water

20 grams | 2 $1/_2$ tablespoons Ultra-Tex 3

450 grams | 1 pound mascarpone cheese

24 | carrot flowers

black cod summer curry

The garden provides an education: unripe figs and their leaves taste and smell just like coconut. From this bit of knowledge we created our own version of curry, pairing steamed black cod with summer vegetables, curry oil, and a cream of unripe figs.

SERVES 6

GREEN FIG VINEGAR

200 grams | 7 ounces underripe green figs

525 grams | 2 ¼ cups Champagne vinegar

GREEN FIG CREAM

800 grams | 3 ⅓ cups heavy cream

400 grams | 14 ounces underripe green figs, stems removed

3 grams | 1 teaspoon Ultra-Tex 3

1 gram | ¼ teaspoon xanthan gum

4 grams | 1 teaspoon green fig vinegar (recipe above)

kosher salt

BRAISED OKRA

27 grams | 2 tablespoons extra virgin olive oil

50 grams | ⅓ cup diced yellow onion

600 grams | 4 cups sliced okra

750 grams | 3 cups dry white wine

710 grams | about 3 cups water

60 grams | 2 cups baby spinach

300 grams | 1 ⅔ cups peeled, seeded, and finely diced tomatoes

50 grams | ¼ cup freshly squeezed lemon juice

27 grams | 2 tablespoons Twin Sisters olive oil

Maldon sea salt

BLACK COD

1 kilogram | 3 ½ cups kosher salt

12 | fresh fig leaves

600 grams | 21 ounces skinned black cod fillet

FOR THE GREEN FIG VINEGAR:

Put the figs and vinegar in a vacuum bag and seal on high to compress. Refrigerate for 24 hours. Strain the vinegar through a chinois and transfer to a squeeze bottle.

FOR THE GREEN FIG CREAM:

Put the cream and figs in a food processor and mix for 1 minute, until the figs are completely pulverized. Transfer the mixture to an airtight container and refrigerate for 12 hours. Strain the cream through a chinois and discard the solids. Measure 400 grams (1 ⅔ cups) and pour into a food processor. Reserve the remaining cream in a saucepan for later use. With the processor running, slowly add the Ultra-Tex and xanthan gum. Once the cream has thickened, strain it through a chinois into a bowl and season with the fig vinegar and kosher salt. Refrigerate in an airtight container.

FOR THE BRAISED OKRA:

Place a rondeau over high heat and add the extra virgin olive oil. When it begins to smoke, immediately add the onion and okra. Cook the vegetables, turning as needed, for about 4 minutes, until evenly charred on all sides. Add the wine and deglaze the pan. Continue to cook for about 10 minutes, until the liquid has evaporated. Add the water and reduce again until the pan is dry. Stir in the spinach, tomatoes, and lemon juice and then remove the pan from the heat. Season with the Twin Sisters oil and Maldon salt. Let cool in the refrigerator for 2 hours, then transfer to a cutting board and mince to a very fine paste.

FOR THE BLACK COD:

Combine the salt and half of the fig leaves in a food processor and mix for 3 minutes, until the leaves are pulverized. Transfer the salt mixture to a container, bury the cod in it, and refrigerate for 35 minutes. Rinse the cod under ice-cold running water to remove the excess salt. Pat dry on paper towels. Cut the cod into 6 equal pieces, about 100 grams (3.5 ounces) each.

To cook the cod, set a bamboo steamer basket over a pot of boiling water. Lay the remaining 6 fig leaves in a single layer in the basket and arrange the cod pieces on top. Cover and steam for 6 to 8 minutes, until the cod is firm and no longer opaque. Remove the cod from the steamer and pull each portion into natural flakes (about 3 flakes per portion).

continued

black cod summer curry *continued*

FOR THE MADRAS CURRY OIL:

Combine the curry powder and oil in a saucepan over low heat and heat at 140°F (60°C) for 20 minutes. Strain the oil through a coffee filter, then transfer to a squeeze bottle.

TO SERVE:

Prepare an ice bath. Bring a saucepan of salted water to a boil over high heat. Add the corn and blanch for 10 minutes, then immerse the corn in the ice bath for 3 minutes. Add the beans to the boiling water and blanch for 15 seconds, then immerse in the ice bath for 1 minute. Pat the corn and beans dry on paper towels. Cut the kernels from the corn in sections.

Place a few piles of the braised okra and a flaked cod portion in each of 6 bowls. Place a small amount of the whipped fig cream in each bowl and garnish with the blanched corn, beans, bell peppers, and fig and okra wedges. Finish with the pole bean flowers and flowering cilantro. Heat the reserved fig cream to 140°F (60°C) and season with kosher salt and fig vinegar. Froth the cream with an immersion blender, then scoop the foam from the top and scatter it on top of each serving. Finish with a few drops of curry oil.

MADRAS CURRY OIL

25 grams | ¼ cup Madras curry powder
200 grams | 1 cup extra virgin olive oil

1 | ear yellow corn, shucked
12 | tiny haricots verts
4 | tiny bell peppers, thinly sliced crosswise
2 | Black Mission figs, quartered lengthwise
2 | okra, quartered lengthwise
pole bean flowers
flowering cilantro

teff pillow sheep's milk cheese

Here is a longtime canapé that usually elicits a smile. Teff is made into a puffed cracker, and the feta and preserved lemon provide a nice contrast to the summer savory and marigolds from the garden.

MAKES ABOUT 50 CRACKERS

TEFF PILLOWS

50 grams | $^1/_2$ cup teff flour

62.5 grams | 5 tablespoons plus $^3/_4$ teaspoon active dry yeast

215 grams | scant 1 cup lukewarm water (90°F/32°C)

407.5 grams | 3 cups bread flour

4 grams | $^3/_4$ teaspoon kosher salt

4 grams | 1 teaspoon sugar

SHEEP'S MILK CHEESE MOUSSE

250 grams | 9 ounces sheep's milk feta cheese

125 grams | $^1/_2$ cup heavy cream

1.5 grams | $^1/_2$ sheet bronze gelatin, bloomed in ice water and wrung gently of excess water

0.5 gram | $^1/_8$ teaspoon freshly squeezed Meyer lemon juice

45 grams | $^1/_4$ cup preserved Meyer lemon peel, in brunoise

kosher salt

summer savory leaves

Mexican marigolds

FOR THE TEFF PILLOWS:

Preheat the oven to 350°F (175°C). Line a sheet pan with parchment paper. Spread the teff flour on the prepared pan and toast in the oven for 12 minutes, until fragrant. Let cool to room temperature.

In the bowl of a stand mixer, combine the yeast and water and let stand for 6 minutes, until the yeast is frothy. Add the teff flour, bread flour, salt, and sugar, fit the mixer with the dough hook, and mix on medium speed for 6 minutes, until elastic and fairly dense. Transfer the dough to a plastic container with a lid and place it in a proof box set at 95°F (35°C) for 12 hours.

Remove the container from the proof box and refrigerate for 12 hours to retard the dough. Transfer the dough to a work surface and punch it down to release the excess gases formed during fermentation. Divide into 6 equal portions and wrap to prevent a skin from forming.

Place an inverted half sheet pan in the oven and preheat to 350°F (175°C). Working with 1 dough portion at a time, allow the dough to sit at room temperature for 10 minutes to warm slightly. Press into a flat disk (about 1 inch/2.5 centimeters thick) and pass through the rollers of a pasta machine set at the widest setting. Lightly flouring the dough before each pass and gradually narrowing the rollers, continue to pass the dough through the rollers until it is about $^1/_{16}$ inch (2 millimeters) thick. Lay the dough sheet on a lightly floured work surface and let rest for about 3 minutes. Meanwhile, line a half sheet pan with parchment paper and spray the paper with nonstick cooking spray. Using a bicyclette (dough divider) about 1 $^1/_4$ inches (3 centimeters) square, cut out shapes and place them on the prepared pan. Spray the cutouts with nonstick cooking spray and season lightly with salt.

Remove the half sheet pan from the oven and invert it onto the sheet pan holding the cutouts, exposing them to the hot surface. Flip the pans together so the hot pan is on the bottom. Remove the top pan and the paper and place the inverted bottom pan with the cutouts in the oven. Bake for 6 minutes, until the crackers have risen fully. Lower the temperature to 320°F (160°C), and continue to bake the crackers for 3 minutes, until evenly toasted. Remove from the oven and transfer to paper towels. Using a router drill, make a small hole in the top of each cracker. Repeat with the remaining dough portions. Store in an airtight container with silica gel packets at room temperature.

FOR THE SHEEP'S MILK CHEESE MOUSSE:

Prepare an ice bath. Put the feta in a food processor and mix for 3 minutes, until smooth, stopping to scrape down the sides of the processor bowl as needed. Combine 18 grams (1 tablespoon plus $^3/_4$ teaspoon) of the cream and the gelatin in a small saucepan and heat over low heat just until the gelatin melts. Add the feta and stir to mix well. Transfer the feta mixture to a bowl and nest the bowl in the ice bath for about 2 hours, until the cheese mixture has cooled and set.

Pour the remaining cream into the bowl of a stand mixer fitted with the whip attachment and whip on high speed until medium peaks form. Using a spatula, lightly fold the cream into the cheese mixture just until combined. Season with the lemon juice, lemon peel, and salt and store in a piping bag in the refrigerator until needed.

TO SERVE:

Preheat the oven to 350°F (175°C). Arrange the crackers on sheet pans and toast in the oven for 2 minutes, until hot. Remove from the oven and fill the hole in each cracker with some of the mousse from the piping bag. Cover the hole with summer savory and marigolds.

daylily wild onion spot prawn caviar

One day, the famed Napa gardener Peter Jacobsen brought me a daylily. The flavor of the petals was delicious—sweet without being overly floral. After several attempts, I settled on this dish, in which beautiful raw spot prawns are chopped, stuffed inside the lily, and then roasted. The dish is garnished simply with caviar, lily bulb and lily petals, and wild onion. When asked which dish I am most happy with, I tend to say this one because of its showcasing of products, its succinct flavors, and its elegant presentation.

FOR THE PICKLED LILY BULB:

Cut a slice off the top and the bottom of the lily bulb and pull apart the layers. Place the bulb layers in a bowl. Combine the water, vinegar, and salt in a small saucepan and bring to a boil over high heat. Remove from the heat, let cool, and pour the liquid over the bulb layers. Let pickle at room temperature for 1 hour.

FOR THE SPOT PRAWNS:

Clean each prawn by removing the head first and then the shell from the body, working carefully so as not to tear the flesh. Reserve the shells. Devein each prawn, then cut the meat very finely into uniform dice and reserve in the refrigerator.

Preheat the oven to 375°F (190°C). Place a roasting rack on a sheet pan and arrange the shells on the rack. Place in the oven for 20 minutes. Remove from the oven, transfer the shells to a saucepan, and add the butter. Place over low heat and heat to 160°F (71°C). Simmer for 2 hours, until the butter clarifies. Strain through a very fine cloth filter into a container and let cool in the refrigerator.

Season the prawn meat with the olive oil and Maldon salt, then spoon the mixture into a piping bag fitted with a small round tip.

To prepare the lilies, cut off the flower where it connects to the stem and discard the stem. Remove the pistils from 4 of the larger lilies and reserve the pistils and the remaining 4 lilies for serving. Pipe the prawn mixture into the 4 lilies, dividing it evenly. Prepare a fire in a wood-burning oven. When the fire is at about 600°F (315°C), put a hot plate in the oven and place the stuffed lilies on the plate. Roast for about 15 seconds, turning frequently, then remove from the oven. Melt a little of the clarified butter, then brush the lilies with the butter and season with Maldon salt.

TO SERVE:

Separate the reserved 4 lilies into petals, reserving the pistils. Lay a roasted lily on each of 4 flat plates. Place some of the caviar and a few pieces of the pickled bulb on top of each lily. Garnish with the lily petals, lily pistils, and wild onion threads.

SERVES 4

PICKLED LILY BULB
1 | lily bulb
500 grams | 2 cups water
50 grams | $^1/_4$ cup white wine vinegar
18 grams | 1 tablespoon kosher salt

SPOT PRAWNS
150 grams | 5.3 ounces live spot prawns
3 grams | $^3/_4$ teaspoon Twin Sisters olive oil
Maldon sea salt
225 grams | $^1/_2$ pound unsalted butter
8 | day lilies

50 grams | 1.8 ounces sturgeon caviar
12 | wild onion threads

green tomato cocktail

Acidic, fresh, smoky—here the ocean meets the land. Soft meets frozen, too, and the oyster meets its country cousin, the oyster leaf. Unripe tomato, which provides a vegetal grounding, is as much of a star as the shellfish is. This dish is an explosive way to begin a meal, containing in a few bites enough flavor and texture to rev the palate and focus the mind.

SERVES 4

TOMATO CLAM SNOW

27 grams | 2 tablespoons extra virgin
    olive oil
30 grams | ¹/₃ cup chopped celery
25 grams | 2 ¹/₂ tablespoons sliced shallot
12 | cherrystone clams, soaked in ice water
    for 20 minutes
650 grams | 2 ³/₄ cups water
480 grams | 2 cups tomato water (page 286)
13 grams | about 4 sheets bronze gelatin,
    bloomed in ice water and wrung gently
    of excess water
liquid nitrogen
kosher salt

GREEN TOMATO VINAIGRETTE

500 grams | 18 ounces green tomatoes
24 grams | 2 ¹/₂ tablespoons freshly
    squeezed lemon juice
2 grams | 1 teaspoon plankton
kosher salt

CLAM PREPARATION

1 | geoduck clam
2 | surf clams, soaked in ice water for 1 hour
Twin Sisters olive oil
Maldon sea salt

FOR THE TOMATO CLAM SNOW:

Combine the oil, celery, and shallot in a rondeau over high heat and sweat for about 3 minutes, just until the fragrance of the vegetables is released. Drain the clams and add them along with the water to the rondeau and bring to a boil. Turn down the heat to a simmer and cook for 6 minutes, until the clams open fully. Remove the clams from the pan, then strain the liquid and reserve the clams and liquid separately.

Combine the tomato water and clam liquid in a saucepan over low heat and heat to just over 100°F (38°C). Remove from the heat, add the gelatin, and allow the gelatin to melt. Whisk briefly and season with salt. Distribute the mixture among small (1-cup/240-milliliter) containers and freeze for about 2 hours, until frozen solid.

Carefully put the liquid nitrogen into a deep metal container (excessive changes in temperature or agitation of the liquid nitrogen may cause it to become volatile). Using a fine-tooth grater, shave the frozen tomato-clam mixture into the liquid nitrogen. Pour the liquid nitrogen through a small strainer to remove the snow and store the snow in a dry plastic container in the freezer until needed.

Shell and trim the cooked clams and reserve in a covered container in the refrigerator.

FOR THE GREEN TOMATO VINAIGRETTE:

Put the tomatoes in a blender and mix on high speed for about 30 seconds, until liquefied. Line a strainer with cheesecloth, place over a bowl, and pour the tomatoes into the strainer. Refrigerate for 24 hours. Season with the lemon juice, plankton, and kosher salt. Refrigerate in an airtight container until needed.

FOR THE CLAM PREPARATION:

Cut the geoduck clam from its shell and discard the intestines. Prepare an ice bath. Bring a large pot of water to a boil and season with salt. Add the clam and blanch for 35 seconds. Remove the clam from the water and shock in the ice bath for 30 seconds, then peel the skin from the clam. Cut the clam in half lengthwise and hold on dry paper towels in the refrigerator.

Drain the surf clams. Insert an oyster shucker or petty knife into the opening of a surf clam, cut as close to the shell as possible, and pull back the top shell to open fully. Cut on the other side of the shell and remove the clam completely. Remove the abductors and reserve for another use. Discard the stomach and mince the remaining clam meat. Repeat with the second surf clam. Season the clam meat with the oil and Maldon salt and refrigerate in a covered container until needed.

continued

FOR THE LOVAGE OIL:

Prepare an ice bath. Line a strainer with cheesecloth and place over a small bowl. Bring a saucepan filled with salted water to a boil, add the lovage leaves, and blanch for 20 seconds. Drain and shock in the ice bath for 30 seconds. Remove the leaves from the water and reserve the ice bath. Wrap the leaves in a piece of cheesecloth and press out the excess water. Transfer to a blender, add the oil, and mix on high speed until the oil reaches a temperature of 170°F (77°C). Strain through the cheesecloth-lined strainer into a bowl, then nest the bowl in the ice bath to cool. Add the lovage stems to the oil and hold in the refrigerator until needed.

FOR THE SEASONED TOMATO WATER:

Strain the tomato water through a very fine cloth filter, then season with Maldon salt.

TO SERVE:

Prepare a fire in a wood-burning oven. When the fire is at about 600°F (315°C), season the geoduck clam with Twin Sisters oil and Maldon salt, place on the oven grate, and grill for 1 minute on each side. Cut the geoduck into slices $1/4$ inch (6 millimeters) thick. Dress the cherrystone clams and geoduck clam with seasoned tomato water, Twin Sisters oil, and Maldon salt and place a few pieces in each of 4 bowls. Put a couple of piles of surf clam, lovage stems with some of the lovage oil, oyster leaves, and lovage sprouts in each bowl. Refresh the tomato clam snow with more liquid nitrogen to separate the individual pieces of snow, then finish the plates with a dusting of the snow. (To discard the liquid nitrogen, carefully pour it back into its original container.)

LOVAGE OIL

20 grams | 1 $1/4$ cups lovage leaves
300 grams | 1 $1/3$ cups Twin Sisters olive oil
40 grams | $3/4$ cup diced lovage stems

SEASONED TOMATO WATER

300 grams | 1 $1/4$ cups tomato water
  (page 286)
Maldon sea salt

12 | green cherry tomatoes, peeled
12 | yellow cherry tomatoes, peeled
2 | Green Zebra tomatoes
oyster leaves
tiny lovage sprouts

foie gras hibiscus radish

Foie gras pairs beautifully with acidic elements. In this case, we marble the foie gras with hibiscus, which creates a visually arresting and surprisingly bright flavor. The foie is served with one of my favorite vegetables, the humble radish, and assorted puffed seeds.

SERVES 8

PRESERVED BABY RADISHES

25 grams | 4 teaspoons kosher salt
11 grams | 2 tablespoons dried hibiscus
16 | baby radishes
5 grams | 1 teaspoon Twin Sisters olive oil

HIBISCUS-CURED FOIE GRAS TERRINE

25 grams | $^1/_4$ cup dried hibiscus
20 grams | 1 tablespoon kosher salt
1.3 grams | $^1/_4$ teaspoon tinted curing mix #1
680 grams | 1.5 pounds grade A foie gras

WHIPPED FOIE GRAS

20 grams | 1 tablespoon kosher salt
1.3 grams | $^1/_4$ teaspoon tinted curing mix #1
680 grams | 1.5 pounds grade A foie gras
50 grams | 3 tablespoons dark chicken jus
 (page 284)
15 grams | 1 tablespoon sherry vinegar
400 grams | 1 $^2/_3$ cups whole milk
400 grams | 1 $^2/_3$ cups heavy cream
10 grams | 2 $^1/_4$ teaspoons powdered agar
kosher salt

GRAIN TUILE

1.4 kilograms | 6 cups water
200 grams | 1 cup farro
200 grams | 1 cup isomalt
100 grams | about 30 sheets bronze gelatin,
 bloomed in ice water and wrung gently
 of excess water
125 grams | $^1/_2$ cup unsalted butter
20 grams | 1 tablespoon kosher salt
90 grams | $^1/_2$ cup amaranth seeds
70 grams | $^1/_2$ cup poppy seeds

FOR THE PRESERVED BABY RADISHES:

Combine the salt and hibiscus in a spice grinder and coarsely grind. Season the radishes with the hibiscus salt, transfer to a vacuum bag, and seal on high. Hold for 24 hours in the refrigerator, then transfer the radishes to a small bowl and season with the oil.

FOR THE HIBISCUS-CURED FOIE GRAS TERRINE:

Combine the hibiscus, salt, and curing mix in a spice grinder and pulse for 10 seconds. Cut the foie gras lobe from the underside to expose the cavity. Remove and discard the veins and any imperfections. Season the lobe with the curing mixture. Press the lobe back together and wrap tightly in plastic wrap. Refrigerate for 12 hours.

Cut the lobe into at least 16 small bars (about $^1/_2$ inch square by 3 inches long (about 1 centimeter by 7 centimeters) that will easily fit into the grain tuiles (recipe below). Keep refrigerated for no longer than 4 hours to avoid oxidation.

FOR THE WHIPPED FOIE GRAS:

Combine the salt and curing mix in a spice grinder and pulse for 10 seconds. Cut the foie gras lobe from the underside to expose the cavity. Remove and discard the veins and any imperfections. Season the lobe with the curing mixture. Press the lobe back together and wrap tightly in plastic wrap. Refrigerate for 12 hours.

Measure 630 grams (1.3 pounds) of the foie gras and transfer to a blender. Combine the jus, vinegar, milk, cream, and agar in a saucepan over high heat. Bring to a boil and boil for 15 seconds while whisking constantly. Remove from the heat and immediately add to the blender. Mix on low speed for 2 minutes, until glossy and slightly thickened. Strain the gel through a chinois into a shallow metal tray. Refrigerate for 4 hours.

Prepare an ice bath. Return the gel to the blender and mix on high speed for about 2 minutes, until the gel develops a sheen. Season with salt, then strain through a chinois placed over a bowl. Nest the bowl in the ice bath to chill the gel. Transfer to a siphon canister and charge with 2 nitrous oxide cartridges. Hold the siphon in the refrigerator until needed.

FOR THE GRAIN TUILE:

Preheat the oven to 330°F (165°C). Combine the water and farro in a rondeau and bring to a simmer over high heat. Cook the farro for 40 minutes, until tender. Drain the farro, reserving the farro and liquid separately.

Weigh 450 grams (2 $^1/_2$ cups) of the cooked farro and 200 grams ($^3/_4$ cup) of the cooking liquid. Combine the farro, cooking liquid, isomalt, gelatin, butter, and salt in a blender and mix on medium speed for 5 minutes, until the farro is completely liquefied. Transfer to a bowl, season with kosher salt, and hold in a warm place.

Place a small rondeau with a lid over high heat. Add a small amount of the amaranth seeds and toast, shaking the pan aggressively, for 10 seconds, then quickly transfer to a bowl. Repeat to toast all of the amaranth seeds. Add the poppy seeds to the bowl and mix together.

continued

Line a sheet pan with a silicone baking mat. Transfer the tuile base to the mat and spread to a thickness of about ⅛ inch (3 millimeters). Evenly distribute the seed mixture over the tuile, coating it generously and reserving the remaining seeds for garnish. Bake the tuile sheet for 8 minutes, just until it begins to color.

Remove from the oven and peel the tuile sheet off of the baking mat. Working quickly, cut the tuile sheet into strips 3½ inches (9 centimeters) wide. Return the strips to the baking mat and return the pan to the oven. Bake the strips for 3 minutes, until the color deepens. Remove the pan from the oven and cut the strips into at least 12 (3½ by 1½-inch/9 by 4-centimeter) rectangles. To shape the warm rectangles, roll the unfinished side of the rectangle around a metal cannoli mold and hold in place until cool, about 15 seconds. (The tuiles may need to be rewarmed in the oven for about a minute if they become too brittle.) Store the tuiles in an airtight container with silica gel packets at room temperature.

FOR THE DAIKON RADISH JAM:

Combine the water and hibiscus in a saucepan, heat to 180°F (82°C), and brew for 5 minutes. Strain the tea through a coffee filter and discard the solids. Set the tea aside.

Combine the oil, daikon, and onion in a small saucepan over medium heat and sweat, stirring constantly, for about 3 minutes, until the onion is translucent. Add the honey and bring to a boil. Add hibiscus tea and simmer for about 15 minutes, until the liquid has completely evaporated. Transfer to a heatproof container and season with salt. Let cool in the refrigerator.

FOR THE HIBISCUS SYRUP:

Prepare an ice bath. Combine the water and hibiscus in a saucepan, heat to 180°F (82°C), and brew for 5 minutes. Strain the tea through a coffee filter and discard the solids. Combine the tea, honey, daikon skins, and corn syrup in a heavy saucepan, place over high heat, and cook, stirring occasionally, until reduced by 90 percent (nappé). Strain the syrup through a chinois and pour into a heatproof container. Nest the container in the ice bath to cool the syrup. Season with salt, then transfer to a squeeze bottle and hold at room temperature.

TO SERVE:

Slip a bar of terrine into the center of each tuile, then fill both ends of the tuile with whipped foie gras. Place 1 tuile on each plate. Place a second bar of the foie gras on the plate and add a few dots of the hibiscus syrup, a couple of piles of daikon radish jam, 2 preserved radishes, and some shaved radish and radish tops. Dress the reserved amaranth and poppy seeds with olive oil and season with Maldon salt. Scatter the dressed seeds over everything.

DAIKON RADISH JAM

350 grams | 1½ cups water
50 grams | ½ cup dried hibiscus
20 grams | 1½ tablespoons extra virgin olive oil
250 grams | 1¾ cups peeled daikon radish, in brunoise, skins reserved and dehydrated at 125°F (52°C) for 10 hours
40 grams | ¼ cup yellow onion, in brunoise
60 grams | about 3 tablespoons raw honey
kosher salt

HIBISCUS SYRUP

1 kilogram | 4¼ cups water
100 grams | 1 cup dried hibiscus
200 grams | ⅔ cup raw honey
80 grams | 2 cups dehydrated daikon radish skins (from daikon radish jam recipe, above)
100 grams | ⅓ cup light corn syrup
kosher salt

baby radishes, shaved
tiny radish tops
reserved amaranth and poppy seeds
Twin Sisters olive oil
Maldon sea salt

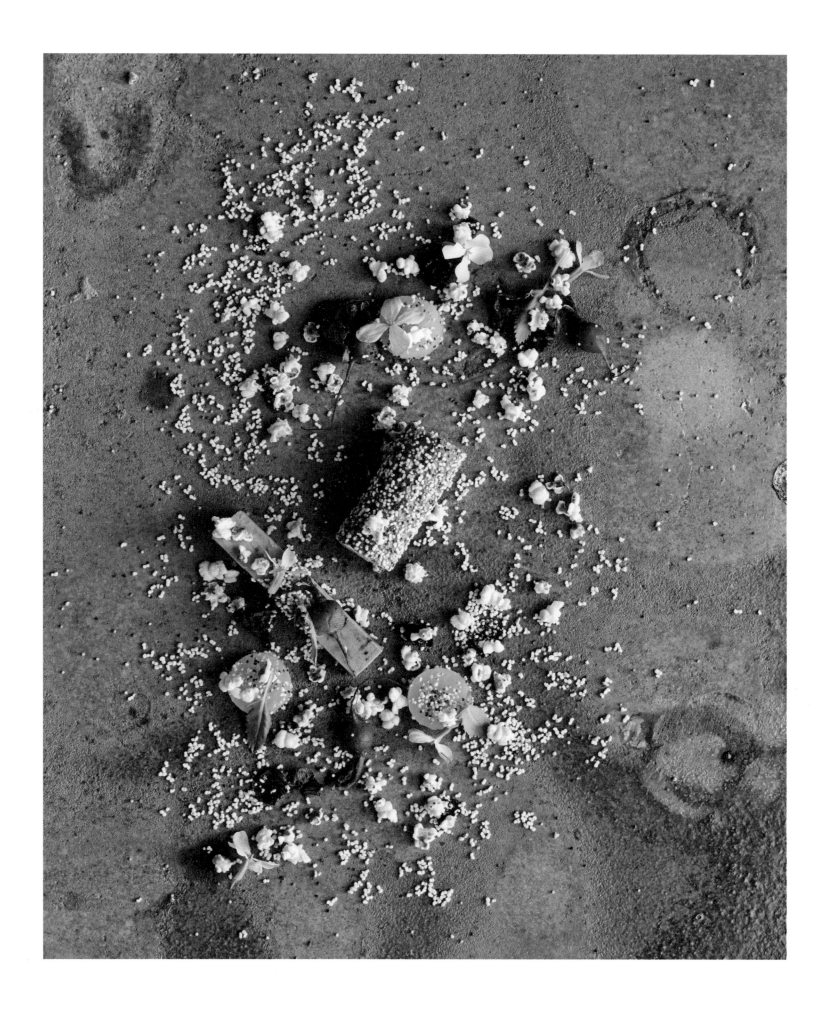

okra flower oyster

When you grow your own vegetables, you can watch the entirety of a plant's life, from the root to the fruit. Here, long after the okra plant had given up producing the vegetable, these flowers began to appear, tender and tasting just like the okra itself. We fill them with raw oyster and serve them as a canapé.

SERVES 4

OYSTER PREPARATION
4 | extra-small Kusshi oysters
sel gris

4 | okra flowers

FOR THE OYSTER PREPARATION:

Shuck the oysters, reserving the liquid and discarding the shells. Rinse the oysters under ice-cold running water to remove any debris from the shells. Lightly dab with paper towels to remove the excess water and transfer to a cutting board. Mince the oysters, working gently to keep the integrity of the flesh. Season with sel gris and just enough of the reserved oyster liquor to moisten. Hold on ice until served.

TO SERVE:

Using a fine-bristled brush, gently clean the inside of each okra flower. Fill the inside of each flower with one-fourth of the oyster and serve.

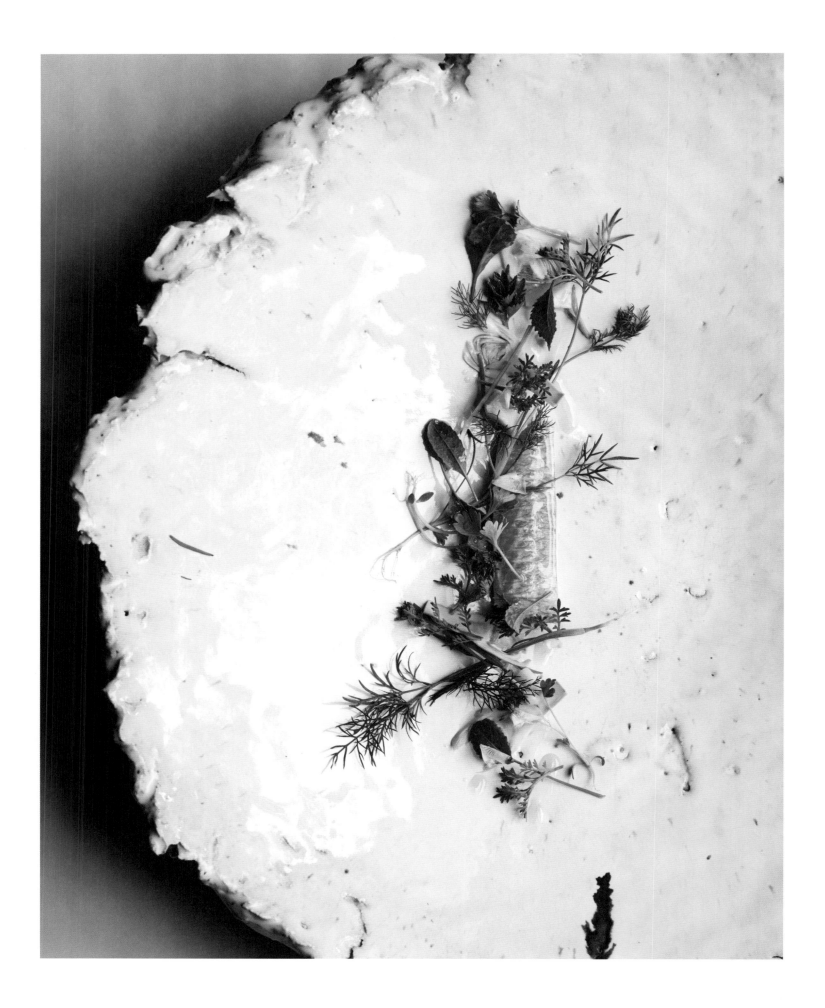

snapper artichoke tiny greens

Tiny, perfect artichokes appear in the Napa Valley Reserve garden in early spring. We prepare them in the style of barigoule and serve them with red snapper. The scales are removed from the snapper, puffed, and served as a garnish along with wild and cultivated greens.

SERVES 4

SNAPPER PREPARATION

390 grams | 14 ounces red snapper fillet,
  scales removed and reserved
800 grams | 2 ³/₄ cups kosher salt
600 grams | 2 ³/₄ cups grapeseed oil

SNAPPER BROTH

200 grams | 7 ounces snapper frames
13 grams | 1 tablespoon ascorbic acid
3.8 kilograms | 4 quarts water
90 grams | 3.3 ounces baby artichokes
30 grams | 2 tablespoons plus ³/₄ teaspoon
  extra virgin olive oil
28 grams | 1 ounce anchovy fillets
80 grams | ³/₄ cup celery, in 1-inch
  (2.5-centimeter) pieces
250 grams | 1 ¹/₂ cups yellow onion, in 1-inch
  (2.5-centimeter) pieces
100 grams | 1 cup green garlic, in 1-inch
  (2.5-centimeter) pieces
3.8 kilograms | 4 quarts fish fumet
  (page 285)
kosher salt

ARTICHOKE PREPARATION

800 grams | 1.8 pounds baby artichokes
13 grams | 1 tablespoon ascorbic acid
30 grams | 2 tablespoons extra virgin olive oil
40 grams | ¹/₃ cup celery, in 1-inch
  (2.5-centimeter) pieces
125 grams | ³/₄ cup yellow onion, in quarters
25 grams | ¹/₄ cup green garlic, in halves
4 grams | 1 ³/₄ teaspoons white peppercorns
1 gram | 1 teaspoon fresh bay leaves
350 grams | 1 ¹/₂ cups dry white wine
2 kilograms | about 8 cups water
10 grams | 2 teaspoons Twin Sisters olive oil
kosher salt

FOR THE SNAPPER PREPARATION:

Put the reserved scales in a container and soak in cold water for 20 minutes. Meanwhile, pour the salt into a container and bury the snapper fillet in it. Place in the refrigerator for 35 minutes. Rinse the snapper under ice-cold running water to remove the excess salt and pat dry on paper towels. Cut the snapper into 4 equal pieces, about 90 grams (3 ounces) each. Store in an airtight container set over ice in the refrigerator until ready to use.

Pour the oil into a small rondeau and heat to 325°F (165°C). Drain the scales and pat them almost, but not completely, dry on paper towels. Add the scales to the hot oil and fry for about 2 minutes. Transfer to paper towels to drain. Line a dehydrator tray with paper towels, spread the fried scales out evenly and dehydrate at 125°F (52°C) for at least 2 hours, until the scales are dry and crispy.

FOR THE SNAPPER BROTH:

Rinse the snapper frames under cold running water for 2 minutes. Pat dry on paper towels and reserve. In a large bowl or other container, dissolve the ascorbic acid in the water. Working with 1 artichoke at a time, use a paring knife to remove and discard the green leaves by peeling them away from the artichoke, exposing the white leaves underneath. Remove the tips of the white leaves and, using a vegetable peeler, peel away the green skin from the stem. Cut the artichoke in half lengthwise and immediately submerge in the acidulated water. Repeat with the remaining artichokes.

Place a stockpot over medium heat, add the olive oil and anchovies, and sweat for about 2 minutes, until fragrant. Remove the artichokes from the acidulated water, and reserve the water. Add the artichokes, celery, onion, and green garlic and sweat for 10 minutes longer, until the vegetables are translucent. Pour in the fumet and bring to a boil. Turn down the heat to a simmer and cook for 1 hour. Meanwhile, prepare an ice bath. When the broth is ready, strain through a very fine cloth filter into a bowl, then nest the bowl in the ice bath to cool the broth. Season with kosher salt.

FOR THE ARTICHOKES:

Trim the artichokes as you did for the broth, adding them to the same acidulated water. Transfer a small amount of the acidulated water to a separate container. Scoop out 4 artichoke halves from the large container and, using a mandoline, shave them into the small container. Refrigerate the small container of artichokes for later use.

Heat the extra virgin olive oil in a large rondeau over low heat. Add the celery, onion, green garlic, peppercorns, and bay leaves and sweat for about 10 minutes, until the vegetables are translucent. Increase the heat to high, add the artichokes and wine and cook until the wine has reduced by half. Add the water and bring to simmer. Reduce the heat to low and cover the surface with a piece of parchment paper. Cook for 15 minutes, until the artichokes are tender. To check for doneness, cut off a piece of the stem; it should cut easily while still maintaining its shape. Remove from the heat.

continued

Prepare an ice bath. Remove 300 grams (10.5 ounces) of the artichokes from the liquid and transfer to a blender. Strain a small amount of the cooking liquid into a small pitcher. Turn the blender on to low speed to start mixing the artichokes, adding a small amount of the cooking liquid at a time until the artichokes become a smooth puree. Increase the speed to high and mix for 1 minute. Turn down the speed to low and slowly add the Twin Sisters olive oil, being careful not to force the puree out of emulsification. Strain the puree through a chinois into a bowl, then nest the bowl in the ice bath to cool the puree. Season with kosher salt and transfer to a squeeze bottle. Store in the refrigerator until ready to serve.

Remove the remaining artichokes from the cooking liquid, cut each half into 3 wedges, and place in a bowl. Strain the cooking liquid through a very fine cloth filter and combine it with the artichoke wedges. Cover and refrigerate until ready to use.

TO SERVE:

Pour about 480 grams (2 cups) of the snapper broth into a shallow saucepan. Add 2 tablespoons of Twin Sisters olive oil and heat over low heat to 120°F (49°C). Add the snapper portions and poach for 12 minutes, until the snapper is firm but still stark white. Meanwhile, dress the shaved artichokes in a small amount of Twin Sisters olive oil and Maldon salt.

Place a few dots of the artichoke puree on each of 4 plates, then put 2 pieces of the braised artichoke on each plate. When the snapper is cooked, lay it on top of the artichoke puree. Lay 5 pieces of the shaved artichoke on each plate. Garnish with the wild garlic, tiny fennel, tiny celery, kale leaves, and wild chervil.

Twin Sisters olive oil
Maldon sea salt
wild garlic with roots intact
tiny fennel with roots intact
tiny celery leaves
Tuscan kale leaves
wild chervil pluches

summer squash conserva

The most underrated and misused vegetable on the planet is summer squash. It is nutty, complex, and unctuous when properly handled. In this play on canned anchovies, we cook down the summer squash slowly and then hang it to remove any excess liquid. We fill a can with the conserva and top it with lightly thickened olive oil, finishing it all with local anchovies and summer herbs.

SERVES 4

SQUASH CONSOMMÉ

200 grams | about 1 ¹/₂ cups diced
    summer squash
25 grams | 2 tablespoons diced tomatoes
5 grams | 2 teaspoons minced garlic
3 kilograms | about 3 quarts water
225 grams | 8 ounces ice
2.5 grams | 1 tablespoon thyme leaves
2.5 grams | 2 tablespooons oregano leaves
2.5 grams | 2 tablespoons summer
    savory leaves
sel gris
tomato water (page 286)

YELLOW SQUASH CONSERVA

50 grams | ¹/₄ cup extra virgin olive oil
20 grams | 2 tablespoons sliced shallot
20 grams | 2 tablespoons minced garlic
6 | Gold Bar squashes, diced
kosher salt
Twin Sisters olive oil

FRESH CURDS

1.9 kilograms | 8 cups whole milk
476 grams | 2 cups heavy cream
238 grams | 1 cup buttermilk (page 284)
22 grams | 1 ¹/₂ tablespoons freshly squeezed
    lemon juice
kosher salt

TEXTURED OLIVE OIL

100 grams | ¹/₂ cup Twin Sisters olive oil
3 grams | 1 teaspoon glice

TOMATO PUREE

400 grams | 3 cups diced red tomatoes
kosher salt
sherry vinegar

FOR THE SQUASH CONSOMMÉ:

Prepare an ice bath. Combine the squash, tomatoes, garlic, and water in a large stockpot. Add the ice and place over high heat. Once the ice melts and the liquid has reached 160°F (71°C), remove from the heat and add the thyme, oregano, and summer savory. Nest immediately in the ice bath to cool. Refrigerate in an airtight container for 24 hours, then strain through a very fine cloth filter. Season with sel gris and tomato water and refrigerate in the airtight container until needed.

FOR THE YELLOW SQUASH CONSERVA:

Heat a rondeau over low heat and add the extra virgin olive oil, shallot, and garlic. Sweat for about 6 minutes, just until fragrant. Add the squash and cover. Cook for 1 ¹/₂ hours, stirring occasionally to keep the squash from burning, until the pan is dry and the squash is very tender. Transfer to a heat-proof container and refrigerate to cool.

Transfer the squash mixture to a food processor and mix until smooth. Wrap the puree in cheese-cloth and place over a perforated hotel tray or other rack-topped pan. Top with a weight of no more than 900 grams (2 pounds) and refrigerate for 24 hours.

Remove from the cheesecloth and season with kosher salt and Twin Sisters oil. Fill 4 sardine-tin serving pieces halfway with the conserva and smooth the surface.

FOR THE FRESH CURDS:

Combine the milk, cream, buttermilk, and lemon juice in a bowl, then season with kosher salt. Pour into vacuum bags and seal on high. Cook the milk mixture in a hot-water bath set at 190°F (88°C) for 2 hours. Meanwhile, prepare an ice bath. Remove the bags from the bath and immerse immediately in the ice bath for 1 hour.

To set up a resting tray for the curds, place a colander above a container. Line the colander with a piece of cheesecloth and pour the curds into the colander. Wrap the entire setup in plastic wrap and store in the refrigerator for at least 6 hours or for up to 24 hours.

Prepare an ice bath. Transfer the strained curds to a blender and mix on medium speed for 30 seconds, until pureed. Strain through a chinois into a bowl, then nest the bowl in the ice bath to cool the puree. Season with kosher salt, then transfer to a squeeze bottle and refrigerate.

FOR THE TEXTURED OLIVE OIL:

Combine the oil and glice in a small saucepan and warm gently over low heat until the glice is melted. Pour evenly over the conserva and let set at room temperature.

FOR THE TOMATO PUREE:

Put the tomatoes in a food processor and mix until smooth. Transfer to a small rondeau, place over low heat, and cook, stirring occasionally, for 2 hours, until thickened. Once thickened, transfer to a blender and mix on high speed for 2 minutes, until the puree is smooth and shiny. Strain through a chinois into a bowl and season with kosher salt and vinegar. Transfer to a squeeze bottle and refrigerate until needed.

continued

FOR THE HERB PUREE:

Prepare an ice bath. Bring a saucepan filled with water to a boil over high heat and season with salt. Add the parsley and blanch for 30 seconds, then drain and shock in the ice bath. Remove the parsley from the ice bath, wrap in a piece of cheesecloth, and press out the excess water. Put the parsley in a blender with the thyme leaves and oregano and mix on high speed for 1 minute, until pureed. Slowly add just enough Ultra-Tex to begin thickening the puree. Strain through a chinois into a bowl, then nest the bowl in the ice bath to cool the puree. Season with kosher salt, transfer to a squeeze bottle, and store in the refrigerator until needed.

FOR THE YELLOW SQUASH BLOSSOM PUREE:

Prepare an ice bath. Bring a saucepan filled with water to a boil over high heat and season with salt. Add the squash peels and blanch for 2 minutes. Add the squash blossoms and blanch for 30 seconds more, then drain and shock in the ice bath. Remove the peels and blossoms from the ice bath, wrap in a piece of cheesecloth, and press out the excess water. Put the peels and blossoms in a blender and mix on high speed for about 2 minutes, until pureed. Add the olive oil and blend for 1 minute more. Strain through a chinois into a bowl, then nest the bowl in the ice bath to cool the puree. Season with kosher salt, transfer to a squeeze bottle, and store in the refrigerator until needed.

FOR THE FRESH ANCHOVIES:

Fillet the anchovies, then rinse under ice-cold running water. Bury the anchovy fillets in the salt for 30 minutes. Rinse the fillets again under running ice-cold water to remove the excess salt, then pat dry on paper towels.

Preheat the broiler to 500°F (260°C). Place the fillets, skin side up, on a sheet pan and warm slightly under the broiler for about 10 seconds, until the skin is blistered.

TO SERVE:

Arrange dots of the tomato, herb, squash blossom, and fresh curd purees in each of 4 bowls. Using a mandoline, shave the raw squash in different shapes, then dress the shavings with a small amount of the squash consommé, some Twin Sisters olive oil, and a little Maldon salt. Arrange the squash shavings, squash blossom strips, and anchovy fillets in a straight line next to the puree. Finish with the oregano and flowering thyme. Serve with the tin of summer squash conserva.

HERB PUREE

40 grams | 2 1/2 cups flat-leaf parsley leaves
20 grams | 1/2 cup thyme leaves
20 grams | 2/3 cup oregano leaves
Ultra-Tex 3
kosher salt

YELLOW SQUASH BLOSSOM PUREE

400 grams | about 3 cups gold bar squash
    peels, 1/4 inch thick
300 grams | 10.5 ounces squash blossoms
50 grams | 1/4 cup Twin Sisters olive oil
kosher salt

FRESH ANCHOVIES

4 | fresh anchovies
400 grams | 1 1/3 cups kosher salt

2 | summer squashes, mixed colors,
    for shaving
Twin Sisters olive oil
Maldon sea salt
2 | squash blossoms, cut lengthwise
    into strips
oregano leaves
flowering thyme

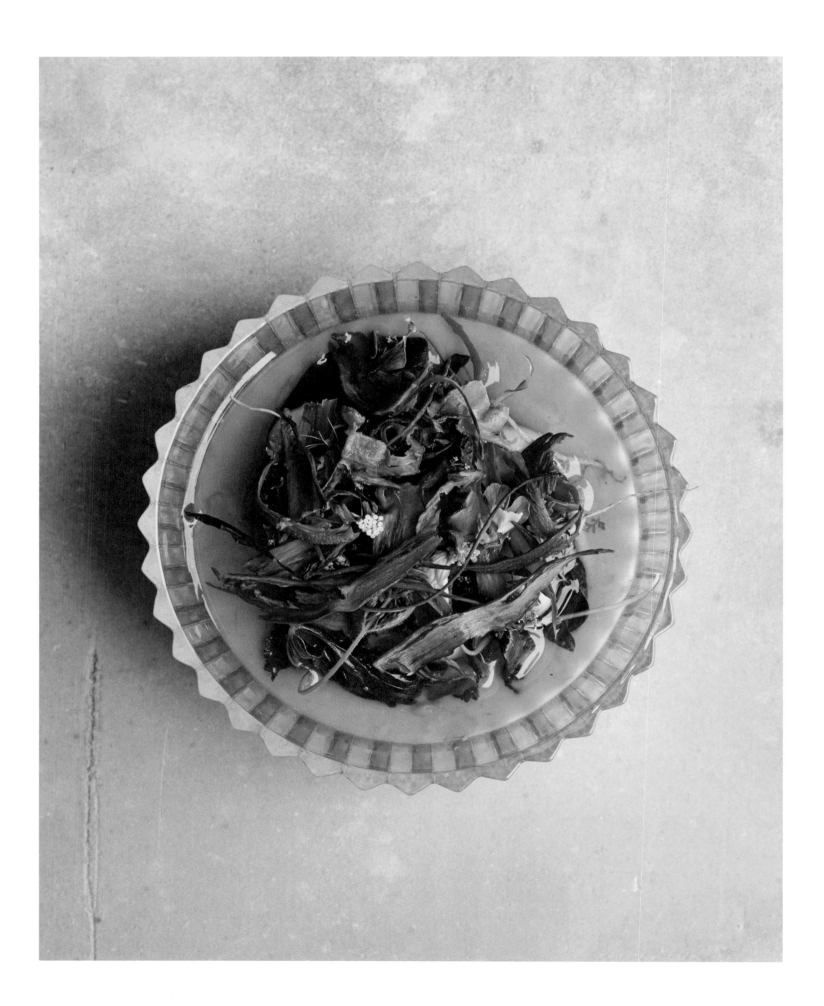

turnip garden dashi

Custard, katsuobushi, and broth—this incredibly intense and entirely vegetal array draws its umami character from smoking and drying the vegetables and braising the lovage leaves.

SERVES 4

CARROT KATSUOBUSHI

300 grams | 1 cup kosher salt
220 grams | 1 cup firmly packed brown sugar
230 grams | 1 cup tamari
3 | large carrots

SMOKED VEGETABLE DASHI

180 grams | 1 ¹/₂ cups diced carrots
200 grams | 1 ¹/₂ cups diced leeks
200 grams | 1 ¹/₂ cups diced turnips
75 grams | 2.5 ounces dried kombu
50 grams | 2 ounces dried matsutake mushrooms
1.8 kilograms | 8 cups water
white soy sauce
sel gris

TURNIP CHAWANMUSHI

700 grams | 5 cups diced turnips
1.5 kilograms | 6 ¹/₃ cups water
325 grams | 1 ¹/₃ cups eggs
8 grams | 1 ¹/₂ teaspoons white soy sauce
kosher salt

BRAISED LOVAGE AND TURNIP LEAVES

20 grams | 1 ¹/₂ tablespoons extra virgin olive oil
50 grams | ¹/₃ cup sliced shallots
100 grams | 4 cups lovage leaves without stems
250 grams | 6 cups turnip leaves without stems
250 grams | 1 cup radish juice
sel gris

BRAISED RADISHES, TURNIPS, AND CARROTS

600 grams | 2 ¹/₂ cups smoked vegetable dashi
    (recipe above)
8 | baby radishes with roots and leaves intact
8 | baby turnips with roots and leaves intact
8 | baby carrots with roots and leaves intact
27 grams | 2 tablespoons Twin Sisters olive oil
sel gris

8 | sun-spotted lovage buds
16 | wild chervil pluches with flowers
8 | phacelia flowers
8 | wild lupine buds

FOR THE CARROT KATSUOBUSHI:

Mix together the kosher salt, brown sugar, and tamari in a bowl to create a paste. Coat the carrots with the paste, place in an airtight container, and cure at room temperature for 36 hours. Gently rinse the cure from the carrots without disturbing the color that has been achieved through the curing process.

Hot smoke (see page 287) the carrots at 140°F (60°C) for 1 hour. Transfer the smoked carrots to a dehydrator tray and dehydrate at 130°F (54°C) for 12 hours, until dry but still pliable. Using a bonito shaver, shave the carrots lengthwise into thin strips. Refrigerate the strips in an airtight container.

FOR THE SMOKED VEGETABLE DASHI:

Cold smoke (see page 287) the carrots, leeks, and turnips for 30 minutes. Transfer the vegetables to a large pot and add the kombu, mushrooms, and water. Bring to a boil over high heat, then turn down the heat and steep at 140°F (60°C) for 2 hours.

Prepare an ice bath. Strain the dashi through a very fine cloth filter into a bowl and season with the white soy and sel gris. Nest the bowl in the ice bath to cool the dashi.

FOR THE TURNIP CHAWANMUSHI:

Combine the turnips and water in a large pot over high heat and bring to a boil. Turn down the heat and simmer at 160°F (71°C) for 2 hours. Strain through a very fine cloth filter and let cool to 100°F (38°C). Measure 975 grams (4 cups) of the broth and pour into a blender. Add the eggs and mix on low speed just until incorporated. Strain the egg base through a chinois into a pitcher. Season the base with the white soy and salt until flavorful.

Fill each of 4 oven-safe service vessels with 150 grams (²/₃ cup) of the chawanmushi base. Wrap tightly with plastic wrap and put into a steam oven set at 200°F (95°C) for 8 to 12 minutes, until the tops of the custards appear slightly set. Let cool in the refrigerator for at least 3 hours.

FOR THE BRAISED LOVAGE AND TURNIP LEAVES:

Combine the oil and shallots in a rondeau over medium heat and sweat the shallots for 4 minutes, until translucent. Add the lovage and turnip leaves and heat until they begin to wilt, then deglaze the pan with the radish juice and cook until the cooking liquid has evaporated. Season with sel gris, transfer to a shallow pan, and let cool in the refrigerator for 1 hour.

FOR THE BRAISED RADISHES, TURNIPS, AND CARROTS:

Heat the smoked vegetable dashi in a saucepan over high heat. Add the radishes, turnips, and carrots and poach at 180°F (82°C) for about 8 minutes, until the vegetables are tender. Season with the oil and sel gris. Hold in a warm place until needed.

TO SERVE:

Arrange the braised radishes, turnips, and carrots in a circular pattern on top of each turnip chawanmushi. Lay the braised lovage and turnip leaves in a composed pattern on top of the vegetables. Garnish each bowl with the carrot bonito, lovage buds, wild chervil, phacelia flowers, and lupine buds. Heat about 200 grams (³/₄ cup) of the smoked vegetable dashi and pour a small amount into each bowl.

tiny vegetables romaine vinaigrette

Here is a dish derived from a food memory: vegetables dipped into ranch dressing. That simple dish has been dressed up: vegetables from the garden, picked when young and tender, are embedded in a whipped romaine crème fraîche. An acidic "snow" and toasted bread create an appealing juxtaposition of temperature and texture.

SERVES 8

TOMATO VINAIGRETTE SNOW

237 grams | 1 cup tomato water (page 286)

3 grams | about 1 sheet bronze gelatin, bloomed in ice water and wrung gently of excess water

100 grams | 6 tablespoons sherry vinegar

8 grams | about 2 cloves garlic

5 grams | 1 ½ teaspoons diced shallot

2.5 grams | about 1 tablespoon thyme leaves

kosher salt

liquid nitrogen

TOASTED BREAD

150 grams | 1 ½ cups cubed levain bread (page 288)

6 grams | 1 ½ teaspoons Twin Sisters olive oil

Maldon sea salt

ROMAINE CRÈME FRAÎCHE

475 grams | 2 cups crème fraîche (page 283)

4.5 grams | 1 ½ sheets bronze gelatin, bloomed in ice water and wrung gently of excess water

100 grams | 3.5 ounces romaine leaves, stems removed

15 grams | 1 tablespoon freshly squeezed lemon juice

3 grams | ½ teaspoon kosher salt

4 | tiny radishes with tops

4 | tiny turnips with tops

4 | tiny carrots with tops

FOR THE TOMATO VINAIGRETTE SNOW:

Combine a small amount of the tomato water with the gelatin in a small saucepan over low heat just until the gelatin melts. Place the remaining tomato water along with the vinegar, garlic, shallot, and thyme in a blender and mix on medium speed for about 1 minute, until liquefied. Strain through a chinois into a container. Skim off and discard the foam from the surface and season with kosher salt. Stir the warm gelatin mixture into the liquid, then distribute among small (1-cup/240-milliliter) containers and freeze for about 2 hours, until frozen solid.

Carefully put the liquid nitrogen into a deep metal container (excessive changes in temperature or agitation of the liquid nitrogen may cause it to become volatile). Using a fine-tooth grater, grate the frozen vinaigrette into the liquid nitrogen. Pour the liquid nitrogen through a small strainer to remove the snow and store the snow in a dry plastic container in the freezer until needed.

FOR THE TOASTED BREAD:

Preheat the oven to 325°F (165°C). Line a sheet pan with parchment paper. Toss the bread with the olive oil and Maldon salt and spread in a single layer on the prepared sheet pan. Bake for 12 minutes, until golden brown. Let cool to room temperature, then transfer to a food processor and mix just to break up the bread into coarse crumbs. Store in an airtight container at room temperature.

FOR THE ROMAINE CRÈME FRAÎCHE:

Warm 30 grams (2 tablespoons) of the crème fraîche and the gelatin in a small saucepan over low heat just until the gelatin melts. Let cool to room temperature. Meanwhile, prepare an ice bath. Bring a pot filled with salted water to a boil over high heat. Add the romaine and blanch for 1 ½ minutes, then drain and transfer to the ice bath to cool for 2 minutes. Remove the romaine from the ice bath, wrap in a piece of cheesecloth, and press out the excess water.

Prepare a fresh ice bath. Put the romaine in a blender and mix on high speed until a smooth, thick puree forms, adding a little water if needed to achieve the correct consistency. Strain through a chinois into a bowl, then nest the bowl in the ice bath and stir occasionally to cool the puree. Measure 75 grams (⅓ cup) of the finished puree.

Put the remaining crème fraîche in the bowl of a stand mixer fitted with the whip attachment and whip on medium speed for about 4 minutes, until thick and airy. Slowly add the gelatinized crème fraîche, followed by the romaine puree. Continue mixing for about 5 minutes, until fully thickened. Season with the lemon juice and kosher salt. Transfer to a piping bag fitted with a small round tip and refrigerate for at least 1 hour before use.

TO SERVE:

Pipe a small amount of romaine crème fraîche into the bottom of 2 jars. Garnish each with a dusting of bread crumbs. Refresh the vinaigrette snow with more liquid nitrogen to separate the individual pieces of snow, then lay a small amount over the bread crumbs in each jar. (To discard the liquid nitrogen, carefully pour it back into its original container.) Arrange two pieces each of the radishes, turnips, and carrots in the jars and finish with more snow. Serve as a shared snack.

sunchoke granola sea lettuce

I love cereal—the interplay of crunchy and milk and the little entertaining bits in between. This sunchoke granola enables me to share the joy of cereal but still charge for it.

FOR THE SUNCHOKE GRANOLA:

Lightly scrub the sunchokes to remove any grit. Combine the water and calcium hydroxide in a large container, then submerge the sunchokes in the mixture. Let stand for 5 hours, stirring occasionally to redistribute the calcium.

Preheat the oven to 300°F (150°C). Rinse the sunchokes very well under running cold water (about 10 minutes). Arrange on a rack in a roasting pan and bake for 1 to 2 hours, until very soft but not too dark. The timing will depend on the size. Let cool to room temperature, then cut in half lengthwise. Using a spoon, scrape the flesh from each sunchoke half, being careful to maintain the original size of each half. Discard the flesh and arrange the cleaned skins on dehydrator trays. Dehydrate the skins at 115°F (46°C) for 8 to 10 hours, until completely dry.

Pour the oil to a depth of 4 inches (10 centimeters) into a deep fryer or deep, heavy pot and heat to 375°F (190°C). Working in batches, add the skins to the hot oil and fry for 15 seconds, until golden brown. Transfer to paper towels to drain and season with salt.

When all of the skins have been fried, once again preheat the oven to 300°F (150°C). Combine the sunchoke skins, sea lettuce, and egg whites in a large bowl and toss to coat the skins, mixing thoroughly to ensure that every piece is well coated. Evenly distribute the skins on a silicone baking mat and bake for 10 minutes, until crispy. Let cool to room temperature, then store in an airtight container with silica gel packets at room temperature.

FOR THE BRAISED SUNCHOKES:

Season the sunchokes with the olive oil and salt, transfer to a vacuum bag, and seal on high. Cook the sunchokes in a steam oven at 200°F (95°C) for 12 to 15 minutes, until very tender. Let cool to room temperature in the bag, then remove from the bag and break each sunchoke into smaller pieces along its natural seams. Refrigerate in an airtight container.

FOR THE SUNCHOKE MILK:

Combine the sunchokes, milk, and cream in a saucepan and bring just to a boil over high heat. Remove from the heat and let stand for 30 minutes. Meanwhile, prepare an ice bath. Strain the mixture through a chinois into a bowl and discard the solids. Nest the bowl in the ice bath to cool the milk. Season with salt and vinegar, cover, and refrigerate until serving.

TO SERVE:

Arrange a small amount of the sunchoke granola and braised sunchoke on each of 4 spoons. Garnish with the roe and sweet clover. Pour a small amount of the milk into the bottom of each of 4 bowls and rest a spoon across the top of each bowl.

SERVES 4

SUNCHOKE GRANOLA

900 grams | about 2 pounds large sunchokes

3.8 kilograms | about 4 quarts water

80 grams | 1/3 cup calcium hydroxide

20 grams | 3 tablespoons sea lettuce, dehydrated at 125°F (52°C) for 12 hours, then finely ground

100 grams | 1/3 cup egg whites

rice bran oil, for deep-frying

kosher salt

BRAISED SUNCHOKES

4 | small sunchokes, peeled

28 grams | 2 tablespoons extra virgin olive oil

kosher salt

SUNCHOKE MILK

100 grams | 3/4 cup peeled and chopped sunchokes

500 grams | 2 cups whole milk

700 grams | 3 cups heavy cream

Maldon sea salt

sherry vinegar

10 grams | 0.3 ounce brook trout roe

12 | sweet clover leaves

trout yellow beets forgotten herbs

This trout dish features some of the more esoteric herbs from the garden—herbs that once played a prominent role in the making of absinthe and other liquors and in the patent medicines of an earlier time. The trout is cured, grilled, and then served with a trompe l'oeil of beets and peaches. The "forgotten herbs" are pressed and dried, creating an obscuring canopy of leaves and stems.

SERVES 6

TROUT

900 grams | 2 pounds McFarland Springs
    rainbow trout (roughly 1 fish)
1 kilogram | 3 ¹/₂ cups kosher salt
600 grams | 4 cups fennel bulbs,
    in small pieces

WHIPPED TROUT CRÈME FRAÎCHE

150 grams | 5.3 ounces trout reserved from
    the cured trout, skin removed
300 grams | 1 ¹/₃ cups crème fraîche
    (page 283)
kosher salt

ROASTED YELLOW BEETS

2 kilograms | 6 ³/₄ cups kosher salt
6 | small yellow beets

PEACHES

800 grams | 5 ¹/₄ cups yellow peaches,
    in small pieces
200 grams | 1 cup sugar
1 gram | ¹/₄ teaspoon xanthan gum
120 grams | ¹/₂ cup water
2 grams | ¹/₂ teaspoon ascorbic acid
2 | ripe yellow peaches

FOR THE TROUT:

To remove the fillets from the trout, use a knife to trace around the outer edge of each fillet, then cut the fillets from the trout. Remove the bones that surround the belly portion and discard.

Combine half of the salt and the fennel in a food processor and mix until the fennel is completely pulverized. Transfer to a bowl, add the remaining salt, and stir to mix. Bury the trout fillets in the salt mixture and refrigerate for 20 minutes. Prepare an ice bath. Remove the fillets from the salt mixture and submerge them in the ice water to halt the curing process. Remove from the ice bath and pat dry on paper towels.

Cut the fillets into square portions each weighing about 60 grams (2 ounces). Reserve all of the remaining tail pieces and any other pieces that are too small or not the appropriate size for use in the trout crème fraîche. You will need 150 grams (5.3 ounces). Store the square trout portions on ice in a metal container in the refrigerator.

FOR THE WHIPPED TROUT CRÈME FRAÎCHE:

Prepare an ice bath. Put the reserved trout and crème fraîche in a blender and mix on high speed for 2 minutes, until a smooth puree forms. Do not mix for much longer than 2 minutes or the puree may become grainy. Using a 60 milliliter (¹/₄ cup) ladle, pass the puree through a chinois placed over a bowl, then nest the bowl in the ice bath to cool the puree. Season with salt, transfer to a small squeeze bottle, refrigerate until ready to use.

FOR THE ROASTED YELLOW BEETS:

Preheat the oven 400°F (200°C). Layer half of the salt in a shallow pan. Pierce a few holes in each beet with a pair of tweezers or a paring knife. Lay the beets in the salt and cover with the remaining salt. Cover the pan with aluminum foil and roast for 25 minutes.

Transfer the beets to a wire rack and let rest for 1 hour. Using a paring knife, peel the beets, then cut the beets into small wedges. Refrigerate in an airtight container.

FOR THE PEACHES:

Combine the peach pieces and 100 grams (¹/₂ cup) of the sugar in a metal bowl. Cover the bowl tightly with plastic wrap, place over a pot of simmering water, and warm the peaches for 4 hours. Remove the bowl from over the water and strain the contents through a chinois into a blender. Discard the solids. With the blender running on the lowest speed, add the xanthan gum slowly so as not to aerate the syrup. Let the syrup cool for 2 hours, then skim off any foam that has formed on the surface.

Warm the water slightly, add the remaining 100 grams (¹/₂ cup) of sugar, and stir to dissolve. Let cool to room temperature, then stir in the ascorbic acid. Cut the whole peaches into wedges to resemble the beet wedges and peel the skin from each wedge. Immerse the wedges in the syrup and refrigerate.

continued

trout yellow beets forgotten herbs *continued*

FOR THE DRIED FORGOTTEN HERBS:

Preheat the oven to 300°F (150°C). Brush 2 sheets of parchment paper with the oil. Lay 1 sheet, coated side up, on a flat surface. Arrange the fennel fronds and rue, wormwood, and anise hyssop leaves on the paper and cover with the second sheet, coated side down. Place the stacked sheets between 2 full sheet pans. Toast for 8 minutes, until the herbs have dried completely. Transfer to dehydrator trays and store in a dehydrator set at 125°F (52°C) until ready to use.

TO SERVE:

Preheat the oven to 400°F (200°C). Heat the extra virgin olive oil in a cast-iron pan over medium heat. Add the trout portions, skin side down, and cook for 1 minute. Transfer the pan to the oven and roast for 3 minutes. Transfer the trout to a cutting board. Trim the sides of each trout portion and lay a portion in the center of each of 6 plates. Mix equal parts peach syrup and Twin Sisters olive oil in a small bowl. Marinate the peaches and beets in the syrup for 2 minutes, then place 3 peach wedges and 2 beet wedges on each plate. Add a couple of dots of trout crème fraîche to each plate and follow with the toasted herbs. Finish with the fennel flowers.

DRIED FORGOTTEN HERBS

40 grams | 3 tablespoons Twin Sisters olive oil
12 | wild fennel fronds
24 | rue leaves
20 | wormwood leaves
16 | anise hyssop leaves

15 grams | 1 tablespoon extra virgin olive oil
Twin Sisters olive oil
wild fennel flowers

pea and white chocolate salad

The gardens serve as the starting point for this dessert, a play on a sweet salad: the bowl, made of white chocolate, is seemingly smashed on the plate, its contents of tiny peas and pistachios spilling out.

SERVES 8

WHITE CHOCOLATE SORBET

270 grams | 9.5 ounces white chocolate
    pistoles (35 percent cacao)
440 grams | 1 3/4 cups water
80 grams | 2/3 cup nonfat milk powder
90 grams | 1/4 cup plus 3/4 teaspoon
    trimoline
10 grams | 2 1/2 teaspoons sugar
5 grams | 1 1/2 teaspoons sorbet stabilizer

WHITE CHOCOLATE GANACHE

680 grams | 1.5 pounds white chocolate
    pistoles (35 percent cacao)
240 grams | 1 cup heavy cream

PEA AND WHITE CHOCOLATE GANACHE

500 grams | 2 cups heavy cream
400 grams | 5 cups pea pods
10 grams | 1 1/2 teaspoons kosher salt
50 grams | 2 tablespoons plus 1 teaspoon
    liquid glucose
500 grams | 1 pound white chocolate
    (35 percent cacao), chopped

PISTACHIO PUREE

150 grams | 1 1/4 cups Sicilian pistachios
250 grams | 1 cup water
30 grams | 2 tablespoons pistachio oil
65 grams | 1/3 cup sugar
kosher salt

WHITE CHOCOLATE POWDER

130 grams | 4.5 ounces white chocolate
    (35 percent cacao), chopped
500 grams | 2 cups water
170 grams | 3/4 cup heavy cream
50 grams | 1/4 cup sugar
4 grams | 1/2 teaspoon liquid glycerin

FOR THE WHITE CHOCOLATE SORBET:

Combine the chocolate, water, milk powder, trimoline, sugar, and sorbet stabilizer in a large saucepan over medium heat. Bring slowly to a boil while whisking constantly. Allow the mixture to boil for 5 seconds, then strain through a chinois into a heatproof plastic container and let sit in the refrigerator for 24 hours. Pour the sorbet base into Pacojet canisters, making sure to fill just to the line on the canister. Freeze for 8 hours, then run through the Pacojet machine once. Store in the freezer for at least 4 hours before use.

FOR THE WHITE CHOCOLATE GANACHE:

Put the chocolate in a heatproof bowl. Put the cream in a saucepan and bring to a boil over high heat. Pour the cream over the chocolate and whisk together until smooth. Pour into a container, let cool to room temperature, and refrigerate until needed or freeze for up to 1 month.

FOR THE PEA AND WHITE CHOCOLATE GANACHE:

Pour the cream into a small saucepan and bring to a boil over medium heat. Pour the cream into a large heatproof plastic container. Add the pea pods and infuse in a warm place for 30 minutes. Strain the liquid through a chinois into a clean saucepan and discard the solids. Add the salt and glucose, place over high heat, and bring to a boil, stirring occasionally. Meanwhile, put the chocolate in a metal bowl. Once the cream mixture has boiled for 10 seconds, pour it over the chocolate. Using an immersion blender, mix on high speed until smooth. Strain the mixture through a chinois into a heatproof container with a lid. Cover and refrigerate for 12 hours, or store in the freezer for up to 1 month.

FOR THE PISTACHIO PUREE:

Put the pistachios in a blender. Combine the water, oil, and sugar in a small saucepan and bring to a boil over high heat, stirring occasionally. Remove from the heat, pour over the pistachios, and mix on high speed for 3 minutes. Season lightly with salt, then strain through a chinois into Pacojet canisters, making sure to fill just to the line on the canister. Freeze for 10 hours, then run through the Pacojet machine twice. Store in the refrigerator.

FOR THE WHITE CHOCOLATE POWDER:

Put the chocolate in a heatproof bowl. Combine the water, cream, sugar, and glycerin in a saucepan and bring to a boil over high heat, using a rubber spatula to incorporate the ingredients evenly. Allow the mixture to boil for 10 seconds, then pour over the chocolate. Use a whisk to emulsify the chocolate into the liquid. Pour into Pacojet canisters, filling just to the line on the canister, and freeze for 6 hours. Run through the Pacojet machine once. Store in the freezer until ready to use, or for up to 1 month.

continued

pea and white chocolate salad *continued*

FOR THE WHITE CHOCOLATE SHELL:

Heat the white chocolate ganache to 110°F (43°C) in a small saucepan. Transfer to a heatproof bowl, add the yogurt and cream, and mix until smooth. Carefully put the liquid nitrogen into a deep metal container (excessive changes in temperature or agitation of the liquid nitrogen may cause it to become volatile). Spray a 120 milliliter (1/2 cup) metal ladle with nonstick cooking spray. Dip it into the liquid nitrogen for 15 seconds and then into the ganache for 15 seconds. Repeat. Once the ladle is covered with two coats of ganache, dip the ladle back into the liquid nitrogen for 20 seconds. Using a kitchen torch, gently heat the inside of the ladle to loosen the shell. Carefully remove the shell by twisting it in one direction and the ladle in the other direction. When the shell is free, drop it back into the liquid nitrogen for 10 seconds, then transfer to a dry plastic container. Repeat to make 4 shells total. Cover the plastic container loosely and store in the freezer for up to 1 month. (To discard the liquid nitrogen, carefully pour it back into its original container.)

FOR THE LEMON-OLIVE OIL CAKE:

Preheat the oven to 325°F (165°C). Line a half sheet pan with a silicone baking mat. Put the trimoline, eggs, and sugar in a food processor and mix for 2 minutes, stopping to scrape down the sides of the processor bowl as needed, until the mixture is smooth and well incorporated. Sift together the flour, baking powder, and salt. With the processor running, slowly incorporate the flour mixture in three batches, mixing well after each addition. Then slowly add the oil, making sure it is fully absorbed into the batter. Finally, mix in the lemon zest.

Pour the batter into the prepared pan and smooth the surface. Bake for 20 to 25 minutes, until golden brown. Let cool in the pan at room temperature for 1 hour. Cut into 1-inch (2.5-centimeter) squares. Reserve at room temperature or store in an airtight container in the freezer for up to 1 month.

FOR THE OLIVE OIL JAM:

Combine the salt, trimoline, and glucose in a saucepan over medium heat and heat to 187°F (86°C). Meanwhile, put the eggs in a food processor and mix until blended. Prepare an ice bath. When the sugars have reached temperature, remove from the heat and, with the processor running, add the sugars to the eggs. As the mixture begins to thicken, slowly add the oil. Pour the mixture into a heatproof bowl and nest in the ice bath until the jam is cool. Transfer to a squeeze bottle and store in the refrigerator.

FOR THE FRESH PEAS:

Prepare an ice bath. Combine the water and kosher salt in a saucepan and bring to a boil over high heat. Add the peas and blanch for 2 minutes, then drain, transfer to the ice bath, and let cool for 2 minutes. Transfer the peas to paper towels and remove and discard the outer shell from each pea.

In a small bowl, combine the lemon juice, olive oil, and sugar and stir until the sugar dissolves. Dress the peas with the lemon vinaigrette and season with Maldon salt.

TO SERVE:

Place a small amount of the pea and white chocolate ganache in the center of each plate. Arrange 3 pieces of the cake around the ganache on each plate. Remove the white chocolate shells from the freezer and break each one into 3 pieces. Prop a piece against each piece of the cake. Scatter the fresh peas, freeze-dried peas, pistachios, tendrils, and flowers around the plate to form a landscape. Place alternating dots of the pistachio puree and the olive oil jam on the plate. Finish with a quenelle of the white chocolate sorbet and a dusting of the white chocolate powder.

WHITE CHOCOLATE SHELL

200 grams | 1 cup white chocolate ganache (page 91)
200 grams | 3/4 cup cultured yogurt (page 284)
200 grams | 3/4 cup heavy cream
liquid nitrogen

LEMON-OLIVE OIL CAKE

84 grams | 1/4 cup trimoline
200 grams | about 4 eggs
204 grams | 1 cup sugar
240 grams | 2 cups all-purpose flour
9.6 grams | 2 teaspoons baking powder
3.6 grams | 3/4 teaspoon kosher salt
240 grams | 1 cup agrumato lemon olive oil
grated zest of 1 lemon

OLIVE OIL JAM

8 grams | 2 teaspoons kosher salt
100 grams | 1/3 cup trimoline
100 grams | 1/3 cup liquid glucose
87 grams | about 5 egg yolks
500 grams | 2 1/3 cups Twin Sisters olive oil

FRESH PEAS

1.9 kilograms | 8 cups water
120 grams | 1/3 cup kosher salt
110 grams | 1/2 cup English shelling peas, shucked
10 grams | 2 teaspoons freshly squeezed lemon juice
15 grams | 1 tablespoon Twin Sisters olive oil
5 grams | 1 teaspoon sugar
Maldon sea salt

freeze-dried peas
Sicilian pistachios
12 | pea tendrils
12 | pea flowers

THE ARTISANS

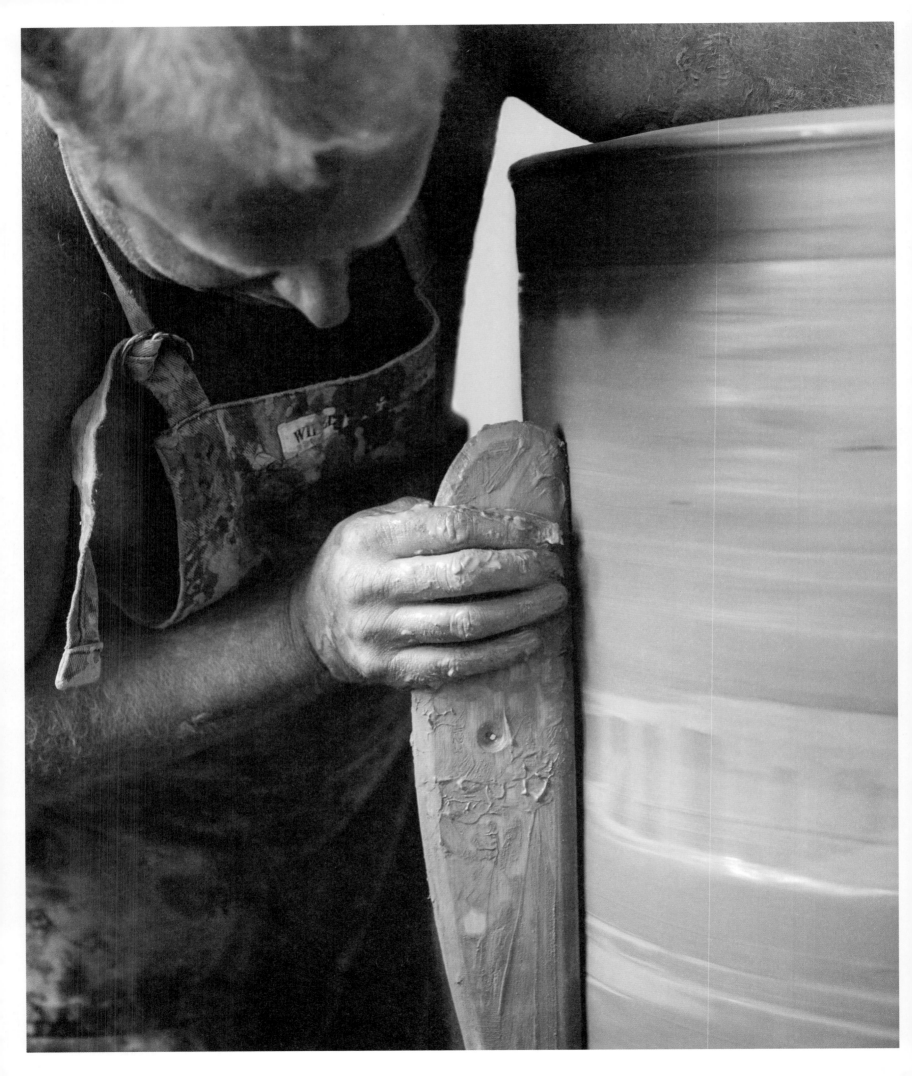

Without extraordinary ideas there can be no extraordinary results.

—KITAOJI ROSANJIN

I remember standing in a plate showroom in San Francisco shortly after starting work at The Restaurant at Meadowood, preparing to spend a sizable amount of money on Hering china. As I studied the displays of stunning plates and bowls that I had seen at other restaurants, I felt surprisingly indecisive. I hemmed and hawed, and then I left. Driving back home at dusk, I entered the part of the valley just before Yountville where the vista suddenly widens and the mountains rise up on either side. I was overwhelmed by a contemplative silence that seemed far too dramatic for the simple question of whether or not to buy that china. I began thinking about the role of the plate in the dining experience, which led me to consider the role of the valley in the creation of that plate, the role I was hoping to play within the valley, and so on.

What is more elegant? An expensive plate made beautifully in a factory in Germany or a handmade piece designed and created by a skilled artisan? This question raised even bigger ones. What did I want this restaurant to be? What kind of chef did I want to be? There was the path that others had forged and tread, where white porcelain begets nicer white porcelain and refinement leads to further refinement. But is there a cost to following the expected path, and what is the end result? Propelled as I always am to improve, improve, improve, the only probable end that I could see by not considering other options was to be an imitator. As I drove through the valley thinking way too much about plates, I realized that I could be great in the manner that greatness is defined by others—by checking the right boxes and covering all the requisite bases—or I could do something else.

I stared out the window at the darkening hills and I thought about the valley surrounding me. People often ask me how Napa influences my work, and while they are probably looking for a simple answer, the truth is decidedly more ephemeral. A place looks a certain way over the course of a year: the grasses and vines grow from a sparse brown in winter to a vibrant green in summer and then slowly change to the oranges and reds of autumn; the rivers swell and recede; the sky is whitish blue in the summer heat and takes on a pallid absence of light in the rainy season. This place has textures, at times craggy, worn, verdant, and soft. These visuals impress themselves on my mind as surely as a favorite passage sticks in my memory. As a chef, I communicate by what I lay on a dining room table. That's why I went to see Lynn.

BEGINNINGS

I took a winding road up Mount Veeder through the dark, moss-covered redwoods, down rows of walnut trees, and past a vineyard to Lynn Mahon's small studio. This drive, with Charlie in the backseat (always!), was the first step toward the creation of something that would eventually mirror the place where I now lived.

The bowl began as a thin piece of clay, formed into a small primitive vessel on Lynn's knee, and finished in a cracked *shino* glaze. I met Lynn through his wife, Anniki, a colleague of mine who had spoken of Lynn's work and his experience studying with the famed ceramist Peter Voulkos. Lynn is quick with a smile and quicker with a hug, and his studio always smells of the fireplace burning in the corner, the ash from which he uses to create texture on his dishes.

The knee bowl was our first foray together; it speaks in form to something at once primitive and pure, as if to say, "This is what a bowl is." That bowl was a beginning; it represented a different look and a different way of looking. This is where our avenue to originality would start at The Restaurant. We were going to try to be what others couldn't be, if only because they weren't working in this particular valley at this moment in time.

Lynn and I have worked together for several years now, designing the plates and serving pieces that contribute to the overall aesthetic of the restaurant. Sometimes I come to Lynn with a dish in mind and he helps design the vessel. At other times, one of his plates serves as a source of inspiration for a recipe. The date plate is a perfect example. A ceramic slab of browns and whites, it had the color palette of a desert, so we began experimenting with ingredients found in that clime: dates and hearts of palm (see page 155). At this point in our collaboration, Lynn knows my weak points. He'll leave some beautiful sample plates in the restaurant kitchen one afternoon; more often than not they are slab pieces, rough-hewn and stunning. I'll plate a dish on them that evening, study them on the dining-room tables, and ask for consensus from the cooks. By morning, I will have called Lynn to ask for thirty more. He has no shame.

I still often travel up Mount Veeder to see Lynn. His family has grown, as has mine; Charlie is bigger but still can't handle the winding roads without occasionally getting sick. In many ways, those twenty-minute drives are a needed respite from the stress

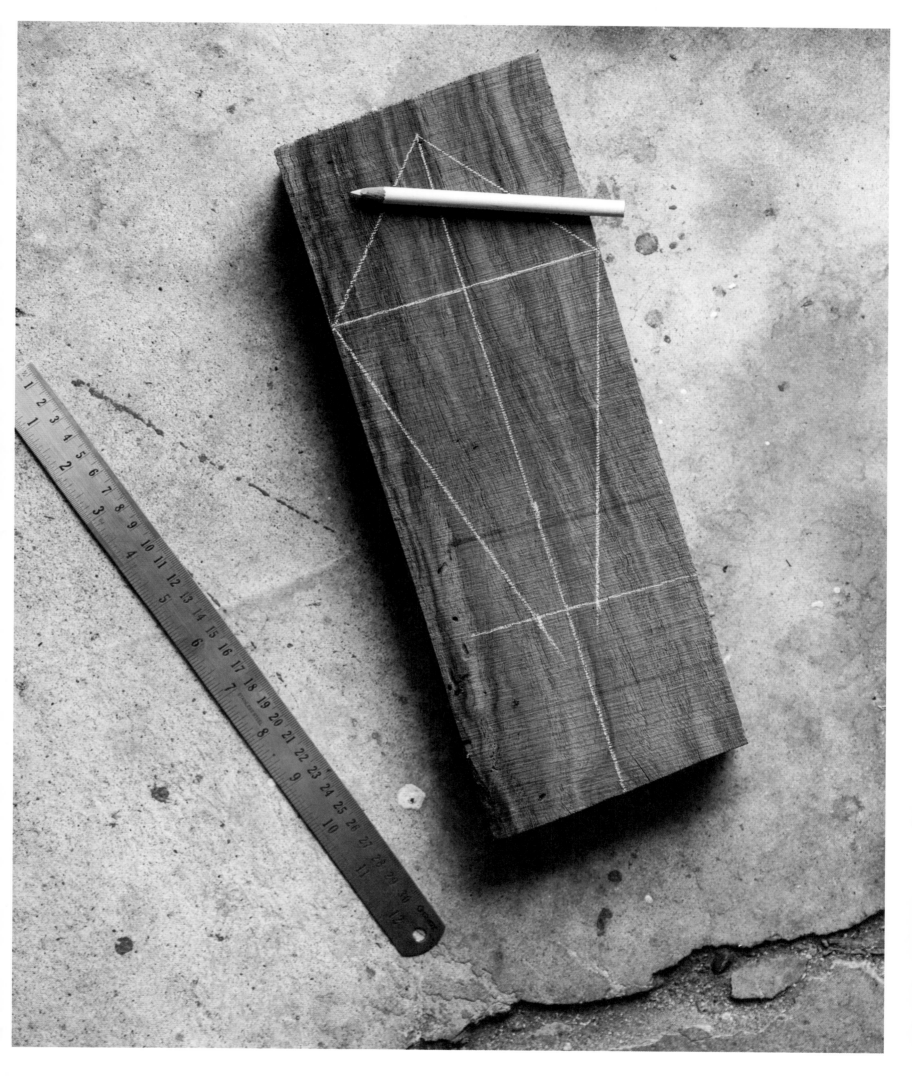

of running a kitchen, so I welcome Lynn's texts that say he has something to show me. Most important, my work with Lynn introduced me to a Napa filled with artists and artisans who, like Lynn, create beauty not from soil and grape must but from ash, clay, and wood. After that first experience of the knee bowl, I started traveling to the studios of these artists, hidden in various corners of the valley, down small overgrown lanes and atop overhanging hills. What I discovered is that these brilliant craftspeople were as thrilled to have the attention and inspiration that our partnership provided as I was to fulfill a vision for the restaurant that was slowly taking form.

Ceramists Nikki and William Callnan came to visit us at the restaurant one day, having heard about our interest in collaborating with artisans in the valley. The Callnans live and work in the town of Angwin, in the hills above Saint Helena, and like us, they are involved in the community, working with Nimbus Arts (cotenants with the Saint Helena Montessori School, see page 38) to teach young people about the joys of art.

On that first visit, they carried boxes dirtied with dried clay and overflowing with newspaper packing material. Among the pieces they laid out was one they called *earth bowl*. The craggy-shaped vessel sat atop three small feet and featured a jagged, organic-looking edge reminiscent of wood and stone and the wilds. It possessed both a graceful lightness and the solidity of clay. Seeing their brown earth bowl on our dining table, a compelling juxtaposition between linen and stone, completely upended my conception of elegance. We have been a different restaurant ever since.

The earth bowl was the beginning of a collaboration that now encompasses an enormous variety of vessels: coffee-service pieces, bread plates, tiny raw clay vases for broths, large "solar" plates for a yogurt dish. I get to be a frequent visitor at their studio, where their wiry dog runs loose among the work and their young son amuses himself with wet clay. The Callnans, along with a number of other talented local artists, continue to contribute their artistry and friendship to the restaurant.

PARTNERS

Our artisans help us both sharpen our language and exponentially increase the sensory impact of our food. When we are at our most successful, the food and its vessel are inseparable in look and texture. Through each course of a meal, the food and its serving piece become a complete vignette—a fully formed idea. I'm not an artist, but I get to work with them. It is my honor to showcase the talents of others. I get to create a self-contained world, the snow globe, as we refer to it, where talent and creative energies flourish. I feel a responsibility not only to find partners whose work makes sense within the context of the restaurant but also to be inspired by the work of others. All of us players are better off for the involvement of those who work alongside us. The contour of a bowl or plate, the sketch of a new shape as the spark of an idea—these things give us a chance to be great by offering the next possible rung on that creative ladder. We offer ideas to the artisans, and they inspire new ideas in us. We exist, together, in this sphere of inspiration. We have all been able to witness this rising and bask in the success of our shared endeavor. Cooks stand over potters and learn how to make bowls; guests fall in love with the shape of an earthenware plate and chopsticks made of ashed madrone. Servers become ambassadors for the work of artists, and our sphere of inspiration grows larger. A restaurant becomes busy. Photographers document its activity. We write these words. People enter the sphere and contribute to it. The sphere, in time, contributes to them.

When I met Richard Carter, I realized we needed a bigger sphere.

RICHARD CARTER

Famed artist and potter, Obi-Wan of high-temperature wood firing, gatekeeper of a nineteenth-century homestead and the legacy of the family born and raised there, Richard is an artist in the bulkiest and most emotive of mediums. He works with clay and stone and their imperfections to produce pieces that are at once romantic and political. He hand digs small rocks from the Sierras and strategically places them in clay spheres, which causes natural fissures during firing. And he is famous for his large tiles with melted metal pouring from them. His kiln firings are weeklong, almost shamanistic gatherings, where soda and salt are dumped into the fires to create natural, unpredictable, glorious glazes. Pieces aren't pulled from his kilns when they cool down. They are excavated from the ashes.

Richard's home has long been a Mecca for aspiring artists who participate in his residency program. A one-time student of the Kansas City Art Institute, Richard is like a celestial object, orbited by the best and brightest in this community and throughout the country. They gather to eat (in the 1980s, Richard was a cook at the original French Laundry) at a picnic table just beyond the old home where scores of children were born and raised for a century and a half. Red hawks fly overhead. Old mortar stones where native people crushed acorns lie near the small creek that pools on the property, serving as relief during the interminably hot summer months, as it has for centuries.

Richard is an artist with whom I share the most important creative trait of all: a sense of wonder. He relishes his reputation as mentor, teacher, and volatile curmudgeon, and refused my initial entreaties to discuss making plates for the restaurant. After several unsuccessful attempts, he now allows me to visit his property often, to participate in kiln firings, and to enjoy the vibe of an artist's residence. Our collaboration has grown to encompass much more than restaurant plates. He has become a historian of the valley and a teacher of the importance of clay. Richard has taught me what clay is, and what the role of ceramics has traditionally been among the chefs of Japan. We discuss *wabi-sabi*, the aesthetic of the imperfect, and Rosanjin, the potter who famously scoffed at Picasso and believed that to serve food on average china was to demonstrate an average character. We have pored over pictures of bowls, both modern and ancient, to understand the full potential for beauty that can come from simple shapes that were historically made (as Richard likes to emphasize) by serfs and slaves. Richard somehow completes the circle for me. He lends a maturity to my thinking and makes me appreciate all the more the artisans with whom I work. While Richard has yet to create vessels for The Restaurant, together we are plotting a path for the future—a nascent collaboration that will distill the ethos of all of the partnerships to date.

WOOD AND FIRE

We have numerous other collaborators at The Restaurant. Rachel Riser, who was originally the restaurant florist, got caught up in the frenzy of our new artisan partnerships and is now a contributing artisan herself. She uses burnt wood as a medium, crafting elegant and masculine serving pieces from the remains of local madrone trees. She has fashioned chopsticks and nests for bowls, and large stumps that hold thin crackers served as a canapé. There is a sleekness to her work that paints natural and rustic elements with a coat of modernity.

Brett Van Natta applies his years as a prosthetics maker to wood serving pieces. Influenced by the surrounding woods of the Mayacamas Mountains, he incorporates earthy textures in his work in clever and stylish ways. He constructs pieces from local walnut that come alive at the table, like a birthday box that springs open when the lid is removed to reveal an individual cake and a card. And his small boxes inspired a series of dishes we call forest *mignardises* (page 125). He greets our absurd requests with a smile and a thank you, his enthusiasm for the possibilities of wood matched by our own.

We have a new glass blower who will contribute his skills, and a merchant of cloth who will soon curate the materials for our food and tables. The sphere has no limits.

CLAY AND COMMERCE

Trends in food have a million mothers, and although I'm sure we have expropriated ideas and techniques from others, I believe the work we have done with our artisans truly stands apart. The same potters who began making plates for The Restaurant now struggle to keep up with demand from our contemporaries, and it is with great pleasure that I watch this unfold. We have done what we promised—from that first knee bowl to the plate lines currently in development—which was to ask these incredible artists to share their abilities with us so we could help share their work with others. The world now knocks on their studio doors.

The interplay between ceramics and food seems fitting to me, as the clay and crops both come from the earth. Beautiful things transcend style and trends and feel as though they have existed forever. Nothing is more timeless than beautiful pottery and thoughtful food. This melding of craft and commerce—that distinctly American notion of creative entrepreneurship exemplified by our artisan collaborators—lies at the heart of Napa Valley. The commingling of sediment and sweat is what brought the world to the valley's doorstep. These talented people and their work will contribute to the soul of this valley in the years to come, and we will continue our efforts to tell the story that a simple plate inspired.

the new luxury

It used to be that a restaurant earning three Michelin stars was expected to populate its menu with ingredients traditionally associated with luxury. Foie gras and truffles and caviar and lobster were featured as justification for the prices and in keeping with the expectations of diners who frequented such establishments. Although my focus is primarily on the ingredients of Napa, I continue to work with truffle purveyors and seek out the best caviar, not because I feel the need to accommodate an expectation but rather because these ingredients have historical value. I see The Restaurant as existing within the traditions of the grand restaurants of the past. There is something celebratory about the experience of eating at such places. They offer drama and elegance and traditions of luxury that transcend any prevailing trends. I am thus less academic in my approach to local cooking than some.

My predecessors changed the paradigm of luxury well before I began cooking. My friend Michel Troisgros's father and uncle began their *nouvelle* cuisine at the eponymous Maison Troisgros in Roanne, France, and ushered in an era of local and light; chef Alain Passard at Arpège in Paris was the first to embrace vegetables at a Michelin three-star level; and the young Turks of Scandinavia have essentially done away with the idea that fine cuisine must be built on a French foundation. These chefs made it easier for me to enter high-end cooking from a different place—and with fewer constraints.

Specificity is the new luxury, and it comes with an appropriate price point. Focusing too closely on the economics of food is debasing to the craft. No one pulls apart the individual pieces of a Maserati or a Birkin bag or a Carolina Herrera gown to determine whether each part, stitch, and piece of fabric justifies the overall price. I like to believe that cooking at the highest levels deserves the same appreciation. We are well past believing that this food is purely for sustenance, just as it's a given that a Maserati is more than simply a mode of transportation. The truth is that specificity costs money.

At The Restaurant, we grow our own vegetables to ensure we have the exact variety we want, harvested when we want by people who share our fervor for quality. Our staff goes willingly into the wilds in search of ingredients that offer a unique flavor and a connection to a shared local history. We spend hours working with our artisan partners designing handmade plates and serving dishes. We have spent years on this food before the dirt is washed off the vegetables or the plates have cooled from their time in the kiln. If we are improving, it is due to the careful sourcing of particular products and the relentless attention paid to those products. We find the best squab and then agonize over how to showcase its most essential flavor. The sturgeon goes in coals, the cod goes in steam, the potato gets cooked in beeswax (which is nearly as expensive as truffles!), and the carrot goes in clay. Specificity begins with the food, extends to its vessel, and then finally rests in the hands of our schooled and generous service staff. This output of time and energy—which cannot be quantified—is (if guests appreciate the stitching) a powerful means of conveying our love and appreciation. This is the stuff of luxury.

That said, it is also true that just because it is expensive for me doesn't mean it has value to you. If you want a steak, then the cost associated with my carrots isn't enough to give them value to you. The same is true of all luxury items. I don't know anything about cars, so I wouldn't buy a Ferrari because something simpler would do for me. Beyond the status statement made by owning certain things, the value comes in appreciating craftsmanship and in its relevance to your priorities.

Food is more difficult to characterize because it ultimately involves something essential: nourishment. No matter how carefully a meal is sourced, prepared, and served, most would agree that it's silly to leave a restaurant hungry. As a chef, I'm tethered to the pragmatic to a degree that few luxury products are, and as a result, the perception of value still plays a role. Traditionally, caviar and lobster say *expensive* while a carrot does not. I'd like to shift perceptions about food so it's less about price (what it costs me to produce) and more about value (how delicious it is and the care and concern that went into its growing, cooking, and serving).

How do I talk about the wonderful garden and the design of the plates without the conversation devolving into absurdity ("Here is your single leaf, sir, waved through mountain air . . .")? I believe the answer is through honesty, passion, and a humble articulation of the underpinnings of our work. We can only invite guests in and share our process with them. An advanced degree in food blogs shouldn't be compulsory to appreciate the beauty of one of our meals any more than an understanding of the mechanics of a car engine is required to enjoy the ride. If as chefs we don't lose sight of our roles as hosts and narrators first and "artists" second, then we can reasonably hope that a new paradigm of luxury will take root and flourish well beyond New York and Copenhagen and Napa. Absent this humility, we will be waving our single leaves to rooms filled only with bloggers and flashing cameras.

yogurt black sesame shiso

William and Nikki designed these bowls for this yogurt amuse-bouche. A larger bowl holds a black, craggy base of small river rocks and fruit blossoms; a smaller bowl holds house-made yogurt and garnishes of tiny black sesame rocks, dots of umeboshi, and piles of shiso that mirror the rest of the dish—Zen and the art of cultured milk.

SERVES 8 TO 10

WHIPPED YOGURT
100 grams | $^1/_2$ cup heavy cream
7.5 grams | 3 sheets silver gelatin,
    bloomed in ice water and wrung gently
    of excess water
800 grams | 3 $^1/_4$ cups cultured yogurt
    (page 284)

BLACK SESAME ROCKS
265 grams | about 1 $^1/_3$ cups sugar
100 grams | $^1/_2$ cup water
465 grams | 3 $^1/_4$ cups black sesame seeds
50 grams | $^1/_4$ cup whole buckwheat
10 grams | 1 tablespoon perilla seeds

UMEBOSHI PUREE
275 grams | 1 $^1/_4$ cups umeboshi plums, pitted

river rocks
tiny branches
30 grams | 2 tablespoons shiso salt
60 | red and green shiso leaves, cut
    into chiffonade

FOR THE WHIPPED YOGURT:
Combine the cream and gelatin in a small saucepan over low heat and heat just until the gelatin melts. Transfer the mixture to a blender, add the yogurt, and mix on high speed for 1 minute, until a smooth puree forms. Pour into a shallow metal pan and place in the freezer for 1 hour, until the surface of the yogurt begins to freeze.

Transfer the yogurt to the bowl of a stand mixer fitted with the whip attachment and mix on high speed for about 8 minutes, until the yogurt thickens (it should look like whipped cream). Place 2 spoonfuls (about 90 grams/$^3/_4$ cup) of the yogurt on the bottom of each of 8 small bowls. Cover lightly with plastic wrap and refrigerate for at least 2 hours, until the yogurt has set up.

FOR THE BLACK SESAME ROCKS:
Combine the sugar and water in a heavy saucepan over medium heat and heat to 239°F (115°C) without stirring. Using a wooden spoon, stir in the black sesame seeds, buckwheat, and perilla seeds. Increase the heat to high and mix quickly to ensure that the sugar crystallizes. Transfer the mixture to a clean saucepan. Place the pan over high heat and mix the contents constantly for about 3 minutes, until the sugar has melted completely and the seeds and buckwheat have formed into clusters and look shiny. Turn the clusters out onto a silicone baking mat and spread them out evenly. Let cool at room temperature for 1 hour. Store the rocks in an airtight container with silica gel packets at room temperature.

FOR THE UMEBOSHI PUREE:
Prepare an ice bath. Place the plums in a blender and mix on high speed for 3 minutes, until a smooth puree forms. Using a small ladle, strain through a chinois placed over a bowl, then nest the bowl in the ice bath to cool the puree. Transfer to a squeeze bottle and refrigerate.

TO SERVE:
Arrange the river rocks and tiny branches in 8 large bowls. Set the bowls of whipped yogurt on top of the rocks. Place dots of the umeboshi puree and a light dusting of shiso salt on the surface of each yogurt portion. Break the black sesame rocks into small clusters and put 4 or 5 pieces on each yogurt portion. Top each yogurt portion with a loose nest of the shiso chiffonade.

bouillon of roasted meats

No other vessel has so directly led to the creation of a dish as this simple bowl and pourer. There is something so poetically essential in these pieces that, when seen halfway through a meal in the guise of a bouillon course, they serve to reinvigorate the senses—reaffirming the spirit of simplicity that exists, a bit more hidden, in all of the courses that precede it and in those that will follow. Clay and essence of fire roasted meats, consumed in that intuitive manner of hands together cradling the warming clay and bringing broth to mouth.

SERVES 10

BOUILLON

460 grams | 1 pound beef oxtail, cut into
4-inch (10-centimeter) sections

900 grams | 2 pounds veal breast cut into
4-inch (10-centimeter) sections

680 grams | 1.5 pounds duck frames, split in
half lengthwise

680 grams | 1.5 pounds chicken frames, split
in half lengthwise

6 kilograms | 6 ½ quarts chicken stock
(page 283)

200 grams | about 1 carrot, peeled and
halved lengthwise

300 grams | about 1 small yellow onion,
halved lengthwise

250 grams | about 2 celery stalks,
halved lengthwise

RAFT

170 grams | 6 ounces boneless skinless
chicken breasts

100 grams | ¾ cup diced carrots

150 grams | 1 cup diced yellow onion

100 grams | 1 cup diced celery

400 grams | 1 ⅔ cups egg whites

30 grams | ½ cup flat-leaf parsley leaves

Maldon sea salt

FOR THE BOUILLON:

Prepare a fire in a wood-burning oven. When the fire is at about 600°F (315°C), line two roasting pans with aluminum foil and place roasting racks into the oven. Arrange the oxtails, veal breast, duck frames, and chicken frames in the pans on the racks, spacing them about 1 inch (2.5 centimeters) apart. Roast for about 15 minutes, then rotate the pans and roast for 15 to 20 minutes longer, until the surface of the bones is evenly colored. Let cool at room temperature for about 2 hours. Meanwhile, arrange the carrot, onion, and celery in a roasting pan and place the pan on the rack. Roast for 7 to 8 minutes on each side, until deep brown. Let cool to room temperature.

In a large stockpot, combine the roasted meats, browned vegetables, and stock and bring to a boil over high heat. Turn down the heat so the liquid simmers at 180°F (82°C) and cook for 15 hours. Strain the stock through a very fine cloth filter into a clean stockpot. Place over medium heat and reduce gently by one-third. Meanwhile, prepare an ice bath. When the stock is ready, strain once more through a very fine cloth filter into a metal bowl, then nest the bowl in the ice bath to chill the stock.

FOR THE RAFT:

Combine the chicken, carrot, onion, celery, egg whites, and parsley in a food processor and mix for 3 minutes, until the ingredients are well incorporated. Put the chilled stock into a rondeau and add the mixture from the food processor. Whisk together until fully incorporated, then place the pan over high heat and bring the mixture to a boil as quickly as possible, stirring for the first 5 to 6 minutes to avoid scorching. When the mixture begins to boil, turn down the heat to a simmer and cook for 10 to 20 minutes, until the solids come together on the surface of the liquid, forming a raft. Lower the heat slightly and continue to simmer gently for 1 hour, until the clarification is complete.

Prepare an ice bath. Ladle the bouillon through a very fine cloth filter into a large metal bowl, then nest the bowl in the ice bath to cool the bouillon. Transfer to an airtight container and refrigerate for up to 4 days, or freeze 1 quart (1 liter) at a time in vacuum bags sealed on high then laid flat on a metal tray, for up to 1 month.

continued

FOR THE SHAVED BEEF FAT:

Cold smoke (see page 287) the beef suet for 1 hour. Combine the parsley, garlic, olive oil, and kosher salt in a blender and mix on high speed for 3 minutes to create a marinade. Rub the smoked beef with the marinade, transfer the beef to vacuum bags, and seal on high. Cook the beef suet in a hot-water bath set at 138°F (59°C) for 1 hour. Meanwhile, prepare an ice bath. Remove the bags and immerse them in the ice bath to cool for 2 hours.

Carefully put the liquid nitrogen into a deep metal container (excessive changes in temperature or agitation of the liquid nitrogen may cause it to become volatile). Using a fine-tooth grater, shave the beef fat into the liquid nitrogen and let sit for 15 seconds. Pour the liquid nitrogen through a small strainer to remove the shavings and store the shavings in a dry plastic container in the freezer. (To discard the liquid nitrogen, carefully pour it back into its original container.)

TO SERVE:

Heat 1 liter (about 1 quart) of the bouillon in a large pot over high heat. When it reaches 150°F (66°C), taste and adjust the seasoning, then pour into a carafe for serving. Mound a small amount of the shaved fat in each of 10 bowls. Garnish each bowl with a few minced chives, chive flowers, and garlic flower petals. Finish with 2 dots of sherry vinegar, then pour about 100 grams (½ cup) of hot broth into each bowl.

SHAVED BEEF FAT

225 grams | 8 ounces beef suet, cut into
 3-inch (7.5-centimeter) squares
30 grams | ½ cup flat-leaf parsley leaves
30 grams | 1 ounce garlic cloves
50 grams | ¼ cup extra virgin olive oil
7.5 grams | 1 ¼ teaspoons kosher salt
liquid nitrogen

5 grams | 1 ½ tablespoons minced chives
30 | chive blossoms
30 | garlic flower petals
sherry vinegar

rutabaga white truffle pecan maple

Rutabaga from the gardens in a crust of salt and soil—here is a humble vegetable prepared in an even more humble fashion. That simplicity is elevated with white truffle, maple, goat's milk, and wild pecans. The brown solar bowl by William and Nikki Callnan (see page 104) works beautifully in shape and color.

SERVES 6

AERATED MAPLE

2 grams | 1 teaspoon powdered gelatin

108 grams | $^{1}/_{2}$ cup plus 2 teaspoons water

345 grams | 1 $^{3}/_{4}$ cups sugar

185 grams | $^{1}/_{2}$ cup liquid glucose

10 grams | 1 $^{1}/_{2}$ teaspoons maple syrup

12 grams | 1 tablespoon baking soda

RUTABAGA

1.6 kilograms | 5 $^{1}/_{2}$ cups kosher salt

300 grams | 1 $^{1}/_{4}$ cups egg whites

100 grams | 1 cup uncultivated soil

10 | dried forest leaves

1 | rutabaga

RUTABAGA PUDDING

470 grams | 3 cups peeled and
    diced rutabaga

500 grams | 2 cups goat's milk

220 grams | $^{1}/_{3}$ cup plus $^{1}/_{2}$ cup goat's
    milk butter

50 grams | 1.8 ounces gellan base
    (page 285)

kosher salt

TOASTED PECANS

50 grams | $^{1}/_{2}$ cup shelled wild pecans

10 grams | 2 teaspoons Twin Sisters olive oil

Maldon sea salt

FOR THE AERATED MAPLE:

Stir together the gelatin and 8 grams (2 teaspoons) of the water in a small bowl. Let stand for 5 minutes to bloom fully. Reserve. Spray a metal pan with a thin coating of nonstick cooking spray. Line the bottom of the pan with parchment paper and coat the paper with cooking spray. Combine the sugar, glucose, and the remaining 100 grams ($^{1}/_{2}$ cup) of water in a wide saucepan and heat slowly, stirring occasionally with a wooden spoon to melt the sugars evenly. Once the sugars have completely dissolved, stop stirring to avoid recrystallization. Increase the heat to high and cook until the mixture reaches 284°F (140°C). Add the maple syrup. Continue cooking, without stirring, until the mixture reaches 302°F (150°C). Immediately add the baking soda and the gelatin mixture and stir briskly with the wooden spoon for 10 seconds. Remove from the heat and pour into the prepared pan. As air pockets develop, do not disturb them, as the sugar structure is very delicate at this stage. Wrap the pan in plastic wrap and let cool for 12 hours at room temperature. Using a paring knife, cut into pieces about 1 inch (2.5 centimeters) square. Store the maple in an airtight container with silica gel packets at room temperature.

FOR THE RUTABAGA:

Preheat the oven to 450°F (230°C). Put the salt in a food processor. With the processor running, slowly add the egg whites, then mix for 3 minutes to form a tight meringue. Turn out the meringue into a bowl, add the soil and foliage, and mix together until well incorporated. Place a small amount of the salt meringue in a metal pan. Place the rutabaga in the salt and cover it completely with more of the salt meringue. Bake for 1 hour, until the rutabaga is tender. Remove the rutabaga from the salt mixture, let cool to room temperature, and cut into 6 wedges, leaving the skin intact. Store in an airtight container in the refrigerator until ready to use.

FOR THE RUTABAGA PUDDING:

Combine the rutabaga, goat's milk, and 100 grams ($^{1}/_{3}$ cup) of the butter in a vacuum bag and season with salt, then seal on high. Cook the rutabaga in a steam oven set at 200°F (95°C) for 40 minutes, until very tender. Meanwhile, prepare an ice bath. Drain the rutabaga, reserving 75 grams ($^{1}/_{3}$ cup) of the cooking liquid. Place the rutabaga, the reserved liquid, the remaining 120 grams ($^{1}/_{2}$ cup) of butter, and the gellan base in a blender and mix on high speed for 3 minutes, until smooth. Strain through a chinois into a bowl, then nest the bowl in the ice bath to cool the pudding. Season with kosher salt, transfer to a squeeze bottle, and reserve in the refrigerator until needed.

FOR THE TOASTED PECANS:

Preheat the oven to 325°F (165°C). Toss the pecans gently with the olive oil and season with Maldon salt. Spread on a small sheet pan and toast in the oven for 8 to 10 minutes, until golden brown and fragrant. Let cool to room temperature, then store in an airtight container at room temperature until ready to use.

continued

BROWNED GOAT'S MILK BUTTER:

Place a saucepan over medium heat and slowly add the butter, agitating the pot to avoid burning the milk solids. Continue to heat the butter until it has browned and has a strong fragrance, then remove from the heat and let cool slightly. Add the maple syrup, season with Maldon salt, and keep warm until serving.

TO SERVE:

Place the rutabaga wedges in a steam oven set at 200°F (95°C) for about 5 minutes, until warmed. Dress the wedges with the browned butter and place a wedge in the center of each of 6 plates. Put a few dots of the rutabaga pudding around the wedges. Place a few pieces of the aerated maple, a few shavings of white truffle, and 3 mustard flowers on each plate. Dress the plate lightly with the browned butter. Break the pecans into small pieces and add to the plate.

BROWNED GOAT'S MILK BUTTER

300 grams | 1 $^1/_3$ cups goat's milk butter, cut into small cubes
60 grams | 3 tablespoons maple syrup
Maldon sea salt

1 | white truffle, thinly shaved
18 | wild mustard flowers

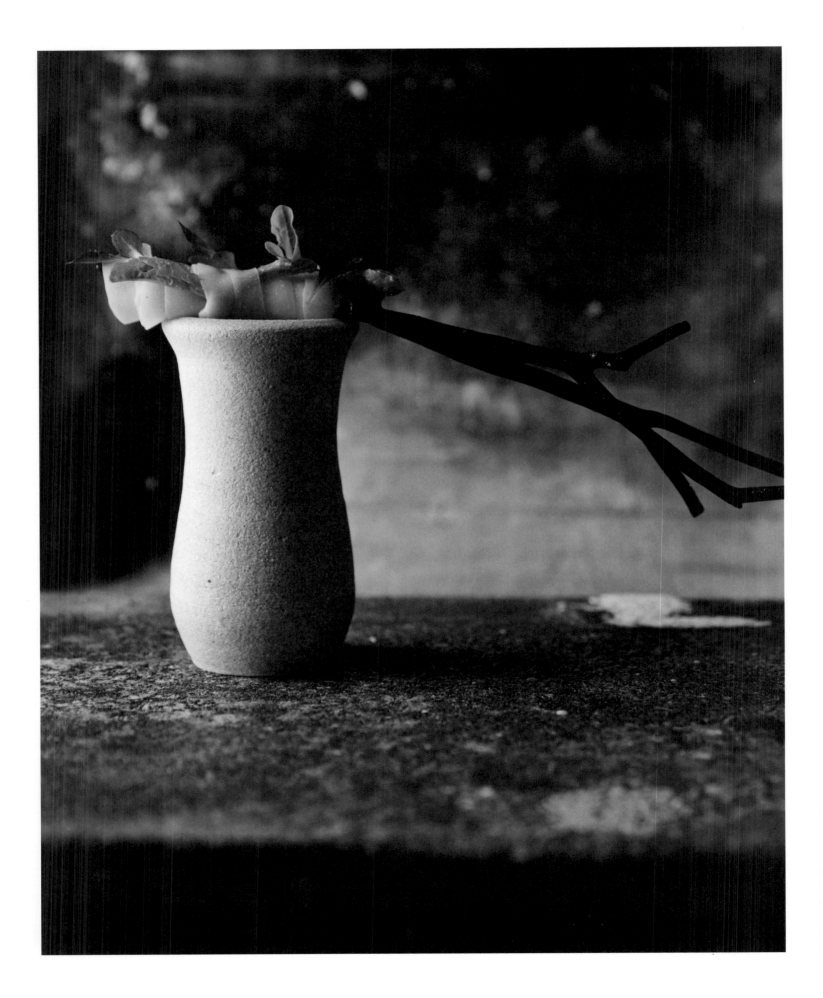

cuttlefish lardo tiny lettuces

*The ashed chopsticks are garnished with ribbons of cuttlefish and cured **lardo** that mimic textures of sea and land in a single bite. A broth bridges the gap in a sip. Hours of work and craft are distilled into the sheen of burnt wood and the feel of an unglazed vase.*

SERVES 6 TO 8

CUTTLEFISH PREPARATION
400 grams | about 14 ounces cuttlefish
kosher salt

PORK STOCK
900 grams | about 2 pounds boneless pork
    shoulder, trimmed of excess fat
60 grams | $^2/_3$ cup diced celery
12 grams | 1 tablespoon sliced garlic
80 grams | $^1/_2$ cup diced yellow onion
20 grams | 1 $^1/_2$ tablespoons extra virgin
    olive oil
4 kilograms | about 4 quarts water
100 grams | 3.5 ounces dehydrated cuttlefish
    (recipe above)
rice vinegar
Maldon sea salt

ESPELETTE OIL
20 grams | $^1/_4$ cup ground Espelette pepper
300 grams | 1 $^1/_3$ cups grapeseed oil

1 | English cucumber
20 | slices Mangalitsa lardo (page 285), cut
    into strips $^1/_8$ inch (3 millimeters) wide
    by 5 inches (13 centimeters) long
20 | tiny red romaine leaves
60 | tiny green leaf lettuce leaves
10 grams | $^1/_3$ cup romaine lettuce juice

FOR THE CUTTLEFISH:
Cut the tentacles and fins from the body of the cuttlefish and set aside. Remove any connective tissue from the body and cut the cuttlefish into planks of about 4 by 6 inches (10 by 15 centimeters), reserving the trim. Arrange the trim, tentacles, and fins on a dehydrator tray and dehydrate at 150°F (66°C) for 24 hours. Reserve for use in the pork stock.

Cold smoke (see page 287) the cuttlefish planks for 30 minutes. Remove from the smoker, season on both sides with kosher salt, transfer to a vacuum bag, and seal on high. Cook the cuttlefish in a hot-water bath set at 138°F (59°C) for 45 minutes. Meanwhile, prepare an ice bath. When the cuttlefish is ready, immerse the bag in the ice bath for 1 hour. Remove the cuttlefish from the bag and freeze for at least 1 hour, until completely frozen.

Place a sheet of parchment paper on a work surface. Using an electric slicer, shave the frozen cuttlefish into very thin strips 5 inches (13 centimeters) long by $^1/_8$ inch (3 millimeters) wide onto the parchment. Store the parchment on a metal tray over ice in the refrigerator until ready to use.

FOR THE PORK STOCK:
Cut the pork shoulder into pieces about 1 inch (2.5 centimeters) square. Combine the celery, garlic, onion, and olive oil in a rondeau over low heat and sweat for 2 minutes, until the vegetables begin to soften. Add the pork, water, and dehydrated cuttlefish, increase the heat to high and bring to a boil. Turn down the heat to a simmer and cook for 3 hours.

Prepare an ice bath. Strain the stock through a very fine cloth filter into a large bowl, then nest the bowl in the ice bath to cool. Season with vinegar and Maldon salt.

FOR THE ESPELETTE OIL:
Combine the Espelette pepper and grapeseed oil in a small saucepan over low heat and heat to 120°F (49°C). Hold at this temperature for 1 hour, then strain through a very fine cloth filter and let cool. Transfer to a squeeze bottle and reserve at room temperature until ready to use.

TO SERVE:
Peel the cucumber, then, using a mandoline, shave the cucumber lengthwise as thinly as possible. Cut the shavings into strips of the same dimensions as the cuttlefish strips. You will need at least 20 strips.

To assemble, lay two sheets of parchment paper on a flat surface and lightly spray with nonstick cooking spray. Lay a strip of cuttlefish on one sheet of parchment. Next, shingle a strip of lardo, overlapping the cuttlefish slightly, followed by a ribbon of cucumber, overlapping the lardo in a similar fashion. Repeat this pattern twice until you have a sheet about 2 inches (5 centimeters) wide. Cover with the second sheet of parchment, sprayed side down, and smooth the surface with a plastic bench scraper to ensure that all of the pieces are firmly in place. Repeat this process with two additional sheets of parchment paper until you have completed 10 shingled sheets. Carefully remove the top sheet of parchment paper from a cuttlefish sheet and use 2 chopsticks to roll up each sheet into a perfect wrap resembling noodles. Arrange the tiny lettuces in the folds of the cuttlefish and cucumber and rest across the rim of a small vase. Finish the pork stock by mixing the lettuce juice with about 500 grams (about 2 cups) of the stock. Pour about 60 grams ($^1/_4$ cup) of the stock into each vase, then finish by adding a few dots of the Espelette oil to each vase.

turnip fermented brown rice
salmon roe

The swooshes of white glaze on the bowl work perfectly with the tiny turnip tails, while the reddish hue mirrors the salmon roe. The dish is as textured as the bowl by Lynn.

FOR THE FERMENTED BROWN RICE:

Combine the rice and cold water in a saucepan, cover, and bring to a boil over high heat. Turn down the heat to a simmer and cook for 50 minutes, until the rice is tender. Transfer the cooked rice to a bowl. In a small bowl, combine the yeast and lukewarm water and let stand for 6 minutes, until frothy. Stir the bloomed yeast, sugar, and cornstarch into the rice. Wrap the bowl tightly with plastic wrap and incubate for 6 days in a proof box set at 110°F (43°C) until the rice is fully fermented, with a strong fragrance and thickened liquid. Store in the refrigerator to retard the fermentation process.

FOR THE HOUSE-CURED SALMON ROE:

Put the salmon roe in a metal bowl. Combine the water, sake, and shiro dashi in a separate bowl and stir to mix. Pour over the salmon roe, cover, and refrigerate for 12 hours.

Inspect the roe carefully for any deflated eggs or sinew and discard. Drain the roe and discard the liquid. Season the roe with the Maldon salt and store on ice in a shallow plastic container in the refrigerator for up to 3 days.

FOR THE PUFFED BROWN RICE:

Combine the brown rice and water in a large saucepan, bring to a boil over high heat, and boil for 30 minutes, whisking occasionally to encourage starch development. Remove from the heat, drain, and transfer the rice to a bowl. Put half of the rice into a food processor and mix for 2 minutes, until a smooth puree forms. Return the puree to the bowl and mix thoroughly. Line a full sheet pan with parchment paper, then spray the parchment with nonstick cooking spray. Arrange small clusters of the rice on the paper. Let dry in a well-ventilated area (80°F to 100°F/27° to 38°C) for at least 24 hours, until completely dry. As the rice clusters begin to dry, turn them upside down to ensure even drying.

Pour the oil to a depth of 4 inches (10 centimeters) into a deep fryer or deep, heavy pot and heat to 375°F (190°C). Working in batches, fry the rice clusters for about 15 seconds, until doubled in size. Transfer to paper towels to drain, then season with kosher salt. Store in an airtight container with silica gel packets at room temperature.

FOR THE RICE-GLAZED TURNIPS:

Combine the rice and water in a saucepan and bring to a boil over high heat. Turn down the heat to a simmer and cook for 2 hours, stirring occasionally with a wooden spoon until very soft. Meanwhile, prepare an ice bath. Transfer the mixture to a blender and mix on high speed for 2 minutes, until liquefied. Pour the liquid through a chinois into a bowl, then nest the bowl in the ice bath to cool the liquid. Season to taste with kosher salt.

Combine 43 grams (3 tablespoons) of the rice puree and the turnips in a vacuum bag and seal on high. Put into a steam oven set at 200°F (95°C) for 10 minutes. Let the turnips cool to room temperature, then remove them from the bag. Put about 448 grams (2 cups) of the rice puree in a pot and bring to a simmer. Using tweezers, dip the cooked turnips into the rice puree to glaze evenly.

TO SERVE:

Put a small amount of the fermented rice at the base of each of 4 narrow bowls. Arrange 6 glazed turnips, root pointing up, in each bowl. Tuck the salmon roe in the crevices around the glazed turnips, then follow similarly with the puffed brown rice clusters. Break up the soy salt and scatter a few pieces in each bowl. Garnish with the daikon flowers and turnip greens.

SERVES 4

FERMENTED BROWN RICE
227 grams | 1 1/4 cups long-grain brown rice
450 grams | 2 cups cold water
3.5 grams | 3/4 teaspoon active dry yeast
120 grams | 1/2 cup lukewarm water
    (90°F/32°C)
8.5 grams | 2 teaspoons sugar
1.5 grams | 1/2 teaspoon cornstarch

HOUSE-CURED SALMON ROE
150 grams | 5.3 ounces salmon roe
315 grams | 1 1/3 cups water
315 grams | 1 1/3 cups sake
53 grams | 1/3 cup shiro dashi (page 286)
7.5 grams | 1 teaspoon Maldon sea salt

PUFFED BROWN RICE
175 grams | 1 cup long-grain brown rice
1.4 kilograms | 6 cups water
grapeseed oil, for deep frying
kosher salt

RICE-GLAZED TURNIPS
52 grams | 1/4 cup white jasmine rice
600 grams | 2 1/2 cups water
24 | baby turnips, tops trimmed with 1/4 inch
    (6 millimeters) stem intact
kosher salt

1 cube | soy salt
16 | wild daikon flowers
16 | turnip greens

forest mignardises

This is as close to naturalism as we get. For me, such cuteness is more fitting in **mignardise** *and pastry than in other parts of the meal. "Twigs," "moss," "leaves"—Brett's black walnut box (see page 106) is stately and elegant enough to hold a dish that has more than its share of quotation marks.*

SERVES 8 TO 10 AS A CANAPÉ

HONEYCOMB

4 grams | 2 teaspoons powdered gelatin
16 grams | 1 tablespoon water, at room temperature
685 grams | scant 3 1/2 cups sugar
370 grams | 1 cup liquid glucose
200 grams | 3/4 cup cold water
20 grams | 1 tablespoon raw honey
20 grams | 1 1/2 tablespoons baking soda

HONEY GEL

600 grams | 3 cups raw honey
200 grams | 3/4 cup water
10 grams | 2 1/4 teaspoons powdered agar

COFFEE TWIGS

450 grams | 2 1/4 cups powdered isomalt
200 grams | 1 2/3 cups all-purpose flour
100 grams | 1/2 cup sugar
10 grams | 1 1/2 teaspoons kosher salt
500 grams | 2 cups egg whites
400 grams | 1 3/4 cups brown butter, melted
10 grams | 5 teaspoons instant coffee powder

FOR THE HONEYCOMB:

Stir together the gelatin and room-temperature water in a small metal bowl. Let stand for 5 minutes to bloom fully. Reserve. Spray a metal pan with a thin coating of nonstick cooking spray. Line the bottom of the pan with parchment paper and coat the paper with cooking spray. Combine the sugar, glucose, and cold water in a wide saucepan over low heat and heat slowly, stirring occasionally with a wooden spoon to melt the sugars evenly. Once the sugars have completely dissolved, stop stirring to avoid recrystallization. Increase the heat to high and cook until the mixture reaches 284°F (140°C). Add the honey and continue cooking, without stirring, until the mixture reaches 302°F (150°C). Immediately add the baking soda and the gelatin mixture and stir briskly with the wooden spoon for 10 seconds. Remove from the heat and pour into the prepared pan. As air pockets develop, do not disturb them, as the sugar structure is very delicate at this stage. Let cool for 12 hours. Using a paring knife, cut into pieces about 1 inch (2.5 centimeters) square. Store the honeycomb in an airtight container with silica gel packets at room temperature.

FOR THE HONEY GEL:

Combine the honey and water in a saucepan, add the agar, and place over high heat. Cook, whisking continuously, until the mixture comes to a boil. Boil for 15 seconds, then pour into a small shallow metal pan. Refrigerate the pan for about 2 hours, until the gel has set. Cut the gel into pieces small enough to fit in a blender, transfer them to the blender, and mix on high speed for 2 minutes, until smooth and shiny. Strain through a chinois into a bowl, then cover and refrigerate for 12 hours to allow the air pockets to escape. Transfer the mixture to a squeeze bottle and return to the refrigerator.

FOR THE COFFEE TWIGS:

Preheat a convection oven to 325°F (165°C). Combine the isomalt, flour, sugar, and salt in a food processor. With the processor running, slowly add the egg whites. Follow with the brown butter and continue to mix for about 2 minutes, until a batter forms. Scrape down the sides of the processor bowl and mix for 30 seconds longer. Transfer about 150 grams (2/3 cup) of the batter to a bowl, add the coffee powder, and stir to dissolve, then reserve to the side. Spread the remaining batter in a thin layer (about 1/16 inch / 2 millimeters) on a full-size silicone baking mat. Scatter the coffee-flavored batter in small amounts evenly over the batter layer, then spread it to the same thickness, creating a streaked pattern. Bake the tuile for 5 minutes, just until the surface is no longer tacky. Using a knife and a straight edge, cut the tuile lengthwise into strips 2 1/4 inches (6 centimeters) wide. Return the tuile to the oven and continue to bake for about 2 minutes, until it turns light amber.

Working quickly while the tuile is hot, tear the strips from the mat in 3-inch (7.5-centimeter) sections and place on a work surface. Immediately roll each strip into cigarette-shaped pieces. If the tuile becomes too brittle, return it to the oven to soften again. Once all of the twigs have been formed, store in an airtight container with silica gel packets at room temperature.

continued

FOR THE DIRTY CARAMEL:

Spray a 7 by 13-inch (20 by 33-centimeter) metal pan with nonstick cooking spray, coating the bottom and sides. Line the bottom of the tray with parchment paper and spray the paper with cooking spray. Pour the cream into a saucepan and heat over low heat to 140°F (60°C). Add the eucalyptus leaves, remove the saucepan from the heat, and steep in a warm place for 30 minutes. Strain the cream into a clean saucepan and add the sugar, corn syrup, and glucose. Place over high heat and, stirring with a wooden spoon, heat to 220°F (104°C). Add the butter and continue to cook until the mixture reaches 240°F (116°C). Remove from the heat, pour into the prepared pan, and let rest for 24 hours at room temperature to crystallize properly.

Using a knife, cut the caramel sheet into 1-inch (2.5-centimeter) squares. In a bowl, combine the ground eucalyptus and cocoa nibs. Toss the squares, a few at a time, in the crumb mixture, then reform the sides of each caramel to maintain a perfect square. Reserve the squares in an airtight container in an area with an ambient temperature of 50°F to 70°F (10°C to 21°C).

FOR THE MAPLE LEAF:

Combine the cream, maple syrup, and corn syrup in a small rondeau and whisk to combine. Place over low heat and, gently stirring, heat slowly until the mixture reaches 238°F (114°C). (Do not heat higher than 240°F/116°C or the fudge will burn.) Immediately transfer the mixture to the bowl of a stand mixer fitted with the paddle attachment. Mix on low speed to start cooling the fudge. When the temperature of the fudge reaches 108°F (42°C), turn it out onto a sheet of parchment paper and top with a second parchment sheet. Roll the fudge through a dough sheeter set at about $^1/_3$ inch (1 centimeter). Using a leaf-shaped metal mold, cut out leaf shapes from the fudge, then press each shape into a silicone leaf impression mold. Arrange the cutouts on thin wooden dowels to form the shapes of dried leaves and place on a dehydrator tray. Dehydrate at 115°F (46°C) for 6 hours, until dry and crispy.

FOR THE MAPLE GEL:

Put the maple syrup and gellan base in a blender and mix on high for about 2 minutes, until a uniform puree forms, stopping occasionally to scrape down the sides of the blender. Pour through a chinois into a container, cover, and refrigerate for 12 hours to allow the air pockets to escape. Transfer to a squeeze bottle.

TO SERVE:

Arrange the Irish moss and young pine in wooden boxes with lids. Put a couple of dots of honey gel on each piece of the honeycomb and garnish with 2 rosemary flowers. Place the honeycomb pieces on one end of the box. Lay the coffee twigs next to the honeycomb and follow with the dirty caramel. To finish the maple leaves, put a few dots of the maple gel on each leaf and dust with a very small amount of candy cap mushroom powder. Place the leaves on the opposite side of the box.

DIRTY CARAMEL

1.2 kilograms | 5 cups heavy cream
75 grams | $^3/_4$ cup fresh eucalyptus leaves
800 grams | 4 cups sugar
30 grams | 4 teaspoons light corn syrup
270 grams | $^3/_4$ cup liquid glucose
15 grams | 1 tablespoon unsalted butter
23 grams | 0.8 ounce eucalyptus leaves, dehydrated at 125°F (52°C) for 24 hours
150 grams | 5.3 ounces cocoa nibs, ground

MAPLE LEAF

600 grams | 2 $^1/_2$ cups heavy cream
1.5 kilograms | 4 $^2/_3$ cups maple syrup
60 grams | 3 tablespoons light corn syrup

MAPLE GEL

100 grams | $^1/_3$ cup maple syrup
250 grams | 8.8 ounces gellan base (page 285)

Irish moss
young pine twigs
16 to 20 | rosemary flowers
10 grams | 5 teaspoons ground dried candy cap mushrooms

abalone beans nasturtium vinegar

The earthenware bowl used here is always referred to in the kitchen as the "abalone bowl," as its glaze and shape seem to work perfectly with whatever abalone dish we are making at the time. The rustic patterns of ash on glaze, the hand-wrought shape—hints of "Japanese caveman"—are trademarks of Lynn Mahon's style (see page 102). In this recipe, we serve the shaved abalone with beans from Rancho Gordo, a Napa-based purveyor of, among other things, the world's best dried beans.

SERVES 4

RED ABALONE

500 grams | about two 8-ounce red abalone in the shell

sel gris

50 grams | 1.8 ounces dried kombu

RANCHO GORDO BEAN PUREE

160 grams | $3/_4$ cup Santa Maria pinquito beans

160 grams | $3/_4$ cup Good Mother Stallard beans

160 grams | $3/_4$ cup Rio Zape beans

5 grams | $2 1/_4$ teaspoons cumin seeds, toasted in a dry pan until fragrant

20 grams | $1 1/_2$ tablespoons extra virgin olive oil

30 grams | 1 ounce peeled carrot, cut into three equal pieces

30 grams | 1 ounce celery stalk, cut into three equal pieces

30 grams | 1 ounce yellow onion, cut into three equal wedges

abalone trim (recipe above)

1 kilogram | about 4 cups chicken stock (page 283)

1 kilogram | about 4 cups water

5 grams | 1 tablespoon plus 2 teaspoons thyme leaves

5 grams | $1 1/_2$ tablespoons epazote leaves

5 grams | $1 1/_2$ tablespoons flat-leaf parsley leaves

kosher salt

Twin Sisters olive oil

FOR THE RED ABALONE:

To remove each abalone from its shell, wedge an offset spatula between the shell and flesh of the abalone and pry gently to release the foot from the shell. Cut off the intestines and the foot from each abalone and reserve them on ice in a metal container in the refrigerator. Rinse the abalone under cool running water, then place between two kitchen towels. Using a butchery mallet, lightly pound each abalone 20 times on each side. Cover and refrigerate for 24 hours.

Remove the abalone from the refrigerator and again pound 20 times on each side. Season them lightly with sel gris and place in a vacuum bag. Arrange the kombu in the bag and seal on high. Cook the abalone in a hot-water bath at 138°F (59°C) for 40 minutes. Remove the abalone from the bag and pat dry on paper towels. Coat one side of 2 sheets of parchment paper with nonstick cooking spray. Lay the abalone on the coated side of 1 sheet and top with the second sheet, coated side down. Freeze for 4 hours.

Line a small sheet pan with fresh parchment paper and spray the parchment with nonstick cooking spray. Using an electric slicer, very thinly slice the frozen abalone and arrange the slices on the parchment. Cover the tray in plastic wrap and store on ice in the refrigerator until ready to use.

FOR THE RANCHO GORDO BEAN PUREE:

Place each type of bean in a separate bowl and add water to each bowl to cover the beans. Let soak for 12 hours. Divide the toasted cumin evenly among 3 small pieces of cheesecloth and tie each into a bundle with kitchen string. Place 3 saucepans over medium heat and divide the extra virgin olive oil, carrot, celery, and onion evenly among the pans. Sweat the vegetables until they have softened but not browned. Drain the beans, keeping them separate and discarding the soaking water. Add each type of bean to a saucepan, then distribute the cumin sachets, abalone trim, stock, and water evenly among the pans. Bring the contents of each pan to a simmer over medium heat and cook at 180°F (82°C) for about 2 hours, until the beans are tender (the timing will depend on the type of bean). Divide the thyme, epazote, and parsley among the pans, then season with kosher salt and remove from the heat. Let the beans cool in their cooking liquid in the refrigerator.

Prepare an ice bath. Remove the cumin sachets, carrot, celery, onion, abalone trim, and herbs from the cooking liquid and discard. Drain each pan of beans, reserving the broth. Cover the broth and refrigerate for making the bean broth. Place half of all of the beans in a blender. Reserve the remaining half, keeping the types of beans separate. Mix on high speed for 3 minutes, until a smooth puree forms, then add a small amount of Twin Sisters olive oil and continue to mix to emulsify the puree. Strain the puree through a chinois placed over a bowl, then nest the bowl in the ice bath to cool the puree. Taste and adjust the seasoning with kosher salt. Transfer the puree to a squeeze bottle and refrigerate until ready to use.

continued

FOR THE RANCHO GORDO BEAN BROTH:

Combine the chicken, carrot, celery, onion, and egg whites in a food processor mix for 3 minutes, until completely incorporated. Put the chilled bean broth into a rondeau and add the mixture from the food processor. Whisk together until fully incorporated, then place the pan over high heat and bring the mixture to a boil as quickly as possible, stirring for the first 5 to 6 minutes to avoid scorching. When the broth begins to boil, turn down the heat to a simmer and cook for 10 to 20 minutes, until the solids come together on the surface of the liquid, forming a raft. Lower the heat slightly and continue to simmer gently for 1 hour, until the clarification is complete.

Prepare an ice bath. Ladle the broth through a very fine cloth filter into a metal bowl, then nest the bowl in the ice bath to cool the broth.

FOR THE NASTURTIUM VINAIGRETTE:

Prepare an ice bath. Place the lime juice, oil, and nasturtium leaves in a blender and mix on high speed for 20 seconds. Slowly add the Ultra-Tex 3 and continue to mix until thickened. Strain through a chinois into a bowl, then nest the bowl in the ice bath to cool the vinaigrette. Season with salt, then transfer the vinaigrette to a squeeze bottle and refrigerate until ready to use.

TO SERVE:

Place a few large dots of the bean puree in the center of each of 4 small bowls. Place the abalone slices in tight curls on the bean puree. Dress the sea beans and the reserved whole beans with the nasturtium vinaigrette and arrange them on the abalone curls. Garnish each serving with nasturtium leaves. Pour about 50 grams (¹/₄ cup) of the bean broth in each bowl.

RANCHO GORDO BEAN BROTH

400 grams | about 14 ounces boneless skinless chicken breast, diced
60 grams | about 2 ounces peeled carrot, cut into three equal pieces
60 grams | about 2 ounces celery stalks, cut into three equal pieces
80 grams | about 3 ounces peeled yellow onion, cut into three equal pieces
90 grams | about 3 egg whites
1.5 kilograms | about 6 cups bean cooking liquid (page 127)
kosher salt

NASTURTIUM VINAIGRETTE

90 grams | ¹/₃ cup freshly squeezed lime juice
180 grams | ³/₄ cup Twin Sisters olive oil
100 grams | 3.5 ounces nasturtium leaves
8 grams | 1 ¹/₂ teaspoons Ultra-Tex 3
Maldon sea salt

sea beans
nasturtium leaves

raw goat sunflower

Lynn brought me this bowl at the same time that sunflowers were beginning to bloom. Call it fate. We created this dish as a wonderful way to use the sunflower petals and seeds, pairing them with almost-raw goat and pickled lime.

SERVES 4

SUNFLOWER SEED PUREE

500 grams | 3 ¹/₂ cups sunflower seeds
150 grams | ²/₃ cup mascarpone cheese
20 grams | 1 ¹/₂ tablespoons Twin Sisters
    olive oil
kosher salt

BRAISED SUNFLOWER HEARTS

4 | large sunflowers
2 kilograms | about 8 cups water
2 grams | ¹/₂ teaspoon ascorbic acid
13 grams | 1 tablespoon extra virgin olive oil
kosher salt
sunflower seed oil

INDIAN PICKLED LIMES

300 grams | 10.5 ounces Indian pickled limes
    in canning liquid
125 grams | 4.4 ounces gellan base
    (page 285)

GOAT PREPARATION

225 grams | 8 ounces goat loin, trimmed of
    fat and sinew
25 grams | 1 ¹/₂ tablespoons sunflower
    seed oil
6 grams | 1 teaspoon shabazi spice
Maldon sea salt

16 | sunflower sprouts
 reserved sunflower petals

FOR THE SUNFLOWER SEED PUREE:

Combine the sunflower seeds with water to cover in a pressure cooker and cook on high pressure for 30 minutes. Meanwhile, prepare an ice bath. Drain the seeds, transfer to a blender, and add the mascarpone cheese and olive oil. Mix on high speed for about 2 minutes, until a thick and shiny puree forms. Strain through a chinois into a bowl, then nest the bowl in the ice bath to cool the puree. Season with kosher salt, transfer to a squeeze bottle, and store in the refrigerator until needed.

FOR THE BRAISED SUNFLOWER HEARTS:

Remove and reserve the sunflower petals. Peel away the outer skin of the sunflower hearts and clean away the thistles. Pour the water into a large bowl, add the ascorbic acid, and stir to dissolve. Immerse the cleaned sunflower hearts in the acidulated water for 10 minutes. Remove the hearts from the water and season with kosher salt and extra virgin olive oil. Place in a vacuum bag and seal the bag on high. Cook in a steam oven set at 200°F (95°C) for 15 minutes, until the hearts are tender. Meanwhile, prepare an ice bath. When the hearts are ready, remove the bag from the steam oven and immerse the bag in the ice bath for 1 hour to chill. Remove the hearts from the bag. Cut two of the hearts into ¹/₄-inch (6-millimeter) cubes and cut the remaining two hearts into thin strips 2 inches (5 centimeters) long and ¹/₁₆ inch (2 millimeters) wide. Reserve all the pieces in an airtight container in the refrigerator until ready to use.

FOR THE INDIAN PICKLED LIMES:

Prepare an ice bath. Cut the lime rind from the pith, reserve the pith, and slice the rind into narrow strips. Add the canning liquid to a blender with the reserved pith and the gellan base and mix on high speed for 2 minutes, until smooth. Strain through a chinois into a bowl, then nest the bowl in the ice bath to cool the puree. Transfer to a squeeze bottle and store in the refrigerator until ready to use.

FOR THE GOAT PREPARATION:

Prepare a fire in a wood-burning oven. When the fire is at about 600°F (315°C), place the loin directly on the hottest spot of the grate. After 5 seconds, rotate the loin a quarter turn and cook for an additional 5 seconds. Repeat until the loin is barely cooked on all sides. Remove from the fire and mince very finely. Season with the oil, shabazi spice, and Maldon salt.

TO SERVE:

Place the marinated goat in a couple of piles on each plate. Arrange a few dots of the sunflower seed puree and pickled lime around the plate. Combine the sunflower heart pieces, sunflower oil, and Maldon salt. Cut the sunflower petals in chiffonade. Scatter the heart pieces, sunflower sprouts, and petal chiffonade over each plate.

sea lettuce laver

An ashed stump of manzanita serves as a holder for these laver chips, a take on the Korean seaweed snacks that I was introduced to by sous chefs Kat and John. When laid on a white cloth, this striking serving piece is at once natural, elegant, and muscular.

Place the sea lettuce in a blender and mix on high speed for about 1 ½ minutes, until reduced to a powder. Set the powder aside. Put the black rice and 900 grams (about 4 cups) of the water in a shallow saucepan with a lid, cover, and bring to a boil over high heat. Turn down the heat to a low simmer and cook for 25 minutes, until the water has been absorbed and the rice is tender. While the rice is cooking, combine the tapioca starch and 150 grams (⅔ cup) of the water in a saucepan, place over medium heat, and bring to a boil, stirring continuously with a rubber spatula. Boil for 1 minute, then cover and remove from the heat.

When the rice is ready, transfer to a blender along with the remaining 450 grams (about 2 cups) of water. Mix on high speed for 3 minutes, until smooth. Add the tapioca gel and continue mixing for about 1 minute, until completely homogenous. Add the sea lettuce powder and mix on high speed for 10 seconds to combine. Measure 250 grams (about ¾ cup) of the blended base, then spread it on full-size silicone baking mats ¹⁄₁₆ inch (2 millimeters) thick. Place the mats in an area with an ambient temperature of 70°F to 90°F (21°C to 32°C) for at least 12 hours, until fully dried.

Pour the oil to a depth of 4 inches (10 centimeters) into a deep fryer or deep, heavy pot and heat to 375°F (190°C). Break the dried laver into 3-inch (7.5-centimeter) squares. Working in batches, add the squares to the hot oil and fry for 8 seconds, until doubled in size. Transfer to paper towels to drain. Season on both sides with kosher salt. Store in an airtight container with silica gel packets at room temperature.

MAKES ABOUT 50 CHIPS

90 grams | 3 ounces dried sea lettuce
285 grams | 1 ½ cups black rice
1.5 kilograms | 6 ⅔ cups water
75 grams | ⅔ cup tapioca starch
kosher salt
grapeseed oil, for deep-frying

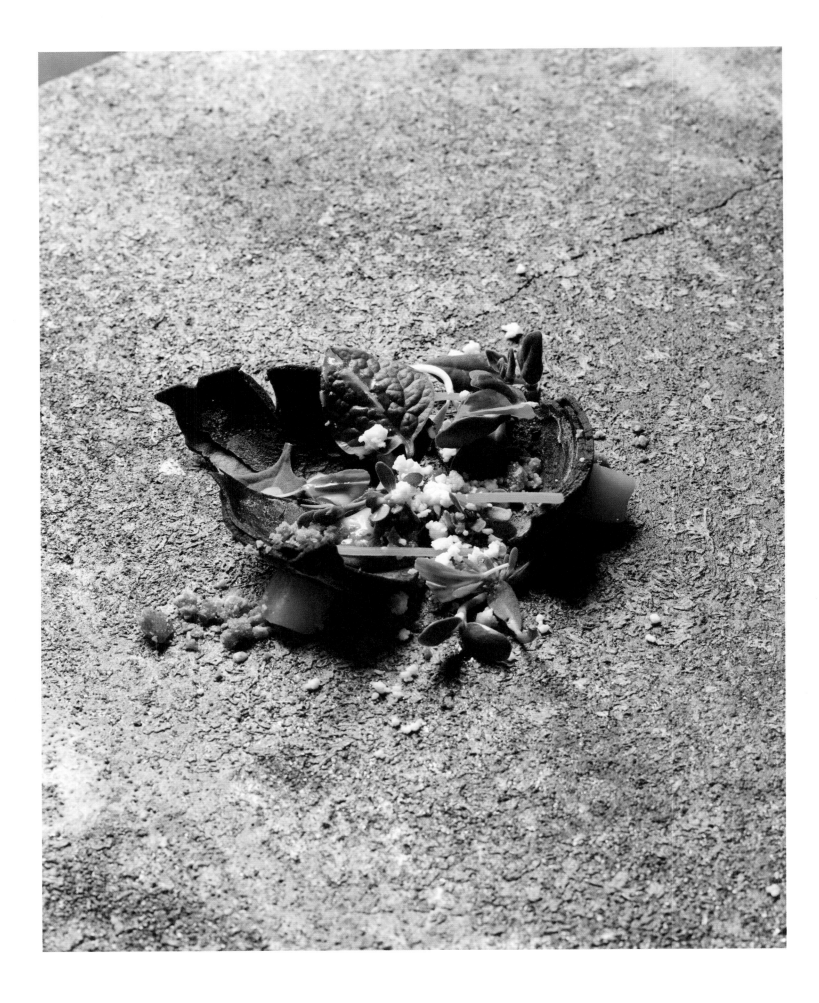

smashed pumpkin mole curds

Inspired by a trip to Mexico City, this pumpkin dish makes use of the complex flavors of an ashed pumpkin mole. We counter the sweetness with pickled raw pumpkin and beautiful succulents from the greenhouse. Lynn Mahon's slab plate (see page 102) serves as a perfect pedestal.

SERVES 4

FRESH RICOTTA

1.9 kilograms | 8 cups whole milk

476 grams | 2 cups heavy cream

238 grams | 1 cup buttermilk (page 284)

22 grams | 1 ¹/₂ tablespoons freshly squeezed
    lemon juice

kosher salt

PUMPKIN SKIN ASH

2 | kabocha squashes

50 grams | 3 ¹/₂ tablespoons brown butter

kosher salt

PUMPKIN MOLE

80 grams | 2.7 ounces dried ancho chiles

80 grams | 2.7 ounces dried guajillo chiles

80 grams | 2.7 ounces dried cascabel chiles

36 grams | about 6 cloves garlic

1 | 3-inch (7.5-centimeter) piece cassia bark

14 grams | 2 tablespoons white peppercorns

25 grams | ¹/₄ cup cumin seeds

4 grams | 2 teaspoons whole cloves

200 grams | 1 ¹/₃ cups pumpkin seeds

25 grams | 1 tablespoon plus 2 teaspoons
    extra virgin olive oil

150 grams | 1 cup diced yellow onions

300 grams | 10.5 ounces pumpkin cubes
    (recipe above)

100 grams | ²/₃ cup golden raisins

675 grams | 2 ³/₄ cups crushed tomato

45 grams | ¹/₃ cup pumpkin skin ash
    (recipe above)

30 grams | 1 ounce unrefined Mexican
    chocolate

FOR THE FRESH RICOTTA:

In a container, stir together the milk, cream, buttermilk, and lemon juice, then season with kosher salt. Pour into vacuum bags and seal the bags on high. Cook in a hot-water bath set at 190°F (88°C) for 2 hours. Meanwhile, prepare an ice bath. Remove the bags from the bath and immerse immediately in the ice bath for 1 hour.

To set up a resting tray for the curds, place a colander above a container. Line the colander with a piece of cheesecloth and pour the curds into the colander. Wrap the entire setup in plastic wrap and store in the refrigerator for at least 6 hours or up to 24 hours. Transfer the strained curds to a container with a lid and discard the whey. Taste for seasoning and add more kosher salt if necessary. Cover and refrigerate.

FOR THE PUMPKIN SKIN ASH:

Prepare a fire in a wood-burning oven. Peel the skin away from the kabocha flesh and reserve the skin. Cut the flesh into uniform small cubes, about 8 cubes total. Reserve the trim for use in the mole. Put the cubes into a vacuum bag, add the brown butter and salt, and seal the bag on high. Cook in a steam oven set at 200°F (95°C) for 15 minutes. Reserve in the bag in the refrigerator.

When the fire is about 600°F (315°C), arrange the reserved skin on a cast-iron tray and roast in the oven for 1 hour, until heavily charred and desiccated. Let the charred skin cool, then transfer to a blender and mix on high speed for about 3 minutes, until pulverized. Store the powder in an airtight container at room temperature.

FOR THE PUMPKIN MOLE:

Heat a griddle over high heat. Arrange all of the chiles and the garlic on the hot surface and toast on all sides for about 3 minutes total, until light brown and fragrant. Add the cassia bark, peppercorns, cumin, cloves, and pumpkin seeds and toast for an additional 2 minutes. Transfer all of the toasted ingredients to paper towels.

Place a stockpot over medium heat. Add the olive oil, onions, pumpkin cubes, and raisins and stir the contents of the pot continuously to keep the onions from caramelizing. Add the toasted chiles, garlic, spices, and pumpkin seeds and continue to stir continuously. Follow with the crushed tomatoes, pumpkin skin ash, and chocolate, continuing to stir. Bring the mole to a simmer over low heat and cook, stirring occasionally to prevent scorching, for about 2 hours. Remove from the heat and let cool slightly. Meanwhile, prepare an ice bath. Working in batches, add the mole to a blender and mix on high speed until a smooth puree forms. Strain the puree through a chinois into a bowl, then nest the bowl in the ice bath to cool.

continued

smashed pumpkin mole curds *continued*

FOR THE FROZEN PUMPKIN SHELL:

Season the diced kabocha squash with kosher salt. Place the kabocha and 200 grams (scant 1 cup) of the brown butter in a vacuum bag and seal the bag on high. Cook in a steam oven set at 200°F (95°C) for about 30 minutes. Let cool slightly, transfer to a blender, and mix on high speed for 30 seconds, until smooth. Add the pumpkin mole, the remaining 75 grams (⅓ cup) of brown butter, and the gelatin and mix on medium speed for an additional 20 seconds. Season with kosher salt and strain through a chinois into a heatproof bowl.

Carefully put the liquid nitrogen into a deep metal container (excessive changes in temperature or agitation of the liquid nitrogen may cause it to become volatile). Spray a 60 millimeter (¼ cup) metal ladle with nonstick cooking spray. Dip it into the liquid nitrogen for 15 seconds and then into the pumpkin mole for 15 seconds. Repeat. When the ladle is covered with two coats of mole, dip the ladle back into the liquid nitrogen for 20 seconds. Using a kitchen torch, gently heat the inside of the ladle to loosen the shell. Carefully remove the shell by twisting it in one direction and the ladle in the other direction. When the shell is free, drop it back into liquid nitrogen for 10 seconds, then transfer to a dry plastic container. Repeat to make at least 6 shells total. Cover the container loosely and store in the freezer until needed. (To discard the liquid nitrogen, carefully pour it back into its original container.)

FOR THE PUMPKIN SEED GRANOLA:

Preheat the oven to 325°F (165°C). Line a large sheet pan with parchment paper. Heat the brown butter in a medium saucepan to about 300°F (150°C). Working in batches, fry the pumpkin seeds for about 20 seconds, until golden brown. Transfer the seeds to the paper-lined sheet pan. Again working in batches, add the bread slices to the brown butter and fry, turning once, for about 20 seconds total, until golden brown. Transfer to the paper-lined sheet pan.

Toast the pumpkin seeds and bread in the oven for 6 minutes. Let cool to room temperature. Transfer to a food processor and mix for 15 seconds. Add the brown rice syrup and pulse just to combine. Season with kosher salt. Line a sheet pan with a silicone baking mat and spread the granola evenly on the mat. Return to the oven and toast for 5 minutes. Let cool to room temperature, then store in an airtight container with silica gel packets at room temperature.

FOR THE PICKLED RAW PUMPKIN:

Using a mandoline, thinly shave the squash. Cut the pieces into julienne, transfer to a container, and add the vinegar. Season with kosher salt and put the entire container into the chamber of a vacuum seal machine. Compress twice with full vacuum and store the squash in the refrigerator.

FOR THE PUMPKIN JUICE VINAIGRETTE:

Warm the brown butter in a small saucepan over low heat. When the butter reaches 130°F (54°C), season it with the pumpkin juice, vinegar, and Maldon salt. Keep in a warm place.

TO SERVE:

Warm the cubed pumpkin in the vacuum bag for about 5 minutes in a steam oven set at 200°F (95°C). Put 2 pieces on each of 4 plates, placing the pieces opposite each other. Put some of the pumpkin seed granola in the center of each plate. Break a pumpkin shell into 3 pieces and arrange the pieces in more or less their original shape in the center of each plate. Garnish with the pickled pumpkin, Red Malabar spinach, purslane, New Zealand spinach, and sunflower sprouts. Scatter the ricotta and more of the granola around each plate, then dress the pumpkin cubes with the pumpkin juice vinaigrette. Finish each plate with a few marigold petals.

FROZEN PUMPKIN SHELL

600 grams | 21 ounces kabocha squash, peeled and diced
kosher salt
275 grams | 1 ⅓ cups brown butter
100 grams | ½ cup pumpkin mole (page 135)
13 grams | 4 sheets bronze gelatin, bloomed in ice water and wrung gently of excess water
kosher salt
liquid nitrogen

PUMPKIN SEED GRANOLA

500 grams | 2 ½ cups brown butter
350 grams | 2 ½ cups pumpkin seeds
200 grams | 7 ounces levain bread (page 288), thinly sliced
20 grams | 1 tablespoon brown rice syrup
kosher salt

PICKLED RAW PUMPKIN

200 grams | 7 ounces kabocha squash, peeled
300 grams | 1 ¼ cups cane vinegar
kosher salt

PUMPKIN JUICE VINAIGRETTE

50 grams | 3 ½ tablespoons brown butter
200 grams | ¾ cup pumpkin juice
30 grams | 2 tablespoons cane vinegar
Maldon sea salt

12 | Red Malabar spinach leaves
16 | garden purslane bunches
12 | New Zealand spinach leaves
12 | sunflower sprouts
marigolds

duck persimmon beet spice bush

In this case, a plate begot a dish. The rust-colored plate by Lynn Mahon (see page 102) inspired me to work within the same autumn color palette: duck, persimmons, and beets dyed orange with a bit of sumac. The smoked and dried duck katsuobushi and the grated spice bush berry contribute to creating that specific "thing unto itself" that we strive for with our collaborations with artisans—it is unclear where the food ends and the clay begins.

SERVES 4

AGED DUCK

130 grams | 1 quart dried spice bush leaves

20 grams | $^2/_3$ cup dried rose geranium
   leaves and flowers

75 grams | $^3/_4$ cup La Boîte Isphahan spice

1 | Muscovy duck

kosher salt

Maldon sea salt

SMOKED DUCK FAT

2 kilograms | about 8 cups rendered duck fat

DUCK KATSUOBUSHI

2 | duck legs (recipe above)

1.2 kilograms | 4 cups kosher salt

200 grams | 1 cup firmly packed
   brown sugar

300 grams | 1 $^1/_4$ cups white soy sauce

DRIED PERSIMMONS

4 | Fuyu persimmons, peeled and halved

1.5 kilograms | 6 $^3/_4$ cups granulated
   piloncillo

750 grams | 3 cups water

10 grams | 0.3 ounce spice bush berries

PERSIMMON PUREE

600 grams | 4 cups peeled and sliced fresh
   Fuyu persimmons

80 grams | 6 tablespoons rendered smoked
   duck fat (recipe above)

70 grams | $^3/_4$ cup dried persimmons
   (recipe above)

150 grams | 5.2 ounces gellan base
   (page 285)

kosher salt

FOR THE AGED DUCK:

Combine the spice bush leaves, geranium, and Isphahan spice in a blender and mix on high speed for about 15 seconds, until pulverized. To prepare the duck, remove the 2 leg quarter portions from the breast. Reserve the legs for later use. Rub the skin of the breast with the spice bush mixture and allow to air-dry in the refrigerator for 2 weeks.

FOR THE SMOKED DUCK FAT:

Hot smoke (see page 287) the duck fat at 160°F (71°C) for 1 hour. Use this duck fat for the remaining steps in the recipe.

FOR THE DUCK KATSUOBUSHI:

Skin the duck legs. Combine the kosher salt, sugar, and soy sauce in a bowl, mixing well. Bury the duck legs in the mixture and cure in the refrigerator for 24 hours.

Remove the legs from the cure, rinse under cool running water, and pat dry. Hot smoke (see page 287) the legs at 180°F (82°C) for 1 hour. Transfer the legs to a dehydrator tray and dehydrate at 125°F (52°C) for at least 24 hours, until completely dry. Using a bonito shaver, shave the legs into long, very thin strips. Reserve the duck bonito in an airtight container at room temperature.

FOR THE DRIED PERSIMMONS:

Combine the persimmons, piloncillo, water, and spice bush berries in a pressure cooker and cook on high pressure for 20 minutes, until the persimmons are tender but still hold their shape. Arrange the persimmons on a dehydrator tray and dehydrate at 125°F (52°C) for 24 hours, until dry but not tacky. Cut the persimmon halves in half crosswise and store in an airtight container at room temperature until ready to use.

FOR THE PERSIMMON PUREE:

Prepare an ice bath. Combine the fresh persimmons and 30 grams (2 tablespoons) of the duck fat in a vacuum bag and seal on high. Cook in a steam oven set at 200°F (95°C) for 15 minutes. Remove the persimmons from the bag and transfer to a blender. Add the dried persimmons, gellan base, and 50 grams (4 tablespoons) of the duck fat and mix on high speed for about 3 minutes, until a smooth puree forms. Strain through a chinois into a bowl, then nest the bowl in the ice bath to cool the puree. Season with salt, transfer to a squeeze bottle, and reserve in the refrigerator.

continued

FOR THE GLAZED YELLOW BEETS:

Put the beets, 45 grams (about ¹/₄ cup) of the duck fat, and a pinch of kosher salt in a vacuum bag and seal on high. Cook the beets in a steam oven set at 200°F (95°C) for 1 hour, until tender. Drain the beets, reserving the beets and liquid separately.

Combine 500 grams (about 2 cups) of the beet liquid, the water, sumac, and Isphahan spice in a saucepan over medium heat and simmer for 10 minutes. Meanwhile, pull the cooked beet quarters apart into small pieces, following the natural seams of the beets. Put the pieces into a saucepan and strain the seasoned beet liquid through a chinois into the pan. Bring to a boil over high heat and cook until the liquid is reduced by 80 percent, about 30 minutes. Transfer the beets and the liquid to a sheet pan and let cool in the refrigerator.

FOR THE SPICE BUSH SYRUP:

Combine the glucose, water, and spice bush leaves in a saucepan and bring to a boil over high heat. Cook until reduced by one-third. Strain the syrup through a chinois and hold warm until needed.

TO SERVE:

Prepare a fire in a wood-burning oven fitted with a grate and heat to 400°F (200°C). Remove the breast half from either side of the duck and season well with kosher salt. Place the breasts, skin side down, on the cooler part of the grate for 4 minutes to render the skin. Remove the breasts from the grate and let rest in an area with a temperature of 100°F (38°C) for 5 minutes. Slice each of the breasts into 2 equal slices and brush the skin side with the spice bush syrup. Season the cut side with Maldon salt and place 1 slice on each of 4 plates. Place the remaining 1 kilogram (5 cups) of duck fat in a saucepan over medium heat and heat to 180°F (82°C). Immerse the beet pieces in the fat for about 2 minutes, until warmed through. Garnish each plate with the dried persimmons, persimmon puree, glazed beets, and duck bonito. Heat a small amount of the duck jus and place a few dots around the duck. Finish with a couple of drops of persimmon vinegar and with fine gratings of spice bush berry.

GLAZED YELLOW BEETS

4 | large yellow beets, peeled and quartered
1 kilogram | 5 ¹/₄ cups rendered smoked
　　duck fat (page 137)
1.5 kilograms | 6 ¹/₃ cups water
100 grams | ³/₄ cup sumac
7 grams | 1 tablespoon La Boîte Isphahan spice
kosher salt

SPICE BUSH SYRUP

300 grams | 1 cup liquid glucose
500 grams | 2 cups water
200 grams | 7 ounces dried spice bush leaves

roasted duck jus (page 286)
persimmon vinegar
1 | dried spice bush berry

époisses last year's pluots

Nothing lightens the mood of an elongated menu like a bit of humor, here evinced in tiny Époisses baskets made of clay—the lid lifted before each guest. I hope that a smile results, overcoming perhaps the disappointment of not getting a whole wheel of Époisses.

SERVES 4

LAST YEAR'S PLUOTS
2 | Pluots, halved
4 grams | 1 teaspoon ascorbic acid
3 grams | $^1/_2$ teaspoon kosher salt
1 kilogram | 4 $^1/_4$ cups water
1 kilogram | 5 cups sugar

ÉPOISSES
400 grams | 14 ounces Époisses de
    Bourgogne cheese
200 grams | $^3/_4$ cup heavy cream
5 grams | 2 teaspoons low-acyl gellan gum
5 grams | 2 teaspoons high-acyl gellan gum
kosher salt

16 | buckwheat flowers
Noble sherry vinegar
Twin Sisters olive oil

FOR LAST YEAR'S PLUOTS:

Sterilize a large glass jar with a lid by submerging the jar in boiling water for 10 minutes. Remove from the water and let cool to room temperature. Leave the pot of water on the stove. Wearing gloves, carefully fit the Pluot halves in the jar along with the ascorbic acid and salt. Combine the water and sugar in a saucepan over high heat and bring to a boil, stirring to dissolve the sugar. Remove from the heat and pour the hot syrup into the jar. Screw the lid onto the jar, tightening it only about 80 percent. Return the pot of water to a boil and submerge the jar in the boiling water for 15 minutes. Remove the jar and immediately tighten the lid fully to secure the pressure in the jar. Let the jar cool overnight in the refrigerator. Transfer the jar to a cool, dark place, such as a root cellar, preferably for 1 year.

FOR THE ÉPOISSES:

Prepare an ice bath. Put the Époisses with rind intact in a blender. Pour the cream into a small saucepan and warm slightly over low heat. Add the gellan gums and mix with an immersion blender until completely dissolved. Increase the temperature to high and, using a rubber spatula, stir until the cream begins to thicken, wiping down the sides of the pot with the spatula as needed. Boil for 30 seconds, then transfer to the blender. Mix on high speed for about 2 minutes, until the mixture is smooth. Using a 60 millimeter ($^1/_4$ cup) ladle, pass the puree through a chinois into a bowl, then nest the bowl in the ice bath to cool the puree. Season with kosher salt, then refrigerate in an airtight container until ready to serve.

TO SERVE:

Put a Pluot half in the middle of each of 4 round vessels. Use a teaspoon dipped in warm water to shape a quenelle of the Époisses. Place it on top of the Pluot and garnish with the buckwheat flowers. Place a few drops of the vinegar around the cheese and drizzle with olive oil.

foie gras black walnut chicory quince

We have a set of plates that are named for their size and their creator: small Lynn, medium Lynn, big Lynn. We stack all three to elevate this dish of shaved foie gras marbled with preserved walnut. Bitter chicory, sweet quince, and wild fennel deliver an English-Christmasy take on duck liver.

FOR THE CURED FOIE GRAS:

Temper the foie gras at room temperature for about 3 hours, until it feels soft. Using a bench scraper, press through a tamis into a large metal bowl. Add the salt and curing mix and whisk until smooth and thoroughly incorporated. Cover the bowl with plastic wrap and set aside.

Combine the walnuts, chicory, wine, water, and cinnamon in a small saucepan over medium-low heat, bring to a simmer, and simmer for 30 minutes, until reduced by one-third. Prepare an ice bath. Remove the mixture from the heat and transfer to a blender. Blend on high speed for about 2 minutes, until smooth. Strain through a chinois into a bowl, then nest in the ice bath and stir to cool.

Spoon the foie gras into a piping bag fitted with a large round tip. Spoon the walnut puree into a second piping bag with a large round tip. Line the bottom and sides of a 6-inch (15-centimeter) square metal pan with plastic wrap. Fill the prepared pan with alternating lines of the foie gras and the walnut puree, changing each line's thickness (the more sporadic the lines, the better). Using a wooden skewer, mix together the foie gras and walnut mixtures, creating a swirl pattern. Cover with plastic wrap and place in the freezer for at least 6 hours.

FOR THE PINCH COOKIE:

Preheat the oven to 325°F (165°C). Line a half sheet pan with parchment paper and spread the all-purpose flour evenly in the lined pan. Bake for 30 minutes, until golden brown. Let cool to room temperature, then transfer to a food processor. Add the sugar, almond flour, salt, and walnut oil and pulse to create a uniform texture. Combine the cinnamon, cardamom, allspice, cloves, and star anise in a small sauté pan over low heat and toast for 2 minutes, until fragrant. Add the spices to the food processor and pulse just to mix. Transfer to an airtight container and store at room temperature.

FOR THE QUINCE PUREE:

Peel and quarter the quince. Combine the quince, sugar, and water in a pressure cooker and cook on high pressure for 25 minutes. Meanwhile, prepare an ice bath. Drain the quinces and transfer to a blender. Mix on high speed for 2 minutes, until a smooth puree forms. Strain through a chinois into a bowl, then nest the bowl in the ice bath and stir to cool the puree. Season with salt, then transfer to a squeeze bottle.

FOR THE WALNUT PUREE:

Place a saucepan over high heat. Add the brown sugar and stir aggressively to avoid scorching. When the sugar is fragrant and has liquefied (after about 15 seconds), add the young walnuts, raw walnuts, and water and turn down the heat to a simmer. Cook for 30 minutes, until tender. Prepare an ice bath. When the walnuts are ready, drain, reserving both the walnuts and the cooking liquid. Transfer the walnuts to a blender and begin mixing on high speed, adding the cooking liquid as needed to create a smooth puree. Strain the puree through a chinois into a bowl, then nest in the ice bath to cool. Transfer to a squeeze bottle.

TO SERVE:

Remove the foie gras from the freezer and temper for 15 minutes. Place a small dollop of quince puree on the bottom of each of 6 bowls. Crumble the pinch cookie on top, then, using a mandoline, shave the foie gras as thinly as possible into the bowls. Garnish with a few dots of walnut puree, young walnut slices, and fennel fronds. Dust additional pinch cookie on top of each serving.

SERVES 6

CURED FOIE GRAS

680 grams | 1.5 pounds grade A foie gras

19 grams | 1 tablespoon kosher salt

1.3 grams | 1/4 teaspoon tinted curing mix #1

200 grams | 7 ounces preserved young walnuts

15 grams | 2 tablespoons instant chicory coffee powder

150 grams | 2/3 cup white port

300 grams | 1 1/4 cups water

10 grams | about 1 Ceylon cinnamon stick

PINCH COOKIE

150 grams | 1 1/4 cups all-purpose flour

150 grams | 3/4 cup sugar

150 grams | 1 1/2 cups extra-fine almond flour

10 grams | 1 1/2 teaspoons kosher salt

120 grams | 1/2 cup toasted walnut oil

1 gram | 1/2 teaspoon ground cinnamon

1 gram | 1/2 teaspoon ground green cardamom

0.5 gram | 1/4 teaspoon ground allspice

0.5 gram | 1/4 teaspoon ground cloves

1 gram | 1/2 teaspoon ground star anise

QUINCE PUREE

450 grams | about 2 large pineapple quince

300 grams | 1 1/2 cups sugar

600 grams | 2 1/2 cups water

kosher salt

WALNUT PUREE

100 grams | 1/2 cup firmly packed light brown sugar

150 grams | 5.3 ounces preserved young walnuts

300 grams | 10.5 ounces raw walnuts

400 grams | 1 2/3 cups water

3 | preserved young walnuts, thinly sliced

5 | wild fennel stalks

poussin baked in bread
nasturtium onion

In preparation for a dinner with the chefs of San Francisco's famed Bar Tartine, we attempted this dish of a bird baked in a nigella seed–studded sourdough. Unlike most new ideas, this one worked right away: the bird was moist and had a subtle yeasty flavor. We played with the garniture, eventually settling on melted onions, a puree of the onions and the bread, and spicy nasturtiums. At The Restaurant, we first show the bird to the table garnished with herbs, serve some of the bread in which it is cooked, and then finally, we bring the plated dish. We use the "cake plate" as a canvas for the muted white of the bird and onion and the vibrant green of the nasturtium.

SERVES 4

POUSSIN PREPARATION

1.5 kilograms | 3.3 pounds levain dough
    (page 288)
150 grams | 1 1/2 cups nigella seeds, toasted
1 | poussin, 450 to 680 grams
    (1 to 1 1/2 pounds)
kosher salt

25 grams | 2 tablespoons rendered
    chicken fat
Maldon sea salt

MELTED WHITE ONIONS

2 | white onions, quartered
kosher salt

BREAD ONION SAUCE

75 grams | 2.5 ounces reserved nigella bread
350 grams | 1 1/2 cups onion cooking liquid
    from melted onions (recipe above)
kosher salt

FOR THE POUSSIN PREPARATION:

Make the levain dough as directed in the recipe up to the point where it has proofed for 2 hours. Line a half sheet pan with parchment paper and spray with nonstick cooking spray. Turn the dough out onto a floured work surface and fold in the nigella seeds, distributing them evenly. Divide the dough in half and shape each half into a disk about 8 inches (20 centimeters) in diameter. Place 1 disk in the center of the prepared sheet pan. Season the poussin on all sides with kosher salt and place in the center of the disk. Place the second disk over the poussin and seal the edges by tucking them under the poussin. Place the pan in a proof box set at 90°F (32°C) for about 30 minutes, until the dough has risen slightly and has a strong, yeasty fragrance. Meanwhile, preheat the oven to 450°F (230°C).

Remove the pan from the proof box and place in the oven. Bake for 30 minutes, until the crust of the bread is a deep golden brown. Let the poussin rest encased in the bread at room temperature for 30 minutes.

FOR THE MELTED WHITE ONIONS:

Put the onions in a vacuum bag, season with salt, and seal on high. Cook in a steam oven set at 200°F (95°C) for 30 minutes, until the onions are very tender but still hold their shape. Remove the bag from the oven, let cool until it can be handled, then open the bag and drain the onions, capturing the liquid in a container. Cover the container and store in the refrigerator until ready to use. Separate the layers of the onion and cut into 1-inch (2.5-centimeter)-wide petals. Store the petals in an airtight container in the refrigerator until ready to use.

FOR THE BREAD ONION SAUCE:

When the poussin has rested for 30 minutes, cut a wide hole in the top of the bread, being careful not to pierce the poussin. Remove the poussin and set aside. Scoop out enough of the insides of the bread to equal 75 grams (2.5 ounces). Place the removed bread in a blender along with the onion liquid and mix on high speed for 2 minutes, until very smooth. Season with salt and hold in a warm place. Reserve the remaining baked bread for serving.

continued

FOR THE NASTURTIUM PUREE:

Prepare an ice bath. Combine the lime juice, olive oil, and nasturtium leaves in a blender and mix on high speed for 20 seconds, until smooth. Slowly add the Ultra-Tex 3 and continue to mix until thickened. Strain through a chinois into a bowl, then nest the bowl in the ice bath to cool the puree. Transfer the puree to a squeeze bottle and refrigerate until ready to use.

TO SERVE:

Slice the breasts and the leg quarters from the rested poussin, then bone the leg quarters. Line a sheet pan with parchment paper. Place 8 pieces of melted onion on the prepared pan and place the pan in a steam oven set at 200°F (95°C) for 3 minutes. Cut 2 diagonal slices from each breast and cut each leg quarter in half. Brush with the rendered chicken fat and season with Maldon salt. Create a circle with the nasturtium puree on each of 4 plates. Place a small amount of the bread onion sauce in the center of each circle and then follow with a slice of breast and half of a leg. Garnish each piece of poussin with an onion petal and a nasturtium leaf. Rip pieces of the crust from the reserved bread and serve alongside.

NASTURTIUM PUREE

90 grams | $^1/_3$ cup freshly squeezed
    lime juice
180 grams | $^3/_4$ cup Twin Sisters olive oil
100 grams | 3.5 ounces nasturtium leaves
8 grams | 1 tablespoon Ultra-Tex 3

8 | tiny nasturtium leaves

chocolate cherry tart

We use a series of William and Nikki's earth bowls (see page 104) to mimic the equally rustic edges of this free-form tart made with chocolate, shortbread, and feuilletine. The pickled cherry dipping dots and salted cherry leaves provide some acidity that nicely prevents the dish from becoming a sugar bomb.

SERVES 4

CHERRY VINEGAR
300 grams | 10.5 ounces Bing cherries
1 kilogram | about 4 cups Champagne vinegar

CHOCOLATE SHORTBREAD
100 grams | 3.5 ounces dark chocolate
(72 percent cacao)
125 grams | 1 cup all-purpose flour
30 grams | $\frac{1}{3}$ cup cocoa powder
1 gram | $\frac{1}{4}$ teaspoon baking powder
4 grams | $\frac{3}{4}$ teaspoon kosher salt
115 grams | $\frac{1}{2}$ cup unsalted butter
132 grams | $\frac{2}{3}$ cup sugar
20 grams | about 1 egg yolk

CHOCOLATE TART SHELLS
300 grams | 10.5 ounces dark chocolate
(72 percent cacao)
80 grams | 2.8 ounces feuilletine
100 grams | 3.5 ounces chocolate shortbread
crumb (recipe above)

FOR THE CHERRY VINEGAR:
Combine the cherries and vinegar in a vacuum bag and seal on high. Macerate in the refrigerator for 36 hours, then strain the cherries from the vinegar, discarding them. Transfer the vinegar to a squeeze bottle and refrigerate until ready to use.

FOR THE CHOCOLATE SHORTBREAD:
Place the chocolate in the freezer for at least 30 minutes while you prepare the dough. Using a tamis, sift together the flour, cocoa powder, baking powder, and salt into a metal bowl. In the bowl of a stand mixer fitted with a paddle attachment, combine the butter and sugar. Mix on medium speed until the sugar is evenly dispersed throughout the butter. Put the frozen chocolate into a food processor and mix until pulverized. Add the chocolate powder to the stand mixer and mix on low speed until fully incorporated, stopping to scrape down the sides of the bowl as needed to ensure an even mixture. Mix in the egg yolk and then add the flour mixture in three batches, mixing for about 20 seconds total, just to incorporate. Remove the dough from the mixer, wrap in plastic wrap, and refrigerate for 1 hour.

Preheat the oven to 325°F (165°C). Roll the chilled dough into a log and place it at one end of a piece of parchment paper. Place another piece of parchment paper on top of the dough and press lightly to flatten. Run through a dough sheeter set to a thickness of about $\frac{1}{32}$ inch (1 millimeter). Remove the dough from the parchment, then lay it on a sheet pan and bake for 12 minutes, until the shortbread is dry and crispy. Let cool to room temperature for 3 hours.

Break the shortbread into manageable pieces and put them into a food processor. Mix to a fine crumb. Transfer to an airtight container and store at room temperature until needed.

FOR THE CHOCOLATE TART SHELLS:
Melt the chocolate in a double boiler over gently simmering water. Heat until the chocolate registers 108°F (42°C). Using a rubber spatula, slowly stir in the feuilletine and shortbread crumbs. Spread the chocolate mixture on a sheet of parchment paper, top with a second parchment sheet, and then pass through a dough sheeter set to a thickness of between $\frac{1}{8}$ inch and $\frac{1}{4}$ inch (4 millimeters). Using a ring cutter 3 inches (7.5 centimeters) in diameter, cut out circles from the chocolate sheet. Using a small bowl (about 3 inches/8 centimeters in diameter) and a spoon, mold the chocolate circle around the bowl to mimic the shape, then place in the freezer. Repeat to make 4 tart shells. Hold in the freezer for at least 2 hours before use.

continued

chocolate cherry tart *continued*

FOR THE CHERRY PÂTE DE FRUIT:

Spray a half sheet pan with nonstick cooking spray, then dust lightly with sugar. Combine the apple pectin and a small portion of the sugar in a small bowl and mix to disperse the pectin evenly. Put the remaining sugar, the cherry puree, and the glucose in a saucepan and place over medium heat. Heat, stirring constantly, to 225°F (107°C), then immediately add the citric acid and pour the liquid into the prepared sheet pan. Allow the liquid to spread out into a thin layer, then dust additional sugar over the top. Hold at room temperature for 2 hours, until cool and set.

Using a ring cutter 1/4 inch (about 6 millimeters) in diameter, punch out small circles from the sheet. Store in an airtight container with silica gel packets at room temperature.

FOR THE DARK CHOCOLATE CRÉMEUX:

 Prepare an ice bath. Pour the cream into a saucepan and heat over low heat to 120°F (49°C). Combine the chocolate and gellan base in a blender, add the hot cream, and mix on high for 3 minutes, until smooth. Strain through a chinois into a bowl, then nest the bowl in the ice bath to cool the mixture. Transfer to a piping bag fitted with a small round tip and refrigerate.

FOR THE GRILLED CHERRY LEAVES:

Prepare a fire in a wood-burning oven. When the fire is at about 600°F (315°C), arrange the cherry leaves on the grate and grill for about 10 seconds, until slightly charred. Flip and char the opposite side for 5 seconds longer. Remove from the oven and arrange on a dehydrator tray lined with paper towels. Dehydrate at 125°F (52°C) for 1 hour before use.

FOR THE DRIED CHERRY PUREE:

Put the cherries in a saucepan, add cold water just to cover, and bring to a simmer over medium heat. Turn down the heat to low and simmer for 20 minutes, until the cherries are tender. Meanwhile, prepare an ice bath. Transfer the cherries and water to a blender and mix on high speed for 3 minutes, until smooth. Strain through a chinois into a bowl, then nest the bowl in the ice bath and stir the puree until cool. Transfer to a squeeze bottle and store in the refrigerator until ready to use.

FOR THE SWEETENED CRÈME FRAÎCHE:

Prepare an ice bath. Combine the crème fraîche, sugar, and gellan base in a blender and mix on medium speed for 2 minutes, until thick and smooth. Do not mix longer, as you do not want to overheat the mixture. Strain though a chinois into a bowl, then nest the bowl in the ice bath and stir the puree to cool. Season lightly with kosher salt, transfer to a squeeze bottle, and store in the refrigerator until needed.

FOR THE ROASTED BING CHERRIES:

Preheat the oven to 280°F (140°C). Line a half sheet pan with parchment paper. Combine the cherries, oil, sugar, and salt in a metal bowl and toss to coat the cherries evenly. Spread the cherries on the prepared sheet pan. Bake for 6 minutes, just until the cherries begin to soften. Let cool at room temperature, then hold in an airtight container at room temperature.

CHERRY PÂTE DE FRUIT

400 grams | 2 cups sugar, plus more for dusting
10 grams | about 2 teaspoons powdered apple pectin
420 grams | 1 3/4 cups Bing cherry puree (page 287)
84 grams | 2/3 cup powdered glucose
6.5 grams | 1 1/4 teaspoons citric acid

DARK CHOCOLATE CRÉMEUX

400 grams | 1 2/3 cups heavy cream
300 grams | 10.5 ounces dark chocolate (72 percent cacao)
30 grams | 1 ounce gellan base (page 285)

GRILLED CHERRY LEAVES

4 | salted cherry leaves

DRIED CHERRY PUREE

400 grams | about 14 ounces dried tart cherries

SWEETENED CRÈME FRAÎCHE

400 grams | 1 3/4 cups crème fraîche (page 283)
50 grams | 1/4 cup sugar
200 grams | 7 ounces gellan base (page 285)
kosher salt

ROASTED BING CHERRIES

6 | Bing cherries, halved and pitted
10 grams | 2 1/4 teaspoons Twin Sisters olive oil
12 grams | 1 tablespoon sugar
kosher salt

PICKLED CHERRY SORBET "DIPPING DOTS"

600 grams | 2 ²/₃ cups Bing cherry puree
  (page 287)
60 grams | ¹/₄ cup cherry vinegar
  (page 149)
simple syrup
liquid nitrogen

FOR THE PICKLED CHERRY SORBET "DIPPING DOTS":

Combine the cherry puree and cherry vinegar in a bowl. Using a refractometer, measure the Brix level naturally occurring in the puree. Adjust the level by adding simple syrup to reach 25° to 27° Brix. Transfer the sorbet base to a large squeeze bottle. Carefully put the liquid nitrogen into a foam-insulated container (excessive changes in temperature or agitation of the liquid nitrogen may cause it to become volatile). Put a second foam-insulated container next to the first one and rest a strainer over the top. Turn the squeeze bottle upside down over the liquid nitrogen and squeeze gently to make dots, moving in a circular pattern so as not to drop the dots in the same place twice. Squeeze about one-fourth of the contents of the bottle, then lightly agitate the sorbet dots using a metal spatula or other long utensil to ensure they don't adhere to the bottom and sides of the container. Pour the contents of the first container through the strainer resting on the second container. Break up any clusters, then store the dots in a dry plastic container in the freezer until ready to use. Repeat until all of the sorbet base has been formed into dots.

TO SERVE:

Place the chocolate tart shells on 4 round plates. Distribute dots of the dark chocolate crémeux, sweetened crème fraîche, and dried cherry puree on the shells. Place 3 roasted cherry halves around the dots in each shell and then scatter a few pieces of the cherry pâte de fruit around the dots. Reintroduce the sorbet "dipping dots" into liquid nitrogen for 10 seconds and, using a slotted spoon, place them in a pile in the center of the shell. (To discard the liquid nitrogen, carefully pour it back into its original container.) Break up the cherry leaves and place a few pieces on top of the dots.

birthday cake

Sous chef Poncho helped come up with this birthday cake recipe, but woodworker Brett Van Natta brought it to life with his birthday box, a box with sides that fall away when the top is removed, revealing the cake inside. Below the cake sits a card wishing the guest a happy birthday. The cake has just enough savory elements to appease the chefs in the kitchen and just enough sweetness to delight the guests in the dining room.

SERVES 10

OLIVE OIL CAKE

42 grams | $^1/_4$ cup trimoline
100 grams | 2 eggs
100 grams | $^1/_2$ cup sugar, plus more
    for dusting
120 grams | 1 cup all-purpose flour
4.3 grams | 1 teaspoon baking powder
1.3 grams | $^1/_4$ teaspoon kosher salt
130 grams | $^3/_4$ cup extra virgin olive oil

CARAMEL MOUSSE

300 grams | 1 $^1/_4$ cups heavy cream
47 grams | $^1/_4$ cup egg yolks
80 grams | $^1/_3$ cup sugar
37 grams | 2 $^1/_2$ tablespoons water
6.6 grams | about 2 sheets bronze gelatin,
    bloomed in ice water and wrung gently
    of excess water
kosher salt

FOR THE OLIVE OIL CAKE:

Preheat the oven to 300°F (150°C). Put the trimoline, eggs, and sugar in a food processor and mix for 2 minutes, until smooth, stopping to scrape down the sides of the processor bowl as needed. Sift together the flour, baking powder, and salt into a bowl. With the processor running, slowly incorporate the flour mixture into the egg mixture in three batches. Then slowly add the oil, mixing until it is fully absorbed into the batter.

Divide the batter evenly between 2 full-size silicone baking mats and spread in an even layer $^1/_{16}$ inch (2 millimeters) thick. Transfer the baking mats to full sheet pans and bake the cakes for 12 to 15 minutes, until golden brown.

The moment the cakes are evenly colored, remove them from the oven and immediately dust them with a thin layer of sugar. Lay a sheet of parchment paper over the sugar, flip the cake upside down, and peel away the baking mat as quickly as possible. At this point, the cakes will have cooled too much and must be returned to the oven for 1 to 2 minutes to rewarm. Using a bicyclette, cut the cake into strips about $^1/_2$ inch by 5 $^1/_2$ inches (12 millimeters by 14 centimeters). Coil each cake strip along the inside of a metal ring mold about 1 $^1/_4$ inches (3 centimeters) wide by 2 inches (5 centimeters) deep, leaving the middle of the ring mold open. If the cake becomes too stiff to handle, return it to the oven to rewarm. Store the filled rings on a half sheet pan in the refrigerator.

FOR THE CARAMEL MOUSSE:

Pour 250 grams (1 cup) of the cream into the bowl of a stand mixer fitted with the whip attachment and whip on medium speed until medium peaks form. Transfer to a covered container and refrigerate until needed.

Rinse the bowl, return it to the mixer, add the egg yolks, and begin whipping on low speed. Meanwhile, combine the sugar and water in a small, heavy saucepan over medium-high heat and cook, stirring occasionally, until a syrup forms that is amber and has the fragrance of caramel. Slowly whisk in the remaining 50 grams ($^1/_4$ cup) cream, then cook for about 30 seconds, until the water has evaporated from the cream. At this point, the yolks in the mixer should have formed medium-stiff peaks. With the mixer still on low speed, slowly add the caramel to the yolks. Once the caramel is incorporated, increase the speed to high to begin cooling the mixture. When the mousse is at about 120°F (50°C), add the bloomed gelatin and continue whipping until the mousse cools to room temperature.

Gently fold the whipped cream into the mousse until just combined. Season with salt and then spoon the mousse into a piping bag fitted with a medium round tip. Pipe 30 grams (about 2 tablespoons) of the mousse into the center of each mold with the cake and freeze for at least 2 hours.

continued

birthday cake *continued*

FOR THE SALTED MILK CHOCOLATE:

Melt 125 grams (1 cup) of the chocolate in a double boiler over gently simmering water. Heat until the chocolate registers 107°F (42°C), then add the remaining 75 grams (²/₃ cup) of chocolate to the melted chocolate to reduce the temperature to 89°F to 92°F (32°C to 33°C). Turn the chocolate out onto a sheet of acetate and spread in a thin, even layer about $1/_{32}$ inch (1 millimeter) thick. Allow the chocolate to crystallize for about 10 minutes, until hard enough to touch but not so brittle that it cracks. Press a ring mold of equal size to the mousse cake (1 ¼ inches wide by 2 inches deep/3 by 5 centimeters) into the chocolate to create perfect disks of tempered chocolate. Season each disk with Maldon salt and hold in an area with an ambient temperature of no more than 75°F (24°C) until needed.

TO SERVE:

To release each cake from its ring mold, gently warm the mold with a kitchen torch and lift it off. Top each cake with a disk of salted chocolate, then place the cake on parchment paper in a wooden box with fall-away sides.

SALTED MILK CHOCOLATE
200 grams | 7 ounces milk chocolate
(40 percent cacao), chopped
Maldon sea salt

hearts of palm dates young coconut

This dessert represents the single most important interaction between food and ceramics. The interplay of the hues of the dates, hearts of palm, and coconut with similar themes on the rough slab plate was the beginning of much of the collaborative work with the artisans that has followed (see page 102).

SERVES 8

HEARTS OF PALM CUSTARD

900 grams | 2 pounds hearts of palm

1.4 kilograms | 6 cups heavy cream

490 grams | 2 cups whole milk

20 grams | 6 sheets bronze gelatin, bloomed in ice water and wrung gently of excess water

8 grams | 1 ¹/₂ teaspoons iota carrageenan

90 grams | ¹/₂ cup sugar

6 grams | 1 teaspoon kosher salt

CARAWAY CAKE

230 grams | 1 cup unsalted butter, softened

230 grams | 1 cup muscovado sugar

200 grams | about 4 eggs

280 grams | ³/₄ cup dark molasses

320 grams | 2 ¹/₂ cups all-purpose flour

6 grams | 1 tablespoon ground ginger

12 grams | 2 tablespoons caraway seeds, toasted in a dry pan until fragrant and ground into a powder

4.5 grams | 1 teaspoon baking soda

80 grams | ³/₄ cup shredded unsweetened dried coconut

150 grams | ²/₃ cup canola oil

FOR THE HEARTS OF PALM CUSTARD:

Dice the hearts of palm into uniform pieces and put them into a large plastic container. Combine the cream and milk in a saucepan and bring to a boil over high heat. Pour the hot cream mixture over the hearts of palm and place in a warm spot to infuse for 1 hour. Strain the hearts of palm from the infusion, place the infusion in a large rondeau, and discard the solids. Add the bloomed gelatin, iota carrageenan, sugar, and kosher salt to the infusion, place over high heat, and bring to a boil, whisking constantly. Boil for at least 20 seconds, until the liquid thickens slightly. Strain the custard base through a chinois into a container and let cool to about 130°F (54°C). Transfer to a sauce gun or large squeeze bottle.

Have ready at least 6 metal cylindrical molds about 1 inch (2.5 centimeters) in diameter and 6 inches (15 centimeters) tall. Seal one end of each mold with plastic wrap and stand the cylinders on that end. Secure the molds together with butcher's twine to ensure they are stable and sealed on the bottom. Pour the custard into the molds to create tube shapes. Refrigerate for at least 2 hours, until set.

Separate the molds from each other, then unmold the custard tubes by removing the plastic from the bottom end of the mold and lifting gently to loosen the custard. Slice each custard tube crosswise into 1-inch (2.5-centimeter) pieces. Using a smaller cylindrical mold, punch out the center of each custard piece so that it resembles a heart of palm and discard the trim. Repeat with the remaining custard portions and store in an airtight container in the refrigerator.

FOR THE CARAWAY CAKE:

Preheat the oven to 325°F (165°C). Line a quarter sheet pan with parchment paper and spray the paper with nonstick cooking spray. Combine the butter and muscovado sugar in the bowl of a stand mixer fitted with the paddle attachment and mix on medium speed until the butter is slightly aerated. Add the eggs, one at a time, mixing well after each addition. Scrape down the sides of the bowl, add the molasses, and mix on low speed until smooth. Using a tamis, sift together the flour, ginger, caraway, and baking soda into a bowl. On medium speed, add the flour mixture to the butter mixture in three batches at short intervals to avoid overmixing the flour. Using a rubber spatula, fold in the coconut and canola oil just until evenly incorporated.

Pour the batter into the prepared sheet pan and smooth the surface. Bake the cake for 12 to 15 minutes, until the center springs back when lightly pressed with a fingertip. Let cool to room temperature in the pan, then invert the pan and peel the parchment away. Cut into roughly 1-inch (2.5-centimeter) cubes. Store the cubes in an airtight container in the refrigerator.

Gather up the trim left over from cutting the cubes, spread on a dehydrator tray, and dehydrate at 125°F (52°C) for 6 hours, until dried. Transfer to a food processor and pulse until uniform crumbs form. Store the crumbs in an airtight container with silica gel packets at room temperature.

continued

FOR THE SORBET SYRUP:

Prepare an ice bath. Combine the sugar and sorbet stabilizer in a bowl and whisk together to distribute the ingredients evenly. Pour the water into a saucepan and warm gently over low heat. Whisk in the sugar mixture and heat, continuing to whisk, until it has dissolved. Add the glucose and increase the heat to high. Whisking constantly, bring the mixture to a boil and boil for 30 seconds. Remove the syrup from the heat, strain through a chinois into a bowl, and then nest the bowl in the ice bath to cool the syrup. Store in an airtight container in the refrigerator until ready to serve, or for up to 1 month.

FOR THE DATE SHERBET:

Put the dates in a metal container and pour boiling water over them just to cover (about 4 kilograms/ 4 quarts). Allow the dates to soften for 2 minutes, then drain them, discarding the water. Pit and peel the dates, discarding both the skin and pits. Place the cleaned dates in a blender and mix on high speed for about 3 minutes, until a smooth puree forms. Strain the puree through a chinois, measure 1 kilogram (4 1/2 cups), and reserve. Combine the milk, cream, and sorbet syrup in a saucepan, place over high heat, and heat to 187°F (86°C). Remove from the heat, add the date puree, and combine with an immersion blender until smooth. Season with the lime juice and pour into an ice cream machine. Run a cycle for 6 to 8 minutes, just until the sherbet is thick but still pourable. Transfer the sherbet to a few plastic containers and hold in the freezer for at least 1 hour before use.

FOR THE CARAMELIZED COCONUT WATER:

Combine the coconut water and sugar in a small saucepan over low heat. When the liquid begins to simmer, shift the pan slightly off the burner to avoid boiling. Reduce the liquid for about 2 hours, until a light syrup forms. Strain through a chinois and let cool to room temperature. Transfer to a squeeze bottle and store in the refrigerator until needed.

FOR THE YOUNG COCONUT, HEARTS OF PALM, AND FRESH DATES:

Break the coconut in half, reserving the coconut water. Slice the flesh away from the shell and cut it into small dice. Slice the heart of palm into thin, round slices. Using a mandoline, shave the dates lengthwise into thin slices. Combine the reserved coconut water and sugar, mix well, and divide evenly among 3 containers. Immerse the coconut flesh, hearts of palm, and dates each in its own container. Refrigerate until needed.

FOR THE CRISPY HEARTS OF PALM:

Fill a small stockpot half full with oil and heat the oil to 325°F (165°C). Meanwhile, cut the heart of palm into 2-inch (5-centimeter) pieces, then, using a mandoline, shave each piece lengthwise into very thin strips (which will then naturally separate into threads). Lightly dust the threads with confectioners' sugar, shaking off the excess, then add to the hot oil and fry for about 15 seconds, until golden brown. Transfer to paper towels to drain and pull the threads apart while still warm. Season with kosher salt, let cool, and store in an airtight container with silica gel packets at room temperature.

TO SERVE:

On a rectangular plate, crumble 2 cubes of the caraway cake and place 2 pieces of the hearts of palm custard, one on its side and one standing on its end. Garnish with the diced coconut, sliced hearts of palm, and sliced dates. Place a few dots of the caramelized coconut water on the plate and pile a few of the cake crumbs next to the custard. Using a teaspoon dipped in warm water, form a quenelle of the date sherbet and place it on top of the cake crumbs, then finish the plate with the crispy hearts of palm and lime zest.

SORBET SYRUP

1 kilogram | 5 cups sugar
18 grams | 1 tablespoon plus 1 teaspoon sorbet stabilizer
1 kilogram | about 4 cups water
450 grams | 1 pound powdered glucose

DATE SHERBET

1.4 kilograms | about 3 pounds Medjool dates
575 grams | 2 1/3 cups milk
75 grams | 1/3 cup heavy cream
600 grams | 1 3/4 cups sorbet syrup (recipe above)
20 grams | 4 teaspoons freshly squeezed lime juice

CARAMELIZED COCONUT WATER

500 grams | 2 cups coconut water
25 grams | 2 tablespoons granulated sugar

YOUNG COCONUT, HEARTS OF PALM, AND FRESH DATES

1 | young coconut
1 | heart of palm stalk
4 | fresh Barhi dates, pitted
25 grams | 2 tablespoons sugar

CRISPY HEARTS OF PALM

rice bran oil, for deep-frying
1 | heart of palm stalk
confectioners' sugar
kosher salt

1 | lime, zest grated

koji manzanita berries

Turned on to koji by our friends at Culture Pickle in Berkeley, we created this sorbet as a refreshing and complex segue into sweeter courses. The nest of ashed manzanita branches, fresh leaves, and berries correspond quietly with the berries that accompany the sorbet.

FOR THE MANZANITA BERRIES:
Combine the vinegar, water, and sugar in a saucepan and bring to a boil over high heat. Transfer to a heatproof metal container and add the manzanita berries. Steep at room temperature for 10 minutes, then store in the refrigerator for at least 24 hours.

FOR THE AMAKASE:
Combine the brown rice and water in a saucepan and bring to a boil over high heat. Cover, lower the heat to a simmer, and cook for 40 minutes, until the rice is soft. When the rice is ready, measure 400 grams (about 2 1/2 cups) of it and place in a heatproof bowl. Add the koji and mix thoroughly, then pack into a glass jar with a lid. Hold in a hot-water bath set at 140°F (60°C) for 12 hours. Remove from the water bath and refrigerate.

FOR THE KOJI SORBET:
Combine the water, glucose, and sugar in a saucepan over medium heat and, without stirring, heat to 160°F (71°C). Transfer to a blender, add the amakase, and mix on high speed for 2 minutes, until smooth. Season with shio koji and kosher salt and mix for 2 minutes longer. Strain through a chinois into a plastic container. Store in an airtight container in the refrigerator for at least 12 hours.

Pour into an ice cream machine and run a cycle for about 4 minutes, until slightly aerated and frozen. Store the sorbet in plastic containers in the freezer.

TO SERVE:
Put a small amount of the manzanita berries and the steeping liquid in the bottom of each bowl. Using a teaspoon dipped in warm water, form a quenelle of the koji sorbet and place on top of the berries.

MAKES 1.5 KILOGRAMS (6 1/2 CUPS); SERVES 20

MANZANITA BERRIES
200 grams | 3/4 cup Champagne vinegar
100 grams | 1/2 cup water
100 grams | 1/2 cup sugar
50 grams | 3/4 cup manzanita berries

AMAKASE
200 grams | 1 cup brown jasmine rice
600 grams | 2 1/2 cups water
200 grams | 1 cup brown rice koji

KOJI SORBET
850 grams | 3 2/3 cups water
200 grams | 1 cup sugar
120 grams | 1/3 cup liquid glucose
400 grams | 1 3/4 cups amakase (recipe above)
shio koji
kosher salt

THE WILDS

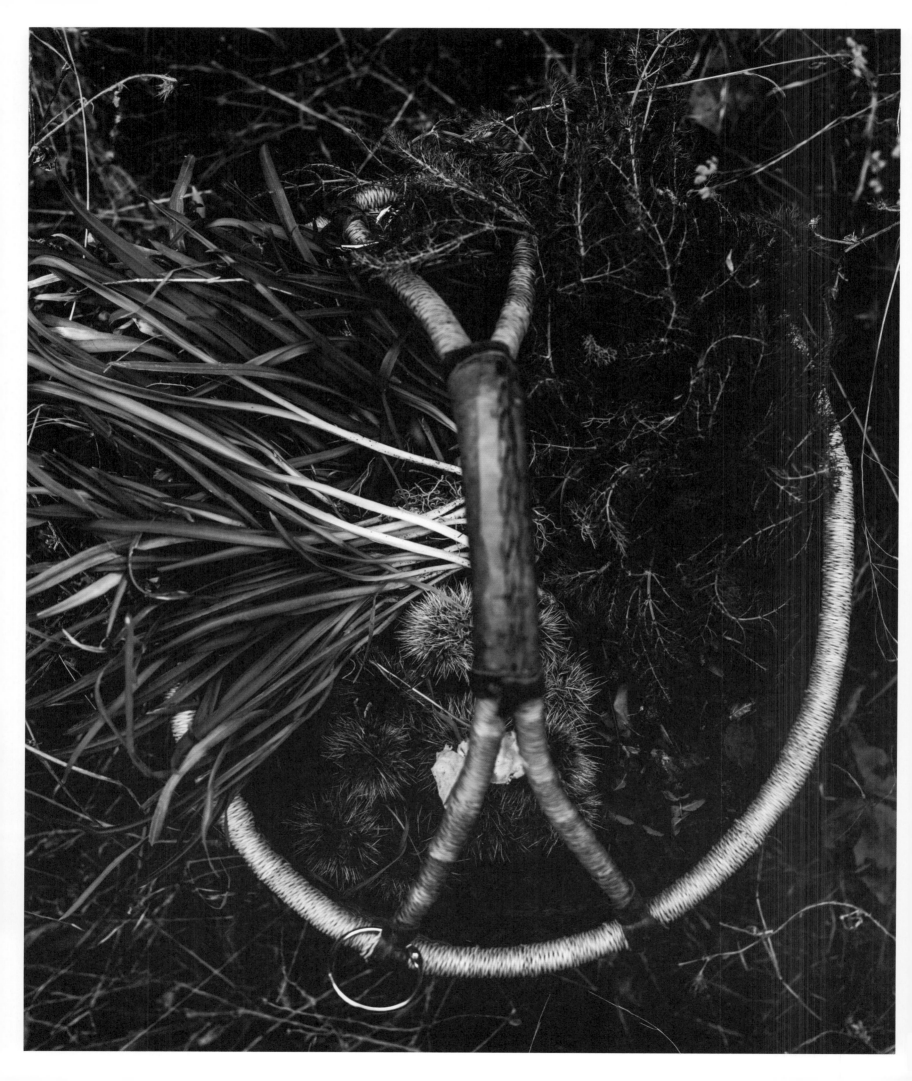

No man ever steps in the same river twice, for it's not the same river and he's not the same man.

—HERACLITUS

I never wanted foraging to be the focus of my work. Before I came to Napa, I thought this trend belonged to others; it was almost a dirty word, an activity that seemed contrived and forced. I assumed other chefs were confusing the hard-to-find with the good, the esoteric with the sublime. A few months in the valley changed my thinking. Wild ingredients can be found in the valley as plentifully as weeds and cigarettes on a city street. You can't help but trip over the wild fennel that grows everywhere in early summer or be transfixed by the yellow mustard flowers that blanket a field in late winter.

The sight of things growing wild here was the spark that led me to reconsider this place and my role in it. Early on I would gather some radish flowers and wild vetch during my walks with Charlie, diligently avoiding any patches that he had watered. Back at the restaurant, we would garnish dishes with the miner's lettuce that I gathered from a sous chef's home on a horse farm at the end of Spring Street. We would tread through open fields, surely mistaken for tourists, while we cut mustard flowers to garnish a beef dish.

There is a giddiness that comes from feeling you have stumbled on something that no one else has, and an excitement that borders on fear when you realize that others might start paying attention to the exciting things happening right in front of them. That's how I felt when I discovered that these wild and delicious ingredients grew throughout the valley; this is the same feeling I still have when I run across a patch of flowering wild mint or a group of matsutakes. Holy shit . . . hurry!

Cameron Rahtz is a better forager than a meat cook, though he continues to disagree with me on this point. He has nevertheless become our resident forager and is regularly found on the coast and along the wooded mountains that ring the valley. Driving a beat-up PT Cruiser that inspires much abuse from the kitchen staff, Cameron arrives in the kitchen with goods and with tales—sometimes more of the latter than the former. We sit around my cutting board and taste the coastal grasses and lamb's quarters, bury our noses in beech roses that smell like ripe, red apples, and check the rock crabs still slick with ocean water. Again, the giddiness hits. We taste the astringent wild rhubarb that grows in the Napa River and its tiny offshoots and even ponder the nopales that grow along the riverbanks. I often join Cameron on his ranges, happy to partake for a few hours in his unabashed excitement while we search for the tiny and the sublime.

We are in constant pursuit of dishes that let us tell a story about the valley. Those manzanita berries, that lemon balm, those pine shoots help us create a series of flavors that, when experienced within the whole of a meal, are singular and essential. These items are not merely garnishment to preexisting ideas; nor are they a means of embellishment or gilding. We don't use the tiny sorrels because they are cute or au courant. We use them because once we know they exist as part of this landscape, we feel compelled to make them part of the story.

My goal is to become fluent in the passing of seasons, to grasp completely the shapes and movements of the *terroir* and gain an understanding of all that time and this place have seen fit to produce. I want to be a student of this area so that I can become a medium of sorts for what grows here, to develop acumen and skill as the years progress and to master the elder flower, the wild plum, and the eucalyptus. I want to be in sync with forces far greater than the ebb and flow of my own popularity or the trends that have created the frenetic maneuverings in the restaurant business.

This is a life's work—this study of a place and the foods that it produces. I can't do this as a concept or as the foundation of a restaurant meant to birth future ones. The ringing phones and demands of life and the restaurant cannot drown out the murmuring, just over that hill, of all that can be found here. This is the greatest challenge of all, and the crux of true success: the restaurant, my career, and my life in the valley are in many ways contingent on my ability to stay tethered here, rather than to spin off into ungrounded celebrity and brand. If I don't know when the acorns begin falling, they will rot on the ground or be stolen by the squirrels. If I don't harvest the onion buds that form after the flowering of the wild onion, they'll disappear until the following year. There are ingredients that pop up quickly and are gone. Manzanita berries go from overly tannic to sweet in the blink of an eye, and radish pods grow tough when the hotter months arrive. If I don't know what is happening in the world around me, then where am I cooking from?

None of this is scalable, and I love that. It is inherently tiny and fluid and precious—the wind and the rains dictate what is found. Thus, everything must always be written in pencil. There is nothing more thrilling than knowing that matsutakes are ending or that watercress has begun flowering in the creek. I cook at the whim of the ingredients around me. Foraging serves as a cultural entry point for my staff—a means of explaining the valley and an opportunity to bridge the gap between chef and server and guest.

Cooks and servers are encouraged (read forced) to trudge along with Cameron on his sojourns. We likely have the only dishwashers in the country who can identify wild spice bush.

The native people who populated this valley created mortars out of boulders they found alongside rivers and used them to grind acorns into flour. The Wappo used the beautiful Indian paintbrush plant to dye their clothing. Legend has it that monks spread mustard seeds so that, come spring, their path to the next mission would be marked by sunny yellow swaths. Families long gathered the wild blackberries that now go mostly untouched. I want to pick up that string that ties us to the past—the past as represented by these early people but also a primeval past that feels palpable on those days when I find myself in the stillness under the shadow of the mountain. It's easy to imagine our ancestors looking for the same matsutakes underneath the scattered fallen leaves, and easier still when looking at a lone madrone heavy with berries to imagine no people at all.

This process will one day make us better chefs and stewards of this land. By cooking without possessing, and living at the whim of the nature around us, we are becoming part of it. As with our gardening operations, the nascent foraging program came alive when the person with the necessary passion took ownership, and the kitchen as a whole helped to create the systems necessary to translate that passion into something functional. It is because of the diligence of my staff that we were able to turn a few leaves of miner's lettuce gathered during my walks with Charlie into a program that connects our food to the living and breathing spirit of this magical place.

history as inspiration

There is a bridge at the south end of Saint Helena that marks where old Chinatown stood. A famous burger stand sits there now, along with a hotel named after the bridge and a small white house that once belonged to Meadowood owner Bill Harlan and his then-young family. The original residents of Saint Helena's Chinatown were the offspring of Chinese immigrants who built the railroads. This community provided labor for the first Napa wineries and constructed the stone walls that run along property lines and the banks of the Napa River. A series of mysterious fires occurred at the end of the nineteenth century, and inhabitants were sometimes lynched amid xenophobic furors, their bodies hung over the bridge. One final fire marked the end of Chinatown in Saint Helena at the turn of the twentieth century.

It is easy to drive over the bridge entering or leaving Saint Helena and not know these things. Why would you? There are few places I have known where the identity of the present is so incongruent with its past. The valley floor is replete with genteel, parceled land dedicated to the cultivation of grapes and wine production. Wealth exists here now, the product of grape growing and the businesses associated with it. But beyond Chinatown, or the old prune-drying facility that stood next door, down to Conn Valley and the hulking ruins of the Franco-Swiss Winery, and past the Bale Grist Mill to the mortar stones along the river, there are ghosts of Napa's past. Some of these stories are common in the American West: brothels and bars; mining encampments on Oat Hill where I now walk with Charlie; jailbreaks and temperance movements. There were also, apparently, a fair number of murders. Scoundrels and dreamers created lives and businesses, most of them now lost to time.

A century ago, the valley was full of spas and baths used for relaxation and for the treatment of tuberculosis. Visitors came to Aetna Springs, the still-active spas of Calistoga, and the most famous spa of all, Soda Canyon, whose cupola could be seen from as far away as San Francisco Bay. The hospital in Saint Helena where my daughter was born is a former sanitarium. A place like Meadowood begins to make sense within the historical context of Napa as a place of retreat and repose. People—miners and soldiers, freed slaves and speculators, winemakers and chefs—have always come to this valley in search of freedom from the constraints of the Old World and the other coast, looking to make their way in an untrammeled valley. This is where my point of connection lies, with this tether to an earlier place and the people who came here with similar dreams. I can only be a big thing by being mindful of my smallness—my food, my journey, my family, and my place in the valley. What do I really know if I walk that bridge and don't understand that bodies were once hung from it? How can I attempt to cook from a place and not be aware of its origins and spirit?

History doesn't give direction as much as it provides a larger lens through which to view a place and therefore a way to see past the elements that seem incongruent with the direction one wants to take. Even a cursory knowledge of the dreams and work of preceding generations provides me with a sense of kinship to the past and makes me want to share that knowledge with my collaborators today. Food can be powerful if it is personal, especially when it is prepared by like-minded people working together and sharing themselves in the process. Imagine how powerful food can be when its creation takes into account the stories and histories of the millions of people who came before us. We are all connected if we allow ourselves to be, simply by remembering. If I think about those residents of Chinatown each time I pass that bridge, they become part of me. Somehow, the food I make will show a trace of them, in much the same way that the stone walls they built still affect the flow of the river.

matsutake plankton almond

After the first early winter rains, matsutakes arrive in our kitchen in abundance. Here we glaze them in plankton, shave them, and then garnish them with Marcona almonds.

SERVES 4

MATSUTAKE MUSHROOMS
20 grams | 3 tablespoons marine
    phytoplankton
100 grams | $1/2$ cup water
4 | matsutake mushrooms, peeled
    and left whole

MARCONA ALMONDS
400 grams | 2 $3/4$ cups Marcona almonds
800 grams | 3 $1/3$ cups water
30 grams | 2 tablespoons crème fraîche
    (page 283)
Maldon sea salt

16 | ice lettuce leaves

FOR THE MATSUTAKE MUSHROOMS:
Combine the plankton and water in a small metal bowl and mix together until smooth. Brush the mushrooms with the plankton slurry, let dry slightly, and then brush to cover well with a second coat. Let the mushrooms dry at room temperature for 4 hours, until the slurry is completely dry.

Using a mandoline, thinly slice about 5 perfect slices from each mushroom. Hold between sheets of parchment paper in the refrigerator. Reserve the remaining slurry for garnishing the plate.

FOR THE MARCONA ALMONDS:
Preheat the oven to 325°F (165°C). Spread the almonds on a sheet pan and toast in the oven for 10 minutes, until golden brown and fragrant. Set aside 12 almonds. Put the remaining almonds in a pressure cooker, add the water, and cook on high pressure for 30 minutes.

When the almonds are ready, prepare an ice bath. Drain the almonds, reserving the liquid. Transfer the almonds to a blender, add the crème fraîche, and mix on high speed for about 1 minute, until smooth. If the puree is not turning freely in the blender, add a little of the reserved liquid. Strain the puree through a chinois into a bowl, then nest the bowl in the ice bath to cool the puree. Season with Maldon salt and transfer to a squeeze bottle.

TO SERVE:
Create random streaks of the reserved plankton slurry on each of 4 plates. Put a few dots of the almond puree on each plate, then top the dots with the whole almonds. Lay 5 matsutake slices on the puree. Garnish the plates with the ice lettuce.

cucumber roasted in madrone dill coastal grasses

Ocean meets land. The Pacific, only about an hour from the valley, provides a wealth of wild edibles. We often travel to the coast and return with a variety of coastal grasses, green and vibrant and tasting of the ocean: sea arrowgrass, wild agretti, sea beans. We snip these grasses over a dish featuring various preparations of cucumber—roasted in madrone leaf, raw, and pickles from the preceding year.

FOR THE DILL PICKLES:

Combine the water and vinegar in a saucepan and bring to a simmer over low heat. Add the kosher salt, dill seeds, bay leaf, allspice, mustard seeds, and peppercorns, cover, and steep over low heat at 140°F (60°C) for 2 hours. Increase the heat to high and bring the liquid to a boil. Meanwhile, place the cucumbers in a metal bowl. When the liquid is at a boil, pour it over the cucumbers and cover the bowl tightly with plastic wrap. Hold in an area with an ambient temperature of 160°F (71°C) for 2 hours. Transfer to the refrigerator to cool for 24 hours.

Remove half of the cucumbers from the liquid and cut them lengthwise into wedges about ¼ inch (6 millimeters) wide. Cut the remaining cucumbers into brunoise. Return all of the cut pickles to the pickling liquid.

FOR THE ROASTED CUCUMBERS:

Pierce the cucumbers evenly with a fork. Bury them in salt in a plastic container and refrigerate for 30 minutes.

Rinse the salt off of the cucumbers and pat dry on paper towels. Using butcher's twine, secure 2 madrone leaves on either side of a cucumber, so that they wrap completely around the exterior. Repeat with the remaining cucumbers. Heat a cast-iron pan over high heat and add the oil. When the oil is smoking, add the wrapped cucumbers and roast for 8 minutes, rotating the cucumbers every 2 minutes so they cook evenly. Transfer to a wire rack to rest for 2 minutes, then snip the butcher's twine.

FOR THE CRÈME FRAÎCHE PUDDING:

Prepare an ice bath. Combine the crème fraîche and gellan base in a blender and mix on high speed for about 3 minutes, until the gellan base is evenly distributed. Strain the pudding through a chinois into a bowl, then nest the bowl in the ice bath and stir to cool the pudding. Season with kosher salt and transfer to a squeeze bottle.

FOR THE BRAISED BORAGE:

Pour the oil in a large rondeau over high heat. When the oil is hot, add the shallot and heat until it begins to sweat. Add the borage leaves and continue to cook for about 4 minutes, until the leaves have wilted. Transfer the leaves to a shallow metal container and refrigerate for 1 hour. Mince the leaves very finely, season with kosher salt, and refrigerate in an airtight container until ready to use.

TO SERVE:

Place the pickle wedges and brunoise in a bowl along with some of the pickling liquid. Season with Maldon salt and Twin Sisters olive oil and add the Mexican sour cucumbers and shaved cucumbers. Let marinate for 5 minutes. Meanwhile, place a few dots of the crème fraîche pudding on each of 4 plates. Follow with a few piles of braised borage. Scatter some pickle wedges, pickle dice, shaved cucumbers, and Mexican sour cucumbers onto each plate. Rewarm the roasted cucumbers and place 1 cucumber on each plate. Garnish with the sea bean tips, dill flowers, dill pluches, agretti pluches, sea arrowgrass, and cucumber flowers.

SERVES 4

DILL PICKLES
240 grams | 1 cup water
120 grams | ½ cup white wine vinegar
18 grams | 1 tablespoon kosher salt
6 grams | 1 ½ teaspoons dill seeds
2 grams | about 1 bay leaf
2 grams | about 3 allspice berries
4 grams | 1 teaspoon yellow mustard seeds
2 grams | about 3 white peppercorns
6 | Dragon's Egg cucumbers

ROASTED CUCUMBERS
4 | small Dragon's Egg cucumbers, about
     2 inches (5 centimeters) long
kosher salt, for burying the cucumbers
8 | madrone leaves
40 grams | 3 tablespoons extra virgin olive oil

CRÈME FRAÎCHE PUDDING
350 grams | 1 ½ cups crème fraîche (page 283)
250 grams | 8.8 ounces gellan base (page 285)
kosher salt

BRAISED BORAGE
40 grams | 3 tablespoons extra virgin olive oil
12 grams | scant 1 ½ tablespoons diced shallot
455 grams | 1 pound borage leaves,
     stems removed
kosher salt

Maldon sea salt
12 grams | 1 tablespoon Twin Sisters olive oil
8 | Mexican sour cucumbers
2 | Dragon's Egg cucumbers, cut into
     thin shavings
8 | sea bean tips, about 1 inch
     (2.5 centimeters) long
4 | dill flowers
8 | dill pluches
16 | agretti pluches
4 | sea arrowgrass stalks, cut into ½-inch
     (12-millimeter) pieces
8 | cucumber flowers

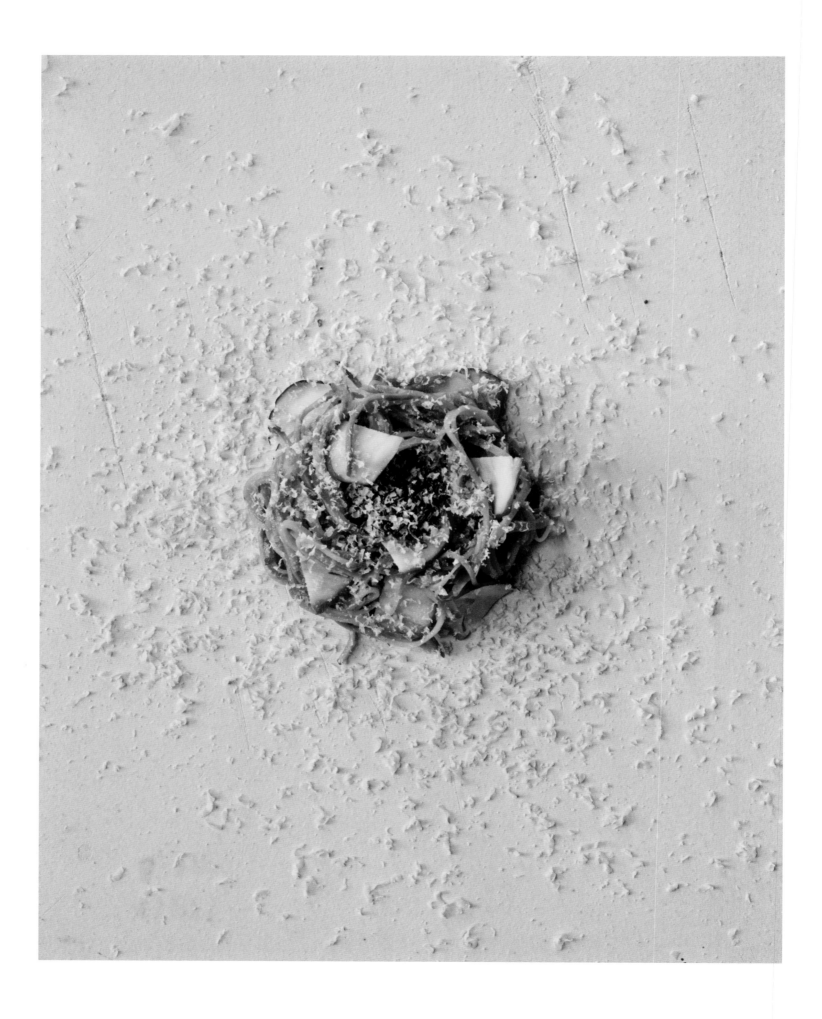

lobster mushroom carbonara

Lobster mushrooms are the most intriguing and complex of all the fungi. Their arrival in the wilds in late summer is as exciting as the first spot prawns or white truffles. Here, we treat the mushrooms like pasta carbonara, pairing them with smoked Monkeyface eel and a grating of cured yolk.

SERVES 4

CURED EGG YOLK

500 grams | 1 ³/₄ cups kosher salt
250 grams | 1 ¹/₄ cups sugar
4 | eggs

LOBSTER MUSHROOM STOCK

20 grams | 1 ¹/₂ tablespoons extra virgin
   olive oil
900 grams | 2 pounds lobster mushroom
   stems and trim
230 grams | 8 ounces dried lobster
   mushrooms
400 grams | about 4 yellow onions, diced
600 grams | about 1 head celery, diced
480 grams | about 3 carrots, peeled
   and diced
65 grams | about 1 head garlic, halved
12 kilograms | about 12 quarts water
230 grams | 8 ounces Parmesan rind
kosher salt

BRAISED LOBSTER MUSHROOMS

40 grams | 3 tablespoons extra virgin olive oil
800 grams | 6 or 7 large lobster mushrooms,
   trimmed
6 kilograms | about 6 quarts lobster
   mushroom stock (recipe above)

FOR THE CURED EGG YOLK:

Combine the salt and sugar in a large metal bowl and mix well. Transfer half of the mixture to a metal tray, forming a layer about ¹/₂ inch (12 millimeters) deep. Using a small ladle, create 8 impressions in the mixture, spacing them about 1 inch (2.5 centimeters) apart. One at a time, carefully crack the eggs and place a yolk in the center of each impression, making sure not to break the yolk. Carefully sift the remaining cure over the eggs, and cover the pan tightly with plastic wrap. Refrigerate for 3 days.

Rinse the yolks in ice-cold water to remove the excess salt, then pat dry on paper towels. Line a dehydrator tray with a silicone baking mat and arrange the yolks on it. Dehydrate the yolks at 135°F (57°C) for 24 hours, until the yolks are firm and slightly dry on the exterior. Store in an airtight container with silica gel packets at room temperature.

FOR THE LOBSTER MUSHROOM STOCK:

Warm the olive oil in a large rondeau over medium heat. Add the mushroom stems and trim and the dried mushrooms and sweat for about 5 minutes, until the mushrooms are lightly browned. Add the onions, celery, carrots, and garlic and continue caramelizing for an additional 10 minutes. Add the water, increase the heat to high, and bring the stock to a boil. Turn down the heat to a simmer and cook the stock for about 3 hours, until flavorful. Add the Parmesan rind and turn off the heat. Steep the rind in the stock for 45 minutes. Prepare an ice bath. Strain the stock through a chinois into a bowl, then nest the bowl in the ice bath to cool the stock. Transfer to an airtight container and store in the refrigerator.

FOR THE BRAISED LOBSTER MUSHROOMS:

Warm the olive oil in a large rondeau over medium heat. Place the lobster mushrooms on the bottom, in direct contact with the hot surface. Cook the mushrooms, turning as needed, for about 8 minutes total, until light golden brown on all sides. Add the stock, increase the heat to medium-high and bring to a simmer. Cover the surface with a piece of parchment paper and simmer for 1 hour, until the mushrooms are tender. Transfer the mushrooms and stock to a metal tray and let cool in the refrigerator.

Remove the mushrooms from the stock and cut half of them into fine julienne. Reserve the julienne in a portion of the cold stock. Cut the remaining mushrooms into ¹/₄-inch (6-millimeter) dice and reserve them in a separate portion of the stock.

continued

lobster mushroom carbonara *continued*

FOR THE MONKEYFACE EEL:

Combine the sugar, salt, and peppercorns in a bowl. Remove the fillets from the eel by tracing around the perimeter of each side with the tip of a knife. Insert the blade into the back portion of the fillet and carefully remove it from the frame of the eel, keeping the skin intact. Bury the fillets in the sugar mixture in a plastic container and refrigerate for 1 hour. Rinse the fillets under running ice-cold water and pat dry on paper towels.

Hot smoke (see page 287) the fillets at 125°F (52°C) for 1 hour. Let cool in the refrigerator, then slice very thinly against the grain. Wrap the slices tightly in plastic wrap and hold on ice in the refrigerator until using.

TO SERVE:

Put about 90 grams (1 cup) of the julienned lobster mushrooms and about 60 grams (¹/₂ cup) of the diced lobster mushrooms in separate small saucepans and add just enough lobster mushroom stock to each pan to cover the mushrooms. Place the pans over low heat and bring to a simmer. Add butter, a couple of pieces at a time, to each pan and stir until the broth thickens slightly and coats the mushrooms. Season the mushrooms with kosher salt. Evenly divide the julienned mushrooms in small piles among 4 bowls. Place some diced mushrooms and a few eel slices on top of the piles. Sprinkle the chives over the eel slices. Using a fine-tooth grater, grate the cured yolks evenly over each serving.

MONKEYFACE EEL

1.5 kilograms | 6 ³/₄ cups firmly packed brown sugar
500 grams | 1 ³/₄ cups kosher salt
10 grams | 1 ¹/₂ tablespoons black peppercorns, crushed
1 | Monkeyface eel

unsalted butter, in small pieces
kosher salt
chives, finely diced

rhubarb buttermilk

Each spring in the valley, the river offers up tiny wild rhubarb that is wonderfully sour and crunchy. We pair it here with what is in essence a macaroon: soft rhubarb crust enveloping acidic buttermilk. We finish with the textures of white chocolate and pistachio and with a bit of sorrel, rhubarb's tamed cousin.

SERVES 10

MACAROON CRUST

212 grams | 2 ³/₄ cups almond flour
212 grams | 1 ³/₄ cups confectioners' sugar
172 grams | ²/₃ cup egg whites
235 grams | 1 cup plus 3 tablespoons
    granulated sugar
150 grams | ²/₃ cup water
40 grams | ¹/₄ cup fresh red currants

BUTTERMILK PARFAIT

75 grams | ¹/₃ cup egg yolks
2.3 grams | 1 sheet gold gelatin, bloomed
    in ice water and wrung gently
    of excess water
40 grams | ¹/₄ cup sugar
150 grams | 5 ounces white chocolate,
    chopped
165 grams | ¹/₂ cup plus 2 ¹/₂ tablespoons
    heavy cream
60 grams | ¹/₄ cup buttermilk (page 284)
50 grams | ¹/₄ cup cultured yogurt
    (page 284)
macaroon crust (recipe above)

BUTTERMILK ESPUMA

250 grams | 1 cup buttermilk (page 284)
50 grams | ¹/₄ cup heavy cream
25 grams | 6 ¹/₄ teaspoons granulated sugar
3 grams | 1 teaspoon heavy cream stabilizer

FOR THE MACAROON CRUST:

Preheat the oven to 325°F (165°C). Line 2 quarter sheet pans with parchment paper and spray the paper with nonstick cooking spray. Combine the almond flour and confectioners' sugar in a food processor and mix for about 2 minutes, until a fine powder forms. Pass the mixture through a tamis into a large bowl. Add the egg whites to the flour mixture and mix with a rubber spatula to create a smooth batter. Combine the granulated sugar and water in a small, heavy saucepan and heat to 248°F (120°C) while stirring occasionally. Let the syrup cool to about 180°F (82°C) and add the currants. When the syrup has turned a deep red, after about 10 minutes, strain it through a chinois into a bowl and discard the currants. Fold the syrup into the batter with a rubber spatula, mixing well.

Divide the batter evenly between the 2 prepared quarter sheet pans and bake for 8 minutes, until the surface is dry but not brown. Let cool in the pans at room temperature for 1 hour. Using a bread knife, even off the top and sides of each macaroon sheet, keeping the sheets the same dimensions. Line a quarter sheet pan with plastic wrap and place a macaroon sheet in the pan. Reserve the second sheet.

FOR THE BUTTERMILK PARFAIT:

Put the egg yolks in the bowl of a stand mixer fitted with the whip attachment and mix on high speed for about 8 minutes, until the yolks have doubled in volume. Meanwhile, combine the gelatin and sugar in a small saucepan and heat to 248°F (120°C). When the egg yolks are ready, pour in the gelatin mixture and continue to whip until the yolks fall in a ribbon when the whip is lifted.

When the egg yolks are nearly ready, heat the chocolate in a double boiler over gently simmering water just until melted, stirring occasionally. Remove from over the heat and fold in the egg yolks, mixing thoroughly. Then fold in 35 grams (2 ¹/₂ tablespoons) of the cream and all of the buttermilk until uniformly combined. Reserve in the refrigerator.

Combine the remaining 130 grams (¹/₂ cup) of cream and the yogurt in the stand mixer fitted with the whip attachment and whip on high speed until stiff peaks form. Fold the cream mixture into the chocolate mixture just until combined, then pour evenly over the macaroon sheet in the sheet pan. Place the reserved macaroon sheet, top side down, on top of the parfait. Line a second quarter sheet pan with plastic wrap, place on top of the stacked macaroon sheets, and press lightly. Freeze in this formation for at least 3 hours, until completely frozen. Using a sharp knife, cut into 1 by 3-inch (2.5 by 7.5-centimeter) pieces. Store in an airtight container in the freezer.

FOR THE BUTTERMILK ESPUMA:

Prepare an ice bath. Combine the buttermilk, cream, and 20 grams (5 teaspoons) of the sugar in a saucepan and heat to 130°F (54°C). Meanwhile, combine the remaining 5 grams (1 ¹/₄ teaspoons) of sugar and the cream stabilizer in a bowl and mix well. Slowly add the warm buttermilk mixture to the sugar mixture while using an immersion blender to dissolve the sugar mixture. Nest the bowl in the ice bath to cool the mixture. Transfer to a siphon canister and charge with 2 nitrous oxide cartridges. Refrigerate for 1 hour before use.

continued

FOR THE RHUBARB PUREE:

Preheat the oven to 325°F (165°C). Put the rhubarb in a metal pan. Combine the simple syrup and verjus in a small saucepan and bring to a boil over high heat. Remove from the heat, pour over the rhubarb, and cover the pan with aluminum foil. Bake for 10 minutes, until very tender. Meanwhile, prepare an ice bath. When the rhubarb is ready, drain it, discarding the liquid, and transfer to a blender. Mix on high speed for about 3 minutes, until a smooth puree forms. Strain through a chinois into a bowl, then nest the bowl in the ice bath to cool the puree. Season with sugar, transfer to a squeeze bottle, and reserve in the refrigerator.

FOR THE COMPRESSED RHUBARB:

Combine the rhubarb, water, and sugar in a shallow plastic container. Put the entire container into the chamber of a vacuum seal machine. Compress twice with full vacuum and store in the refrigerator for at least 1 hour before use.

FOR THE CARAMELIZED WHITE CHOCOLATE SALAD:

Preheat the oven to 250°F (120°C). Put the white chocolate in a metal pan, cover with aluminum foil, and bake for 20 minutes, until the chocolate is golden brown. Remove from the oven and let cool to room temperature. Refrigerate the chocolate to crystallize it. Break into small pieces about the size of a pistachio. (If not using right away, store in an airtight container in a cool, dry area.) Combine the white chocolate pieces, pistachios, and sorrel stems in a small bowl. Add the compressed rhubarb pieces and dress with a small amount of the rhubarb liquid.

TO SERVE:

Lay a portion of rhubarb on its side in the center of each of 10 dark plates. Arrange the white chocolate salad in a cascade over the rhubarb, then add a few dots of the rhubarb puree to each plate. Garnish with the rhubarb batons; French, blood, and wood sorrel leaves; and the sorrel flowers. Discharge a few dots of the buttermilk espuma onto each plate.

RHUBARB PUREE

500 grams | 4 cups diced rhubarb,
in $1/_2$-inch (12-millimeter) pieces
200 grams | $2/_3$ cup simple syrup
50 grams | $1/_4$ cup red verjus
sugar

COMPRESSED RHUBARB

60 grams | $2/_3$ cup finely diced rhubarb
480 grams | 2 cups water
120 grams | $2/_3$ cup sugar

CARAMELIZED WHITE CHOCOLATE SALAD

100 grams | $3/_4$ cup white chocolate pieces
50 grams | $1/_2$ cup pistachio halves
20 grams | 5 teaspoons minced French
sorrel stems
compressed rhubarb (recipe above)

20 | wild rhubarb batons, 1 $1/_2$ inches
(4 centimeters) long
20 | tiny French sorrel leaves
20 | tiny blood sorrel leaves
20 | wood sorrel leaves
20 | wood sorrel flowers

brie flax elderberry honey

Here, I use a technique that employs the coagulating effect of flaxseeds to create a skin around an unctuous puree of Brie. A puree of barely set honey is then piped into the Brie. When the dish is cut, the cheese and honey ooze out, commingled. The dish is finished with a sauce made from the wild elderberries that grow throughout the valley and with the elder flowers that precede them.

SERVES 4

BRIE MORNAY

500 grams | about 1 pound triple-cream
    Brie cheese, rind removed
200 grams | $^3/_4$ cup heavy cream
200 grams | $^3/_4$ cup whole milk
Ultra-Tex 3
kosher salt

HONEY PUREE

600 grams | 1 $^3/_4$ cups raw honey
200 grams | $^3/_4$ cup water
9 grams | 2 teaspoons powdered agar

SABLE COOKIE

260 grams | about 2 cups all-purpose flour
1 gram | $^1/_2$ teaspoon baking powder
1.5 grams | $^1/_4$ teaspoon kosher salt
140 grams | $^2/_3$ cup unsalted butter,
    at room temperature
100 grams | $^1/_2$ cup sugar
60 grams | 1 egg

FLAX CRUST

3 | underripe yellow peaches, pitted
4 | underripe Black Mission figs
400 grams | about 3 $^2/_3$ cups golden
    flaxseed meal
280 grams | 1 $^3/_4$ cups sable crumbs
    (recipe above)
100 grams | $^1/_2$ cup granulated piloncillo
kosher salt

FOR THE BRIE MORNAY:

Prepare an ice bath. Put the Brie in a blender. Combine the cream and milk in a saucepan and bring to a boil over medium-high heat. Pour the hot cream mixture over the cheese and mix on high speed for about 2 minutes, until smooth. Slowly add just enough Ultra-Tex for the cheese to create a ribbon when streamed on top of itself. Strain through a chinois into a bowl, then nest the bowl in the ice bath until the mixture is cool. Season with kosher salt, spoon into a piping bag fitted with a round tip, and refrigerate until ready to use.

FOR THE HONEY PUREE:

Combine the honey, water, and agar in a small saucepan and bring to a boil over medium heat. Pour into a metal container and refrigerate for about 1 hour, until the mixture is stiff. Meanwhile, prepare an ice bath. Transfer the honey mixture to a blender and mix on high speed for about 30 seconds, until smooth. Strain through a chinois into a bowl, then nest the bowl in the ice bath and stir the puree until cool. Transfer to a squeeze bottle and store in the refrigerator until ready to use.

FOR THE SABLE COOKIE:

Combine the flour, baking powder, and salt in a bowl and stir to mix. Combine the butter and sugar in the bowl of a stand mixer fitted with the paddle attachment and mix on low speed for about 30 seconds to aerate the mixture. Add the egg and mix until combined, then scrape down the sides of the bowl. Add the flour mixture in three batches, mixing briefly after each addition so as not to overwork the flour. Wrap the dough in plastic wrap and refrigerate for at least 1 hour.

Preheat the oven to 350°F (175°C). Line a half sheet pan with parchment paper. On a floured surface, roll out the dough about $^1/_4$ inch (6 millimeters) thick. Transfer the dough to the prepared sheet pan and bake for 10 to 12 minutes, until light golden brown. Let cool on the pan on a wire rack. Break the sable into small pieces and freeze them for at least 2 hours, until solid.

Working in batches, transfer the sable pieces to a blender and mix on high speed until pulverized. Work quickly—no more than 15 seconds per batch—so as not to force the butter out of the sable. Store the ground sable in an airtight container with silica gel packets at room temperature.

FOR THE FLAX CRUST:

Prepare a fire in a wood-burning oven. Cut the peaches and figs into thin slices. When the fire is at about 600°F (315°C), arrange the fruit slices in a cast-iron pan, place in the center of the oven, and roast for about 15 minutes, until the fruit has charred but is still intact.

Line a dehydrator tray with a silicone baking mat, arrange the fruit slices on the mat, and dehydrate at 115°F (46°C) for about 12 hours, until completely dry. Transfer the dried fruit to a blender and mix on high speed until pulverized. Weigh 87 grams ($^1/_2$ cup) of the fruit powder and transfer to a large bowl. Add the flaxseed meal, sable crumbs, piloncillo, and salt and stir to mix well. Reserve at room temperature.

continued

FOR THE ELDERBERRY PUREE:

Put the elderberries in a food processor and mix for 2 minutes just to break up the berries. Transfer to a saucepan, place over low heat, bring to a simmer, and cook, stirring occasionally, for about 40 minutes, until about half of the liquid has evaporated. Meanwhile, prepare an ice bath. When the berries are ready, transfer to a blender and mix on high speed for about 2 minutes, until a very smooth puree forms. Strain through a chinois into a bowl, then nest the bowl in the ice bath until the puree is cool. Transfer to a squeeze bottle.

TO SERVE:

Spray the insides of 4 metal cylinders 1 $\frac{1}{2}$ inches (4 centimeters) in diameter and 2 inches (5 centimeters) tall with nonstick cooking spray. Dredge each cylinder in the flax crust, making sure to cover the insides with an even layer of the crust. Spray a silicone baking mat with nonstick cooking spray, then dust lightly with the flax crust. Place the mat on a sheet pan. Arrange the cylinders on the prepared mat. Check to make sure that the interior of each cylinder is evenly coated with the crust. Place the sheet pan holding the mat on a scale, then pipe 25 grams (1 ounce) of the Brie Mornay into each cylinder. Insert the tip of the honey puree squeeze bottle into the center of a cheese portion and squeeze a small amount of the puree into the cheese. Repeat to stuff the remaining cheese portions. When all of the cheese portions have been stuffed, dust additional flax crust over the cylinders, evenly coating the surface of the cheese. Refrigerate for at least 1 hour or for up to 3 hours before unmolding, as the flax needs ample time to create a shell around the cheese.

Circle a small amount of the elderberry puree on the bottom of each of 4 plates. Unmold the Brie from the cylinder, flipping it upside down onto the plate to hide the incision created by the honey. Garnish with the elderberries and elder flowers.

ELDERBERRY PUREE

400 grams | about 2 cups elderberries
simple syrup

24 | elderberries
elder flowers

halibut acorn truffle celery

Here is the essence of culinary vertical alignment: oak used in the cooking of celery root, acorns from that oak encrusting local halibut, and a jus made from truffles that grow, yes, under oaks.

SERVES 4

HALIBUT PREPARATION

1.6 kilograms | 5 $^1/_2$ cups kosher salt

90 grams | 2 cups celery leaves

15 grams | $^1/_3$ cup thyme leaves

450 grams | 1 pound halibut fillet,
     skin removed

CELERY ROOT PUREE

2 kilograms | about 8 cups heavy cream

300 grams | 10.5 ounces oak chips

700 grams | about 1.5 pounds celery root,
     peeled and finely diced

kosher salt

BRAISED CELERY ROOT

350 grams | 12 ounces peeled and diced
     celery root

40 grams | 3 tablespoons extra virgin olive oil

kosher salt

100 grams | $^1/_3$ cup dark chicken jus
     (page 284)

25 grams | 3 tablespoons black truffle,
     in brunoise

ACORN GRAVY

320 grams | 1 $^1/_3$ cups water

6 grams | 0.3 ounce dried kombu

22 grams | 1 $^1/_2$ tablespoons unsalted butter

22 grams | 2 tablespoons plus
     2 $^1/_4$ teaspoons acorn flour

kosher salt

FOR THE HALIBUT PREPARATION:

Combine 450 grams (1 $^1/_2$ cups) of the salt and the celery and thyme leaves in a food processor and mix for 1 minute, until the leaves are pulverized and fully mixed with the salt. Transfer to a bowl and mix in the remaining salt. Bury the halibut fillet in the seasoned salt and refrigerate for 10 minutes. Rinse the fillet in a bowl of ice water and pat dry on paper towels. Cut the fillet into rectangular portions about 2 inches (5 centimeters) wide by 5 inches (13 centimeters) long. Scale each portion to about 100 grams (3.5 ounces). Store in an airtight container in the refrigerator.

FOR THE CELERY ROOT PUREE:

Combine the cream and oak chips in a stockpot. Bring to a boil over high heat, turn down the heat to a simmer, and cook for 20 minutes, until the cream is infused with the flavor of oak. Remove from the heat and strain the cream, discarding the chips. Return the cream to the pot, add the celery root, and bring to a boil. Cook for about 15 minutes, until the celery root is soft. Meanwhile, prepare an ice bath. When the celery root is ready, drain and discard the cream. Place the celery root in a blender and mix on high speed for about 3 minutes, until a very smooth puree forms. Strain through a chinois into a bowl, then nest the bowl in the ice bath to cool the puree. Season with kosher salt, transfer to a squeeze bottle, and refrigerate until needed.

FOR THE BRAISED CELERY ROOT:

Season the celery root with the olive oil and salt. Transfer the celery root to a vacuum bag, seal on high, and cook in a steam oven set at 200°F (95°C) for 25 to 30 minutes, until very tender. Remove the celery root from the bag and finely mince it. Transfer the celery root to a saucepan and warm gently over low heat. Add the chicken jus and increase the heat to a boil. Reduce the residual liquid until the mixture is fairly dry. Add the truffle and season with kosher salt. Hold in an airtight container at 120°F to 130°F (49°C to 54°C) for up to 1 hour.

FOR THE ACORN GRAVY:

Combine the water and kombu in a small saucepan over low heat and simmer for 15 minutes. Meanwhile, melt the butter in a small sauté pan over low heat. Add the acorn flour and mix together with a spatula. Once the mixture has thickened, cook, stirring, for 4 minutes to toast the flour. Transfer to a metal container and let cool in the refrigerator. When the kombu stock is ready, strain it through a fine-mesh strainer into a clean saucepan.

Once the acorn roux has cooled completely and stiffened, break it up into small pieces and whisk the pieces into the kombu stock. Place over medium heat and bring to a boil, whisking constantly. When the gravy has thickened, season with kosher salt and strain through a chinois. Hold in an airtight container at 120°F to 130°F (49°C to 54°C) for up to 1 hour.

continued

FOR THE TRUFFLE JUS:

Heat the chicken jus in a small saucepan over low heat to about 180°F (82°C). Add the truffle and season with sherry vinegar and salt. Hold in an airtight container at 120°F to 130°F (49°C to 54°C) for up to 1 hour.

FOR THE ROASTED CUTTING CELERY:

Pour the olive oil into a cast-iron pan over high heat. Add the celery pieces and sauté until the celery begins to brown slightly. Remove from the pan and season with kosher salt. Pat dry on paper towels.

FOR THE PICKLED TINY CELERY:

Prepare an ice bath. Combine the vinegar, water, and sugar in a small saucepan and bring to a simmer over low heat, stirring until the sugar dissolves. Remove from the heat and nest the pan in the ice bath to cool the pickling liquid. Use the cooled liquid to dress the tiny celery. Season with Maldon salt.

TO SERVE:

In a bowl, whisk the egg whites until frothy, then pour into a shallow container. Combine the flour, sugar, and chanterelle, shiitake, and black trumpet powders in a bowl and stir to mix well.

One at a time, submerge the halibut portions in the egg whites and then coat evenly with the acorn flour mixture. Heat a cast-iron pan over medium-high heat and add the olive oil. When the oil is hot, gently lay the fish portions in the pan and cook evenly, turning them once, for about 4 minutes on each side, until the exterior of the fish is dry and the acorn mixture has completely adhered to the fish. Pat dry on paper towels and pull each portion apart into 3 large flakes. Place the flakes on a plate and garnish with a few dots of the celery root puree, braised celery root, acorn gravy, and truffle jus. Place a couple of pieces of the cutting celery on the plate and finish with the pickled tiny celery.

TRUFFLE JUS

200 grams | ²/₃ cup dark chicken jus (page 284)
50 grams | ¹/₃ cup black truffle, in brunoise
sherry vinegar
kosher salt

ROASTED CUTTING CELERY

25 grams | 1 tablespoon plus 2 teaspoons extra virgin olive oil
3 | cutting celery stalks, cut into 4-inch (10-centimeter) pieces
kosher salt

PICKLED TINY CELERY

300 grams | 1 ¹/₄ cups white wine vinegar
200 grams | ³/₄ cup water
50 grams | ¹/₄ cup sugar
12 | tiny celery with roots intact
Maldon sea salt

300 grams | 1 ¹/₄ cups egg whites
300 grams | 2 ¹/₃ cups acorn flour
20 grams | 1 ¹/₂ tablespoons ground turbinado sugar
125 grams | 1 cup chanterelle mushroom powder
125 grams | 1 cup shiitake mushroom powder
125 grams | 1 cup black trumpet mushroom powder
40 grams | 3 tablespoons extra virgin olive oil

asparagus egg foraged greens

When blessed with asparagus freshly harvested from the garden, a little dirt still clinging to the stalks, we do little to it. Christine, the soil, and time have done all the hard work already. We present a single spear at the table, shiny with olive oil and garnished with cured bantam eggs and tiny wild greens.

SERVES 4

CURED BANTAM EGGS

1 kilogram | 3 $\frac{1}{2}$ cups kosher salt

500 grams | 2 $\frac{1}{2}$ cups sugar

20 grams | $\frac{1}{3}$ cup flat-leaf parsley leaves

20 grams | $\frac{1}{2}$ cup minced chives

8 | bantam eggs

ASPARAGUS

4 | extra-large asparagus

2 kilograms | 8 $\frac{1}{2}$ cups butter stock
    (page 283)

kosher salt

50 grams | 3 tablespoons freshly squeezed
    lemon juice

Maldon sea salt

ASPARAGUS PUREE

1.9 kilograms | 8 cups water

120 grams | $\frac{1}{3}$ cup kosher salt, plus more
    for seasoning

560 grams | 1.3 pounds asparagus

20 grams | $\frac{1}{3}$ cup flat-leaf parsley leaves

50 grams | $\frac{1}{4}$ cup extra virgin olive oil

8 grams | 1 tablespoon Ultra-Tex 3

miner's lettuce

chickweed

vetch

asparagus fronds

fava bean flowers

blue bachelor's button flowers

FOR THE CURED BANTAM EGGS:

Combine the kosher salt, sugar, parsley, and chives in a food processor and mix for 2 minutes, until the herbs have completed pulverized into the salt. Transfer half of the mixture to a metal pan, forming a layer about $\frac{1}{2}$ inch (12 millimeters) deep. Using a small ladle, create 8 depressions in the layer, spacing them about 1 inch (2.5 centimeters) apart.

Place the eggs in a small saucepan, add water to cover, and place over high heat. Bring to a simmer and cook for 4 minutes. Remove the eggs from the heat and place under cool running water until cold. Gently crack the shell and carefully peel each egg. Place an egg in the center of each depression making sure not to break the yolk. Carefully sift the remaining cure evenly over the eggs, and cover the pan tightly with plastic wrap. Refrigerate for 3 days.

Rinse the eggs in ice-cold water to remove the excess cure and pat dry on paper towels. Line a dehydrator tray with a silicone mat and place the eggs on the mat. Dehydrate at 135°F (57°C) for 12 hours. The eggs will be firm and feel slightly dry on the exterior. Transfer to an airtight container and store in the freezer until serving.

FOR THE ASPARAGUS:

Using a paring knife, score an incision about 2 inches (5 centimeters) from the tip of each asparagus. Using a vegetable peeler and starting at the incision, peel each asparagus to the bottom of the stalk, creating a uniform surface. Remove the tough lower end of the asparagus and discard. Pour the stock into a saucepan and bring to a simmer over medium heat. Season with kosher salt, add the asparagus, and cook for 3 $\frac{1}{2}$ minutes, until just tender. Remove the asparagus from the stock and brush with the lemon juice. Season with Maldon salt.

FOR THE ASPARAGUS PUREE:

Combine the water and salt in a saucepan and bring to a boil. Remove the tough lower end of the asparagus and discard, then cut the asparagus into small uniform pieces. When the water is boiling, add the asparagus and blanch for 2 minutes. Add the parsley and continue cooking for 2 minutes longer. Drain the asparagus and parsley and hold in a strainer. Do not chill. Press down on the spears lightly to remove excess liquid.

Prepare an ice bath. Transfer the asparagus and parsley to a blender and mix on high speed. Once the puree moves freely, add the oil a little at a time to maintain the emulsification. Finish with the Ultra-Tex, making sure to continue to mix until fully hydrated. Strain the puree through a chinois into a bowl, then nest the bowl in the ice bath and stir the puree until chilled. Season with kosher salt and transfer to a squeeze bottle.

TO SERVE:

Place a cooked asparagus spear on each plate. Using a mandoline, shave the bantam eggs and gently place the shavings on top of the asparagus. Finish with dots of the asparagus puree and with miner's lettuce, chickweed, vetch, asparagus fronds, fava bean flowers, and bachelor's buttons.

goat's cheese wild radish pumpernickel

In early spring, before the temperature rises, wild radishes flower throughout the valley in pink, yellow, and white. At the same time, the radishes themselves—green pods that are at once spicy and fresh—have appeared and will remain tender for only a month or so. This dish features the wild pods and flowers with their cultivated kin, with everything paired with various forms of goat's milk.

FOR THE GOAT'S MILK BUTTER:

Temper the goat's milk butter at room temperature for 1 hour. Using a stand mixer fitted with the whip attachment, whip the butter on high speed until it doubles in volume. Add the nori and continue mixing until the nori is evenly dispersed. Season with Maldon salt and hold at room temperature until needed.

FOR THE WHIPPED GOAT'S MILK CHEESE:

Put the cheese and oil in the bowl of a stand mixer fitted with the whip attachment and mix on high speed for 2 minutes, until fully incorporated. Roll the cheese into 8-gram (1 1/2-teaspoon) spheres and reserve in the refrigerator.

FOR THE PUMPERNICKEL TUILE:

Juice the radishes, then combine the radish pulp and juice in a small saucepan. Place over high heat and reduce until the pulp is dry. Line a dehydrator tray with a silicone baking mat, spread the radish pulp on the mat, and dehydrate at 125°F (52°C) for about 6 hours, until completely dry.

Combine the ground pumpernickel and nori in a food processor. With the machine running, add the egg whites and continue to mix. Meanwhile, combine the gelatin and radish juice in a small saucepan over low heat and heat until the gelatin melts. Add the gelatin mixture, flour, isomalt, and kosher salt to the whipping egg whites and continue to mix for about 2 minutes, until the mixture is completely homogenized.

Preheat the oven to 325°F (165°C). Line a half sheet pan with a silicone baking mat. Pour 250 grams (1 cup) of the tuile base onto the mat and spread evenly about 1/16 inch (2 millimeters) thick. Bake for 8 to 12 minutes, until light brown. Remove from the oven and, while still hot, cut into four 5-inch (13-centimeter) squares. Let cool to room temperature, then store in an airtight container in a cool, dry area.

TO SERVE:

Place 3 spheres of the whipped goat's milk cheese on each of 4 white plates. Arrange a few of the larger aged goat cheese crumbles on each plate, and then place 2 small quenelles of the whipped goat's milk butter on each plate, positioning one on each end. Break each pumpernickel tuile square into 5 or 6 pieces and arrange them on top of the other elements on the plate to form a tectonic plate effect. Garnish with the remaining goat cheese crumbles, Easter egg radishes, wild radish leaves and pods, and daikon flowers.

SERVES 4

SEASONED GOAT'S MILK BUTTER
200 grams | 1 cup goat's milk butter
15 grams | 2/3 cup ground nori
Maldon sea salt

WHIPPED GOAT'S MILK CHEESE
250 grams | 1 cup fresh goat's milk cheese
20 grams | 1 1/2 tablespoons Twin Sisters olive oil

PUMPERNICKEL TUILE
6 | large radishes
120 grams | 1 cup ground dried pumpernickel rye bread (page 289)
7 grams | 1/4 cup ground nori
130 grams | 1/2 cup egg whites
18 grams | about 5 1/2 sheets bronze gelatin, bloomed in ice water and wrung gently of excess water
64 grams | 1/4 cup French breakfast radish juice
10 grams | 1 tablespoon plus 1 1/2 teaspoons all-purpose flour
10 grams | 2 tablespoons isomalt, ground to a powder
10 grams | 2 teaspoons kosher salt

50 grams | 1.8 ounces aged goat cheese (Andante Dairy étude), crumbled
16 | Easter egg radishes, tops removed
16 | wild radish leaves
16 | wild radish pods
40 | daikon radish flowers

beef pine hamachi sorrels kohlrabi

A guest at The Restaurant once asked if she could wear this dish, our version of surf and turf, as a bracelet. I'm not sure if she was serious. We begin by curing strip loin in pine and then shave it paper-thin and top it with a slice of raw hamachi. We counter the fattiness with pickled kohlrabi, raw tiny onion, and caviar. We serve the dish with sorrel nori, which is made by pureeing sorrel and then drying it. The result looks like traditional nori but is incredibly tart and nuanced. Some people say this dish is very Scandinavian. I prefer to say that the cured meat, caviar, crème fraîche, and onion make it Eastern European. Either way, it can be worn as jewelry.

SERVES 4

CURED BEEF PREPARATION

280 grams | 10 ounces Wagyu strip loin
945 grams | 4 cups kosher salt
125 grams | $^2/_3$ cup sugar
25 grams | $^1/_2$ cup young pine shoots
2 grams | 1 teaspoon allspice berries
2 grams | $^1/_2$ teaspoon coriander seeds
2 grams | 1 teaspoon whole cloves
2 grams | 1 teaspoon white peppercorns
15 grams | 1 tablespoon vodka
150 grams | 5.3 ounces mature pine needles
300 grams | 1 $^1/_3$ cups grapeseed oil

SORREL NORI

30 grams | 1 $^3/_4$ cups French sorrel, in 1-inch
    (2.5-centimeter) pieces
3 grams | 1 sheet bronze gelatin, bloomed in
    ice water and gently wrung
    of excess water
4 grams | 1 $^1/_2$ teaspoons Ultra-Tex 3
kosher salt

FOR THE CURED BEEF PREPARATION:

Remove any fat and connective tissue from the strip loin. Combine the kosher salt, sugar, and pine shoots in a food processor and mix for 2 minutes, until the pine shoots are pulverized. Toast the allspice berries, coriander seeds, cloves, and peppercorns separately in a sauté pan over low heat for about 2 minutes, until fragrant. Let the spices cool, then transfer to a spice grinder and grind to a powder. Add the ground spices to the food processor, then add the vodka and mix for 2 minutes, until well incorporated. Put a small amount of the salt mixture in a metal pan. Lay the strip loin on the salt mixture and then pack the remaining cure around the loin. Be sure there are no gaps in the salt mixture to avoid oxidation. Cover the container tightly with plastic wrap and store in the refrigerator for 30 hours.

Rinse the beef under cold running water and pat dry with paper towels. Place in a vacuum bag and seal on high. Freeze for 8 hours.

Combine the pine needles and grapeseed oil in a small saucepan, heat to 120°F (49°C), and hold for at least 4 hours at that temperature. Strain the oil and let cool to a temperature of 40°F (4°C).

Cut 10 pieces of parchment paper, each 5 inches (12 centimeters) square. Using a pastry brush, brush one side of each piece with the pine oil, then stack the pieces, oiled side up, so that both sides of each piece are coated with oil. Pull the beef from the freezer. Using an electric slicer, shave it lengthwise into slices $^1/_{32}$ inch (1 millimeter) thick. Cut the beef slices into pieces 5 by 2 inches (13 by 5 centimeters). Stack the pieces between the prepared parchment squares and wrap tightly with plastic wrap. Store in the freezer to avoid oxidation until ready to use. Place any leftover beef in a vacuum bag sealed on high and store in the freezer for up to 1 month.

FOR THE SORREL NORI:

Bring a saucepan filled with salted water to a boil, add the sorrel, and blanch for 2 minutes. Drain the sorrel, transfer to a blender, and add the gelatin. Mix on low speed for 1 minute. The sorrel should not be smooth. With the blender running on low speed, add the Ultra-Tex and mix until it is fully absorbed, about 1 minute. Season the puree with kosher salt, then transfer to a silicone baking mat and spread in an even layer $^1/_{16}$ inch (2 millimeters) thick. Transfer the mat to a dehydrator tray and dehydrate the sorrel at 125°F (52°C) for at least 6 hours, until dry and crisp.

continued

FOR THE PICKLED KOHLRABI:

Put the kohlrabi in a large heatproof bowl. Combine the vinegar, water, sugar, dill, and kosher salt in a small saucepan and bring to a boil over high heat, stirring to dissolve the sugar. Remove from the heat and pour over the kohlrabies. Hold at 180°F (82°C) for 1 hour, then cool in the refrigerator.

TO SERVE:

Cut the hamachi into 4 thin strips each about 5 inches (12 centimeters) long. Lay a beef slice on each of 4 flat plates and center a piece of hamachi on top of each beef slice. Place a few dots of crème fraîche on top of the hamachi and a few slices of pickled kohlrabi resting on top of the crème fraîche. Garnish with the sea beans, dill pluches, small piles of caviar, green onion slices, and leaves of wood, French, red-veined, and silver sorrel. Break the nori into jagged pieces (about 1 inch/2.5 centimeters square) and put a few pieces on each plate.

PICKLED KOHLRABI

12 | baby kohlrabi, thinly sliced

250 grams | 1 cup rice vinegar

125 grams | $\frac{1}{2}$ cup water

125 grams | $\frac{2}{3}$ cup sugar

10 grams | 0.4 ounce fresh dill

6 grams | 1 teaspoon kosher salt

120 grams | 4.3 ounces hamachi loin

100 grams | $\frac{1}{2}$ cup crème fraîche (page 283)

16 | tiny sea beans

16 | dill pluches

15 grams | 0.5 ounce sturgeon caviar

2 | tiny onions, thinly sliced

12 | tiny red wood sorrel leaves

12 | tiny French sorrel leaves

12 | tiny red-veined sorrel leaves

12 | silver sorrel leaves

frog mallow cress

An excuse to go frogging, this is an ode to the setting where frogs are found: a murky pond replete with scum from wild mallow. The thickening power of mallow, the original ingredient of marsh-mallows, has been utilized for centuries.

SERVES 8

FROG BROTH

16 | frog legs

35 grams | 1 ounce flat-leaf parsley sprigs

40 grams | 1.3 ounces morning glory sprigs

25 grams | 2 ¹/₂ tablespoons sliced shallot

1 kilogram | 4 ¹/₄ cups water

30 grams | ¹/₂ cup watercress leaves

kosher salt

BRAISED BORAGE

35 grams | 2 ¹/₂ tablespoons extra virgin
olive oil

60 grams | ¹/₃ cup sliced shallots

450 grams | 1 pound borage leaves

kosher salt

BORAGE MALLOW

9 grams | 2 teaspoons guar gum

590 grams | 2 ¹/₂ cups water

45 grams | ¹/₂ cup dried mallow root

60 grams | about 2 egg whites

50 grams | ¹/₄ cup sugar

150 grams | ²/₃ cup braised borage
(recipe above)

kosher salt

FOR THE FROG BROTH:

Cut off the lower leg muscles from each frog leg and store in a container in the refrigerator. Remove the leaves from both the parsley and the morning glory, reserving both the leaves and the stems. Combine the upper frog leg portions, shallots, parsley stems, morning glory stems, and water in a pressure cooker and cook on high pressure for 40 minutes. Strain through a very fine cloth filter into a saucepan, place over high heat, and cook for 1 to 2 hours, until reduced by about one-third. Remove from the heat, add the watercress and the reserved parsley and morning glory leaves, and let steep for 30 minutes. Meanwhile, prepare an ice bath. Remove the leaves from the broth, season the broth with kosher salt, and nest the pan in the ice bath until the broth is cold. Transfer to an airtight container and store in the refrigerator.

FOR THE BRAISED BORAGE:

Warm the olive oil in a large rondeau over medium heat. Add the shallots and sweat for about 3 minutes, until translucent. Add the borage, increase the heat to high, and cook for about 4 minutes, until the leaves have wilted and released their natural juices. Season the leaves with kosher salt, drain in a colander for 30 seconds, then transfer to a sheet pan and cool in the refrigerator for about 1 hour.

Transfer the leaves to a cutting board and mince to a very fine paste. Store in an airtight container in the refrigerator until ready to use.

FOR THE BORAGE MALLOW:

Whisk together the guar gum and 295 grams (1 ¹/₄ cups) of the water in a bowl. Combine the mallow root and the remaining 295 grams (1 ¹/₄ cups) water in a saucepan over low heat and bring to a simmer. Cook for 30 minutes to extract the thickening properties of the mallow. Strain through a very fine cloth filter into a clean saucepan. Add the guar gum gel, place the pan over high heat, and whisk together the mixtures. Set the pan aside in a warm place.

Put the egg whites in the bowl of a stand mixer fitted with the whip attachment and whip on medium speed until soft peaks begin to form. Slowly add the sugar and continue to whip until a meringue forms and begins to thicken. Meanwhile, return the pan holding the mallow gel to high heat and bring to a boil. When then gel is boiling rapidly, remove it from the heat, add it to the meringue, and mix on high speed for about 3 minutes, until the gel is fully mixed with the whites. With the mixer running, add the braised borage and mix until well incorporated. Season with kosher salt. Spoon into a piping bag fitted with a small round tip and refrigerate until ready to use.

continued

FOR THE FROG RAVIOLI:

Prepare an ice bath. Combine 340 grams (12 ounces) of the frog meat, 30 grams (about 1 white) of the egg whites, and the sodium phosphate in a food processor and mix for about 30 seconds, until the egg white has been completely absorbed by the frog meat. Slowly add the cream until a light, uniformly textured mousse forms, stopping to scrape down the sides of the processor bowl as needed. Pass the mousse through a tamis into a metal bowl, then nest the bowl in the ice bath to cool the mousse. Mince the remaining 110 grams (4 ounces) of frog meat, fold it into the mousse, and season with kosher salt. To test the mousse for salt and texture, drop a small amount into salted boiling water and leave for about 45 seconds. Remove and let cool slightly in a small bowl nested in an ice bath. The mousse should taste fully seasoned and be slightly spongy. Transfer the mousse to a piping bag fitted with a small round tip and store in the refrigerator until ready to use.

To make the pasta dough, combine the flour, egg yolks, the remaining 30 grams (about 1 white) of egg whites, and the borage in the food processor and mix for about 2 minutes, until a smooth dough forms. Turn the dough out onto a lightly floured work surface and knead until the dough is uniform. Wrap in plastic wrap and refrigerate for 1 hour.

To assemble the ravioli, divide the dough into 4 equal portions and keep the unused portions covered to prevent drying. Working with 1 dough portion at a time, press the dough into a flat disk (about 1 inch/2.5 centimeters thick) and pass through the rollers of a pasta machine set at the widest setting. Lightly flouring the dough before each pass and gradually narrowing the rollers, continue to pass the dough through the rollers until it is about $^1/_{16}$ inch (2 millimeters) thick. Lay the dough sheet on a lightly floured work surface and cut lengthwise into strips about 10 inches (25 centimeters) long by 3 inches (7.5 centimeters) wide. Pipe a line of the mousse about $^1/_2$ inch (12 millimeters) wide and about $^1/_4$ inch (6 millimeters) in height down the center of a dough strip, then brush the edges of the strip with the egg wash. Starting from a long side, roll the dough around the mousse to form a loose cylinder, pressing to seal the long edge and the ends of the cylinder. Repeat with the remaining dough and mousse until you have 8 cylinders.

Prepare an ice bath. Bring a large pot of salted water to a gentle boil, add the filled pasta cylinders, and cook for 6 to 7 minutes, until the pasta is tender and the filling is cooked through. Carefully transfer to the ice bath to cool for 1 minute, then transfer to paper towels and pat dry. Cut each cylinder crosswise into 6 pieces $^1/_2$ inch (12 millimeters) wide for a total of 48 pieces. Store in a covered container in the refrigerator until ready to use.

TO SERVE:

Warm 350 grams (1 $^1/_2$ cups) of the frog broth in a saucepan over medium heat. When the broth begins to simmer, whisk in the butter a few pieces at a time. Add the reserved frog leg meat and pasta pieces and warm gently for 3 minutes. In a separate saucepan, heat 230 grams (1 cup) of the frog broth over medium heat and bring to a simmer, then taste and adjust the seasoning if needed. Place about 8 pieces of the frog leg meat and 6 pieces of the pasta in each of 4 bowls. Add a few large dots of the borage mallow to each bowl, and garnish each serving with the morning glory, watercress, and mallow. Pour an equal amount of the hot broth into each bowl.

FROG RAVIOLI

450 grams | 1 pound boneless frog meat

60 grams | about 2 egg whites

10 grams | 2 teaspoons sodium phosphate

75 grams | $^1/_3$ cup heavy cream

kosher salt

360 grams | 3 cups all-purpose flour

220 grams | 1 cup egg yolks

150 grams | $^2/_3$ cup braised borage
     (page 199)

equal parts egg and water, for egg wash

50 grams | 4 tablespoons diced
     unsalted butter

20 | morning glory leaves

30 | watercress pluches

30 | tiny mallow leaves

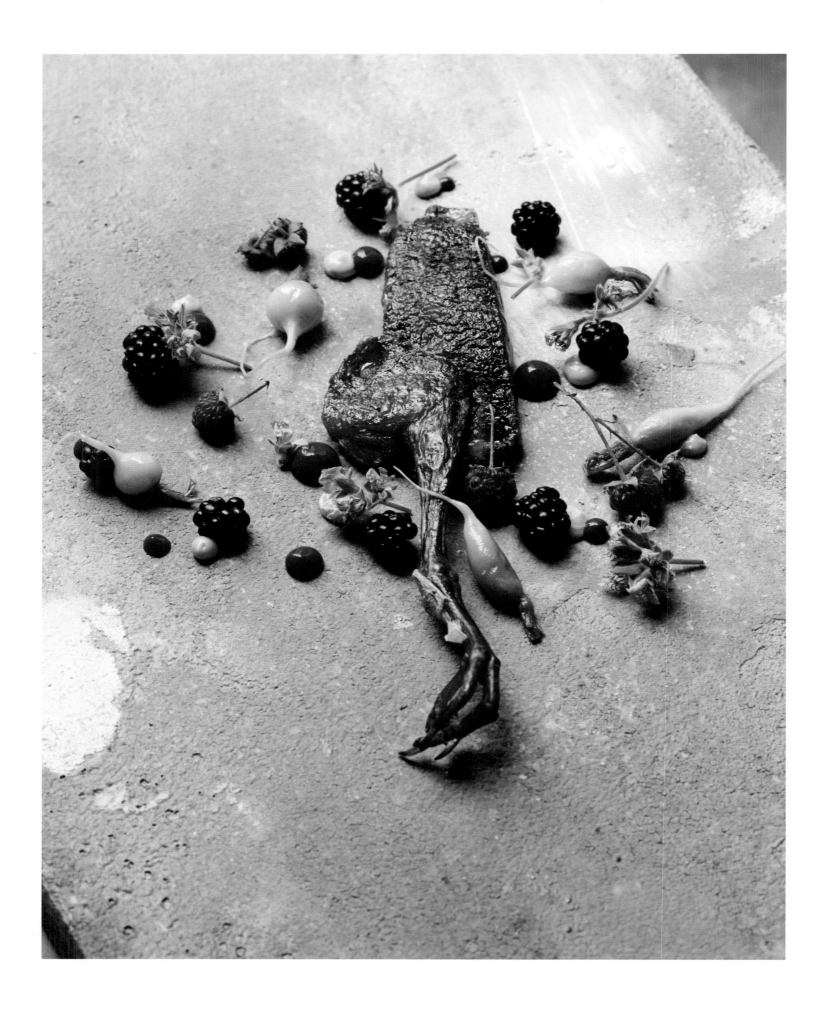

squab wild blackberry wild potpourri

The squab, from our friend Phillip Paine, is rubbed with a potpourri of dried and wild edibles, and then left to age before seeing its time over the fire. This dish illustrates the varying speed of the wild blackberries' maturation by using the tart, unripe ones for a puree and barely warming the juicy ones, mimicking their time in the sun's light.

SERVES 4

NAPA VALLEY POTPOURRI

2 grams | 1 tablespoon dried wild bay leaves
65 grams | 2 cups dried spice bush leaves
20 grams | 2/3 cup dried rose geranium
    leaves and flowers
20 grams | 2/3 cup dried wild fennel fronds
25 grams | 3/4 cup dried pine needles
6 grams | 3 tablespoons dried sweet clover

AGED SQUAB

2 | whole squabs
12 grams | 2 tablespoons Napa Valley
    potpourri (recipe above)

kosher salt
20 grams | 1 1/2 tablespoons rendered squab
    fat (page 283), melted
Maldon sea salt

FOIE GRAS BUTTER

190 grams | 6.6 ounces grade A foie gras
4.5 grams | 3/4 teaspoon foie gras cure
    (page 286)
200 grams | 3/4 cup whole milk
3.5 grams | 3/4 teaspoon powdered agar
kosher salt

BRAISED RADISHES

20 | medium-size Easter Egg radishes
50 grams | 1/4 cup rendered squab fat
    (page 283)
kosher salt

WILD BLACKBERRY PUREE

400 grams | 2 1/2 cups underripe
    wild blackberries
red wine vinegar
kosher salt

48 | underripe and ripe wild blackberries
20 | rose geranium flowers

FOR THE NAPA VALLEY POTPOURRI:

Combine the bay leaves, spice bush leaves, geranium leaves and flowers, fennel fronds, pine needles, and sweet clover in a spice grinder and grind for about 3 minutes, until pulverized. Store in an airtight container with silica gel packets at room temperature.

FOR THE AGED SQUAB:

Season the squabs on all sides with the potpourri. Tie a piece of butcher's twine around the neck of each squab and hang the squabs in the refrigerator with ample air circulation for 2 weeks.

Remove the frame from each squab and retain the 2 breast and leg portions, each in a single piece. Store the breast and leg portions between parchment paper in the refrigerator.

FOR THE FOIE GRAS BUTTER:

Temper the foie gras at room temperature for 3 hours. Pass the foie gras through a tamis and season with the foie gras cure. Place in a vacuum bag, seal on high, and refrigerate for 24 hours.

Transfer the foie gras to a blender. Pour the milk into a small saucepan and warm slightly over medium heat. Whisk in the agar, increase the heat to high, and bring the milk to a boil while whisking constantly. Remove from the heat and pour the milk into the blender. Mix on high speed for 2 minutes, until very smooth and shiny. Strain through a chinois into a metal pan and refrigerate for 2 hours.

Prepare an ice bath. Cut the foie gras into cubes and return to the blender. Mix on high speed for about 2 minutes to reliquefy. Strain through a chinois into a bowl, then nest the bowl in the ice bath to cool the foie gras. Season with kosher salt, transfer to a squeeze bottle, and store in the refrigerator.

FOR THE BRAISED RADISHES:

Season the radishes with the fat and kosher salt. Place in a vacuum bag and seal on high. Cook the radishes in a steam oven set at 200°F (95°C) for 15 minutes, until very tender. Hold the radishes in the bag in a warm place.

FOR THE WILD BLACKBERRY PUREE:

Prepare an ice bath. Put the blackberries in a blender and mix on high speed for about 4 minutes, until a smooth puree forms. Strain through a chinois into a bowl, then nest the bowl in the ice bath to cool the puree. Season with the vinegar and kosher salt, and transfer to a squeeze bottle.

TO SERVE:

Prepare a fire in a wood-burning oven with a grate and heat to 600°F (315°C). Season both the skin side and the flesh side of the squab portions with kosher salt, place on the grate skin side down, and char for 2 minutes. Remove from the oven, brush with the rendered squab fat, and season with Maldon salt. Lay the squab portions on 4 plates. Scatter a few dots of blackberry puree and foie gras butter around each squab portion. Garnish with the braised radishes, wild blackberries, and rose geranium flowers.

surf clam abductor walnut caviar

The abductor muscle of the surf clam is made tender and meaty by its hard work opening and closing the clam shell and flavorful by its life in briny water. Here we pair it with our valley walnut—wood, oil, and shavings of the nut made to look like wood shavings.

Insert an oyster shucker or petty knife into the opening of a surf clam, cut as close to the shell as possible, and pull back the top shell to open fully. Cut on the other side of the shell and remove the clam completely. Repeat with the second clam. Remove the abductors from each clam and reserve the rest of each clam for another use. Rinse the abductors under cold running water and pat dry on paper towels. Reserve in the refrigerator until needed.

Preheat the oven to 325°F (165°C). In a small pan, toast the walnuts for 6 minutes, until fragrant. Remove the pan from the oven and let the walnuts cool.

Increase the oven temperature to 400°F (200°C). Place the abductors on a walnut plank and warm in the oven for 1 minute. Remove the plank from the oven and brush the abductors with the walnut oil. Place a small pile of caviar on each abductor. Using a mandoline, shave the walnuts evenly over the top of the wood plank.

SERVES 4

2 | surf clams, soaked in ice water for 1 hour
6 | walnut halves
25 grams | 1 tablespoon toasted walnut oil
30 grams | 1 ounce white sturgeon caviar
walnut wood, for roasting

orange peel mushroom
herring escabeche

The beauty of "writing everything in pencil" is that certain things arrive at the same time—from the garden or the wilds—in such a way as to appear to be the work of Providence. In this case, citrus peel mushrooms arrive at the same time as herring from San Francisco Bay. We use a traditional escabeche liquid to pickle some fall vegetables and then offset the acidity and crunch with the fattiness of a potato infused with whipped cream. The result is a visually arresting tableau of a very specific moment in time.

SERVES 4

ESCABECHE VEGETABLES

6 grams | 1 tablespoon allspice berries

12 grams | about 2 cloves garlic

2 grams | ¹/₂ teaspoon white peppercorns

2 grams | ¹/₂ teaspoon coriander seeds

2 grams | 1 teaspoon fennel seeds

2 grams | ¹/₂ teaspoon mustard seeds

400 grams | 1 ²/₃ cups white wine vinegar

60 grams | ¹/₄ cup water

75 grams | ¹/₃ cup sugar

10 grams | 2 tablespoons thyme leaves

1.5 grams | ³/₄ teaspoon diced habanero

32 | tiny wild orange peel mushrooms

1 | Gravenstein apple

3 | tiny onion sprouts

2 | rainbow chard stems

2 | fingerling potatoes

POTATO CREAM

300 grams | 10.5 ounces russet potatoes

450 grams | 1 pound kosher salt

450 grams | 2 cups heavy cream

6.5 grams | about 2 sheets silver gelatin, bloomed in ice water and wrung gently of excess water

20 grams | 1 ¹/₂ tablespoons crème fraîche (page 283)

kosher salt

FOR THE ESCABECHE VEGETABLES:

Combine the allspice berries, garlic, peppercorns, coriander, fennel, and mustard seeds in a saucepan with a lid over low heat for about 1 minute, until fragrant. Add the vinegar, water, sugar, thyme, and habanero and bring to a simmer. Turn down the heat to very low, cover, and steep at 130°F (54°C) for 3 hours. Pour the contents of the pan into a container and let cool in the refrigerator for at least 12 hours. Strain through a chinois into a container.

Clean the mushrooms of any debris and submerge in a small amount of the escabeche liquid. Peel the apple and slice into half-moons directly into a small amount of the escabeche liquid. Thinly slice the onion sprouts, followed by the chard stems, making the stem slices about 1 inch (2.5 centimeters) long, and drop them each into their own batch of liquid. Put the prepared mushrooms, apples, onion sprouts, and chard stems in separate containers in the chamber of a vacuum seal machine and compress with full vacuum just once, then transfer to the refrigerator. Thinly slice the potatoes directly into a small amount of the escabeche liquid in a small saucepan and bring just to a boil over high heat. Remove from the heat and let cool to room temperature. Store the potatoes in an airtight container in the refrigerator.

FOR THE POTATO CREAM:

Preheat the oven to 325°F (165°C). Peel the potatoes, leaving a layer of flesh about ¹/₄ inch (6 millimeters) thick attached to the skin. Spread the kosher salt in a thin layer on a quarter sheet pan. Arrange the potato skins, skin side down, on the salt. Roast the skins for 45 minutes, until golden brown and dry.

Remove the potato skins from the oven, let cool just until they can be handled, then dust off the salt. Put the skins in a saucepan, add the cream, and bring to a simmer over low heat. Turn down the heat to low and steep at 120°F (49°C) for 1 hour. Transfer the contents of the pan to a container and refrigerate for 24 hours.

Strain the cream into the bowl of a stand mixer and discard the potato skins. Transfer a small amount of the cream to a small saucepan, add the gelatin, and heat over low heat just until the gelatin melts. Add the gelatin mixture and crème fraîche to the cream in the mixer bowl and fit the mixer with the whip attachment. Mix on medium speed until the cream holds a stiff peak. Taste and adjust the seasoning with salt if needed, then store in an airtight container in the refrigerator.

continued

FOR THE FRESH HERRING PREPARATION:

To remove the skin of the herring, trace the perimeter of the fish with the tip of a boning knife. Insert the knife under the skin in one corner of the fish and gently peel the skin away in a single piece. Repeat on the other side of the fish, then repeat with the remaining herring. Discard the skin. Slice the fillets from each fish, being careful not to burst the roe sack in the stomach cavity, then remove the roe sacks. Reserve the heads and bones for making the glaze. Bury the fillets and the roe in the salt in a plastic container and refrigerate for 10 minutes for the fillets and 45 minutes for the roe. Rinse the fillets and roe under ice-cold running water and pat dry on paper towels. Slice the herring fillets crosswise into diagonal slices ¹/₂ inch (12 millimeters) thick. Slice the roe into very thin strips. Store the fillets and roe on ice in the refrigerator.

Combine the herring heads and bones, celery, shallot, parsley, dill, and water in a pressure cooker and cook on low pressure for 25 minutes. Meanwhile, prepare an ice bath. When the stock is ready, strain through a very fine cloth filter into a bowl, then nest the bowl in the ice bath to cool the stock. Weigh the cooled stock and calculate 4 percent of the weight. Weigh the calculated amount in kuzu root starch and whisk it into the stock until completely dissolved. Transfer the mixture to a saucepan, place over high heat, and bring to a boil, stirring constantly to avoid scorching. Boil for 15 seconds, until the glaze thickens, then pour into a bowl and nest in an ice bath to cool completely. Season with salt, then transfer the glaze to an airtight container and store in the refrigerator.

FOR THE HERB PUREE:

Prepare an ice bath. Bring a saucepan filled with salted water to a boil over high heat. Add the dill, lovage, parsley, and chives and blanch for 35 seconds, agitating the herbs constantly to ensure even blanching. Drain the herbs and transfer to the ice bath for 2 minutes. Remove the herbs from the ice bath, wrap them in a piece of cheesecloth, and press out the excess water. Place the blanched herbs, olive oil, and gellan base in a blender and mix on high speed for 1 minute, until a smooth puree forms. Strain through a chinois into a bowl and season with salt. Transfer to a squeeze bottle and hold at room temperature.

FOR THE APPLE PUREE:

In a bowl, dissolve the ascorbic acid in the water. Core an apple but leave the skin intact, then immerse in the acidulated water to prevent browning. Repeat with the remaining 2 apples. Drain the apples and pass them through a juicer. Strain the juice through a chinois. Weigh the juice and calculate 1.5 percent of the weight. Weigh the calculated amount in agar and combine with the apple juice in a small saucepan. Bring to a boil over high heat, stirring occasionally. Boil for 15 seconds, then pour into a shallow heatproof container and let cool in the refrigerator for 2 hours, until set.

Cut the sheet into small pieces and transfer to a blender. Mix on high speed for about 20 seconds, until a smooth puree forms. Strain through a chinois into a bowl and adjust the seasoning with sugar and salt if needed. Transfer to a squeeze bottle.

TO SERVE:

Place a small amount of the potato cream in the center of each of 4 plates. Dip the herring fillets and roe and the pickled mushrooms, apples, onions sprouts, chard stems, and potatoes in the herring glaze and arrange in the center of each plate. Garnish with the herb puree, apple puree, green onion chiffonade, dill pluches, and kale leaves.

FRESH HERRING PREPARATION

4 | whole fresh herring with roe
450 grams | 1 pound kosher salt
40 grams | ¹/₃ cup diced celery
30 grams | 3 tablespoons diced shallot
2 | flat-leaf parsley sprigs
4 | dill stems
2 kilograms | about 8 cups water
kuzu root starch

HERB PUREE

60 grams | 2 ounces dill
50 grams | 1.8 ounces lovage leaves
30 grams | 1 ounce flat-leaf parsley leaves
30 grams | 1 ounce chives
40 grams | 3 tablespoons extra virgin olive oil
250 grams | 1 cup gellan base (page 285)
kosher salt

APPLE PUREE

13 grams | 1 tablespoon ascorbic acid
2 kilograms | about 8 cups water
600 grams | about 3 large Gravenstein
    apples
powdered agar
sugar
kosher salt

2 | green onion tops, cut in chiffonade
12 | dill pluches
8 | tiny kale leaves

sweetbread wild garlic agretti

Charred coals of sweetbread are garnished with wild agretti and difficult-to-find wild garlic.

SERVES 4

BLACK GARLIC MARINADE

50 grams | 1 3/4 ounces whole green garlic

18 grams | 2 tablespoons Korean black
    garlic cloves

60 grams | 1/4 cup water

6 grams | 1 tablespoon vegetable ash
    (page 289)

1 gram | 1/4 teaspoon squid ink

VEAL SWEETBREADS PREPARATION

475 grams | 2 cups whole milk

475 grams | 2 cups water

60 grams | 1/3 cup kosher salt

400 grams | 14 ounces heart-type veal
    sweetbreads

black garlic marinade (recipe above)

extra virgin olive oil

PICKLED WILD GARLIC CLOVES

12 | tiny cloves wild garlic

250 grams | 1 cup white wine vinegar

150 grams | 2/3 cup water

kosher salt

GARLIC MILK JAM

25 grams | about 5 garlic cloves

245 grams | 1 cup whole milk

250 grams | 8.8 ounces gellan base
    (page 285)

kosher salt

POACHED GREEN GARLIC

4 | whole green garlic

27 grams | 2 tablespoons extra virgin olive oil

kosher salt

FOR THE BLACK GARLIC MARINADE:

Prepare a fire in a wood-burning oven. When the fire is at about 600°F (315°C), arrange the green garlic directly on the coals and char heavily for about 4 minutes, turning once halfway through the cooking process. Transfer the garlic to a blender and add the black garlic, water, vegetable ash, and squid ink. Mix on high speed for 3 minutes, until smooth. Transfer to a container and let cool in the refrigerator for at least 3 hours.

FOR THE VEAL SWEETBREADS:

To make a brine, combine the milk, water, and kosher salt in a plastic container with a lid. Cut the sweetbreads into 2-inch (5-centimeter) pieces and submerge them in the liquid. Cover and refrigerate for 24 hours.

Remove the sweetbreads from the brine and pat dry with cloth towels, making sure that the exterior is very dry. Discard the brine. Mix together the black garlic marinade and sweetbreads in a bowl. Arrange the pieces in a single layer with the marinade in vacuum bags and seal on high. Cook the sweetbreads in a steam oven set at 200°F (95°C) for 18 minutes. Remove the bags from the oven and press between 2 metal pans topped with a weight of at least 2.3 kilograms (5 pounds). Refrigerate for at least 4 hours or for up to 24 hours.

FOR THE PICKLED WILD GARLIC CLOVES:

Using a knife, remove the bulb portion of each garlic, then carefully separate into individual cloves. Discard the remaining shell. Put the cloves in a heatproof container. Combine the vinegar and water in a small saucepan and bring to a boil over high heat. Pour over the garlic cloves and hold at about 190°F (88°C) for 10 minutes. Season with kosher salt and refrigerate for at least 24 hours.

FOR THE GARLIC MILK JAM:

Combine the garlic cloves and milk in a small saucepan, bring to a boil over medium-high heat, remove from the heat, and let steep at 200°F (95°C) for 20 minutes. Strain through a chinois into a blender and discard the garlic. Add the gellan base to the blender and mix on high speed for 2 minutes, until smooth. Strain through a chinois into a container and let cool in the refrigerator. Season with kosher salt, then transfer to a squeeze bottle and store in the refrigerator until needed.

FOR THE POACHED GREEN GARLIC:

Trim off the bulb end of each garlic, cutting about 1/4 inch (6 millimeters) from the roots. Portion each stem by cutting at the point where it turns from white to green, discarding the upper portion. Place the stems in a bowl and season with the olive oil and kosher salt. Arrange the stems in a vacuum bag and seal on high. Cook the stems in a steam oven set at 200°F (95°C) for 20 minutes. Meanwhile, prepare an ice bath. When the stems are ready, immerse the bag in the ice bath for 30 minutes. Remove the garlic from the bag and cut into 1-inch (2.5-centimeter) pieces. Line a sheet pan with paper towels and arrange the garlic on the towels.

continued

FOR THE ROASTED WILD AGRETTI:

Heat a cast-iron pan over high heat. When the pan is hot, add the olive oil and then quickly add the agretti and char for about 1 minute, until crispy. Remove from the pan, pat dry on paper towels, and season with kosher salt.

TO SERVE:

Put the bags of sweetbreads in a hot-water bath at 138°F (59°C) for 12 minutes. Remove the pieces from the bags and discard the liquid. Heat a cast-iron pan over high heat and add the olive oil. Add the sweetbreads and roast, turning once, for 1 ½ minutes on each side. Place 2 pieces of sweetbread on each of 4 white plates. Garnish each plate with a few dots of the garlic milk jam around the center, then place pieces of green garlic next to the sweetbreads. Drape the roasted wild agretti over the sweetbreads and finish with a few pickled garlic cloves and some watercress pluches.

ROASTED WILD AGRETTI

20 grams | 1 ½ tablespoons extra virgin olive oil

140 grams | 5.3 ounces wild agretti, stems removed

kosher salt

40 grams | 2 tablespoons extra virgin olive oil

24 | wild watercress pluches

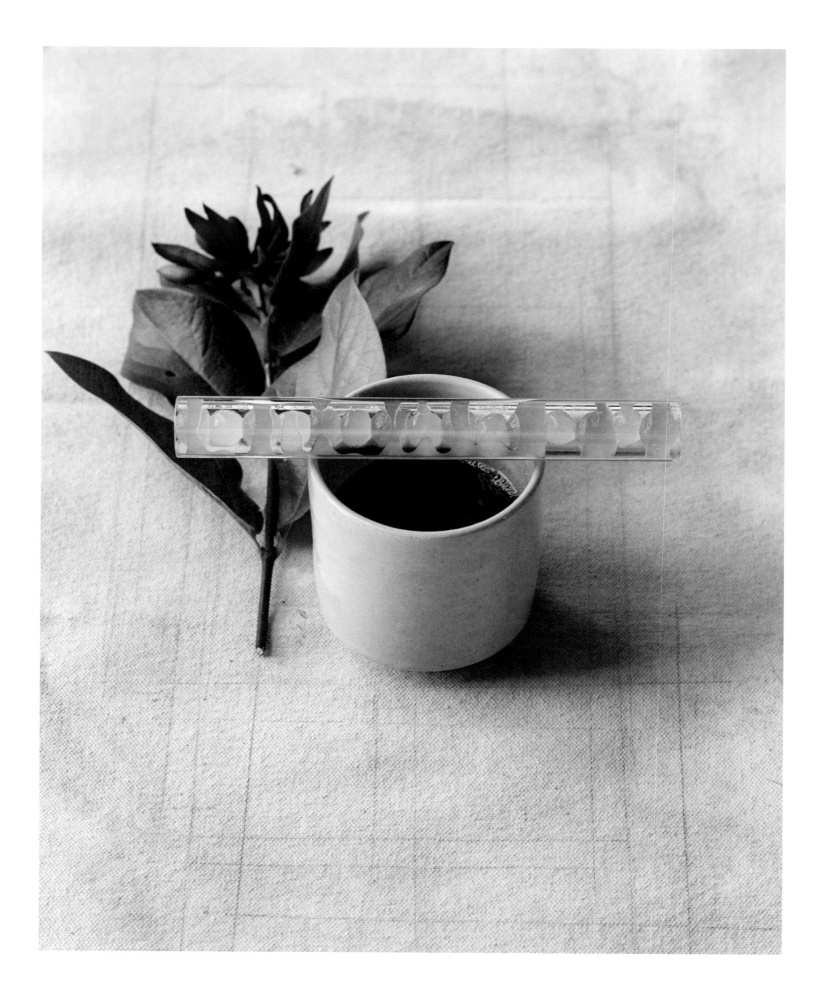

spice bush bubble tea

Spice bush (**Calycanthus occidentalis**), *which grows throughout the valley, was once prized by Native Americans for its medicinal value. Although the flowers and buds smell of Christmas spice, the leaves themselves have a fresh melonlike flavor. This pre-dessert calls for the leaves, pairing them with melons in a play on Taiwanese bubble tea.*

SERVES 8

CANARY MELON ICE

1 kilogram | 4 cups canary melon puree
50 grams | 2 $^1/_2$ tablespoons trimoline
25 grams | $^1/_4$ cup powdered glucose
13 grams | about 4 sheets bronze gelatin, bloomed in ice water and wrung gently of excess water
liquid nitrogen

SPICE BUSH PEARLS

8.3 kilograms | about 8 quarts plus 1 $^1/_4$ cups water
150 grams | 1 cup large tapioca pearls
300 grams | 1 $^1/_2$ cups sugar
300 grams | 1 $^1/_4$ cups water
70 grams | 2.5 ounces spice bush leaves

COMPRESSED CANARY MELON

680 grams | 1.5 pounds peeled and seeded canary melon
1 | lime

25 grams | about 2 $^1/_2$ tablespoons finger lime cells

FOR THE CANARY MELON ICE:

Combine the melon puree, trimoline, glucose, and gelatin in a saucepan. Place over medium heat and whisk just to melt the sugars and gelatin. Strain through a chinois into small plastic containers that hold about 250 grams (1 cup) each. Freeze for 8 hours.

FOR THE SPICE BUSH PEARLS:

Pour 8 kilograms (about 8 quarts) of the water into a stockpot and bring to a boil over high heat. Add the tapioca pearls while stirring constantly. Cook the pearls, stirring occasionally, for 10 to 15 minutes, until they have turned from white to clear. Meanwhile, combine the remaining 300 grams (1 $^1/_4$ cups) of water and the sugar in a small saucepan and heat over medium heat just until the sugar dissolves. Pour the syrup into a blender, add the spice bush leaves, and mix on high speed for about 2 minutes, until liquefied. Strain through a chinois into a container and reserve. When the tapioca pearls are ready, drain them in a colander, then rinse with cold running water to remove excess starch and to cool. Place the pearls in a container and pour in spice bush syrup to cover. Keep at room temperature until needed.

FOR THE COMPRESSED CANARY MELON:

Using a Parisian scoop (about the same size as the cooked tapioca pearls), cut at least 50 spheres from the melon. Juice the remaining melon trim, then combine the melon spheres and enough of the juice to coat the spheres in a vacuum bag and seal on high. Store in the refrigerator for at least 1 hour before use. Measure the remaining juice, then calculate 20 percent of that measure and measure that amount of spice bush syrup. Add the measured syrup to the remaining juice and season with lime juice until flavorful. Store in a very cold environment (about 36°F/2°C) for at least 2 hours before serving.

TO SERVE:

Carefully put the liquid nitrogen into a deep metal container (excessive changes in temperature or agitation of the liquid nitrogen may cause it to become volatile). Using a fork, shave the melon ice into the liquid nitrogen. Pour the liquid nitrogen through a small strainer to remove the shavings and store the shavings in a dry plastic container in the freezer until needed. (To discard the liquid nitrogen, carefully pour it back into its original container.) For each serving, alternate 5 of the tapioca pearls and 5 of the melon spheres in 8 glass straws. Pile a small amount of the shaved ice at the bottom of 8 small cups. Place a few piles of the finger lime cells on the ice. Pour about 60 grams (2 ounces) of the seasoned melon juice into each cup and balance the straw across the rim of the cup.

wild grape blue cheesecake

Wild grapes (Vitis vinifera) *grow throughout the valley. Their fame lies in their hardy resistance to phylloxera, the vine-destroying pest that wrought havoc on European vines in the late nineteenth century and those in the valley at the end of the twentieth century. In this dish, we use the tannic wild grapes to offset the creaminess of an Italian blue cheese and pay homage to my preferred dessert: the humble cheesecake.*

FOR THE BLUE CHEESECAKE:

Preheat the oven to 325°F (165°C). Combine the brown sugar and butter in the bowl of a stand mixer fitted with the paddle attachment and mix on medium speed for about 2 minutes, until the butter is well incorporated into the sugar. Add the flour and pulse for 15 to 20 seconds just to combine. Using a rubber spatula, fold the pecans and then the salt into the dough.

Put the dough between 2 pieces of parchment paper and roll out 1/8 inch (3 millimeters) thick into a rectangle that will fit in a full sheet pan. Place the dough, still sandwiched between parchment, between 2 full sheet pans. Bake for 12 to 15 minutes, until the crust is a light golden brown. Remove from the oven, remove the top pan, then peel off the top sheet of parchment. While the crust is hot, using a quarter sheet pan as a template, cut the crust to the same dimensions as the pan. Cover the bottom and sides of the quarter sheet pan with plastic wrap, allowing it to extend over the sides. Carefully transfer the trimmed dough to the prepared pan and let cool to room temperature.

Crumble 90 grams (3 ounces) of the blu del Moncenisio cheese and scatter it evenly over the crust. Combine the cream cheese and the remaining 450 grams (1 pound) of blu del Moncenisio cheese in the bowl of a stand mixer fitted with the paddle attachment. Pour the cream into a saucepan and warm over low heat. Slowly whisk the iota carrageenan into the cream, continuing to whisk until fully dissolved. Continuing to whisk, increase the heat to high and add the gelatin. Bring to a boil and maintain a boil for at least 10 seconds. Pour the hot cream mixture into the stand mixer with the cheeses and pulse to incorporate the cheese into the liquid. Once the mixture is homogenous, pour it over the crust. Let stand at room temperature until the cake begins to set. Transfer the pan to the refrigerator and allow the cake to set fully, about 3 hours.

FOR THE WILD GRAPE GLAZE:

Combine the grapes, sugar, and water in a heatproof bowl and cover tightly with plastic wrap. Set the bowl directly on top of a pot of simmering water, pressing down lightly on the bowl to form a seal and maintain the heat. Poach the grapes for 2 hours. Remove the plastic wrap and inspect the liquid that has formed in the bowl. It should be a light purple and have all the flavor of a grape. Strain the liquid through a very fine cloth filter and then measure 500 grams (about 2 cups) of it. Transfer to a saucepan and place over low heat. Add the gelatin, heat just until the gelatin melts, and mix gently. Remove from the heat and let cool slightly. Pour a thin layer of the glaze evenly over the set cheesecake and return the cake to the refrigerator to set the glaze.

TO SERVE:

Preheat the oven to 325°F (165°C). Spread the walnuts on a small sheet pan and toast for 6 minutes. While the nuts are still warm, thinly shave them on a mandoline. Let cool to room temperature. Lift the finished cheesecake from the sheet pan. Heat a long-bladed knife with a kitchen torch, then cut the cheesecake lengthwise into 10 even strips each about 1/2 inch by 8 inches (12 millimeters by 20 centimeters). Position each strip on its side on a plate and garnish it with the shaved walnuts, wild grapes, and bachelor's buttons.

SERVES 10

BLUE CHEESECAKE

75 grams | 1/3 cup firmly packed brown sugar

150 grams | 2/3 cup unsalted butter

150 grams | 1 1/4 cups pastry flour

150 grams | 1 1/3 cups chopped pecans

7 grams | 1 teaspoon kosher salt

540 grams | 1 pound, 3 ounces blu del Moncenisio cheese

250 grams | about 1 cup cream cheese

850 grams | 3 1/2 cups heavy cream

3.5 grams | 3/4 teaspoon iota carrageenan

12.5 grams | 5 sheets silver gelatin, bloomed in ice water and wrung gently of excess water

WILD GRAPE GLAZE

500 grams | about 1 pound wild grapes

50 grams | 1/4 cup sugar

200 grams | 3/4 cup water

10 grams | 4 sheets silver gelatin, bloomed in ice water and wrung gently of excess water

20 | Hartley walnut halves

100 | wild grapes

50 | blue bachelor's button flowers

MATERIA PRIMA

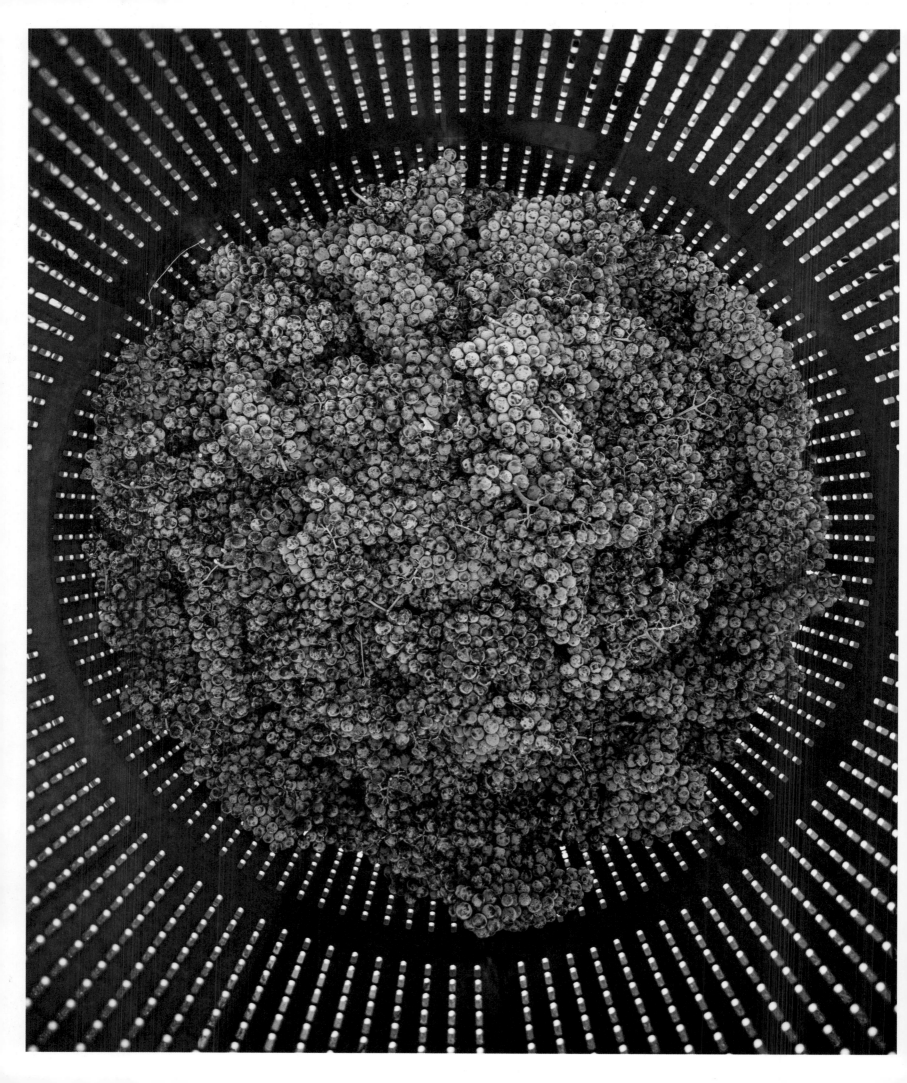

A place belongs forever to whoever claims it hardest, remembers it most obsessively, wrenches it from itself, shapes it, renders it, loves it so radically that he remakes it in his own image.

—JOAN DIDION

What can we do that no one else can? This is the fundamental question, the beating heart of my work. When I pose this question to myself and to my team, I'm not asking what our skills enable us to do or suggesting that we possess a level of talent that others do not. I'm wondering, rather, what we can do owing to our place in the world that others cannot because they are not here. I am not even close to the full realization or exploration of this idea. I catch glimpses of an answer in certain dishes and lose it in others. There are seasons when the menu reads like a haiku written in the dialect of the valley. Other times, meals just look and sound and taste like good food. This answer is like an amorphous figure in the distance. I get close enough sometimes to make out its basic shape, but it moves as I do. I give it a name: *specificity*, or even *style*. I wonder what we are gathering and squeezing from our life experiences that we can point to as our own, that we can set before a guest knowing the dish could have only been found here.

Local is certainly part of it, exemplified by all the ideas I've already shared: working closely with our growers and artisans, foraging the wilds of the valley. There is one final piece to this: the *materia prima* of Napa, those products and ingredients that we source and preserve and utilize that are found in this narrow stretch of land between the Palisades and the Mayacamas.

VITIS VINIFERA

It seems logical to begin with the grape. Napa Valley is America's preeminent wine-growing region, and as you might imagine, I witness throughout a year the various mutations and stages of the grape plant—bud break, the flowering of the vines, *véraison*, harvest, and the slow coloration of the leaves. I smell the fermentation in the air after harvest as nature and yeast do their things. As a chef, the grape is something that I can consider mine. I use the leaves as wrappers, pickle the tiny grape shoots, squeeze the unripe juice for verjus, and utilize the fruits themselves. I use the dried vines as serving pieces and as fuel. I immerse myself in this most Napa of things.

Using grapes in our cooking at The Restaurant ties us to the activities of the valley. When I first arrived here, I operated with very little attention to the movements of wine production. They seemed irrelevant to the tasks at hand. I was here to cook. Over the last several years, however, I have come to better understand the physiology of wine and the incredible passions inherent in those who craft the product. There is a spiritual connection between the winemakers, past and present, and our cooking. To make wine is to coax from the grape the maximum amount of character. This requires many elements outside the grape itself: soil, *terroir*, climate, microbiology. It also requires diligence, passion, and a team that follows suit. This mirrors exactly my tasks as a chef. When I work with grapes, I understand this and I am finally part of the enormous economic and human force that hums around me. To continue to ignore this would be self-delusional. To embrace it is to cook with open eyes.

DIRT

Grapes thrive here in part because of the geological makeup of the soils. Volcanic activity that occurred as recently as five million years ago spread a layer of volcanic ash all over the valley. There is still an active volcano about twenty miles to the north, as well as gushing geysers (the unhappy result of someone trying to dig a well) and a petrified forest where large redwoods lie like stone. Spas new and old with names like Dr. Wilkinson's and Indian Springs have catered to visitors for a century. Calistoga was historically where people flocked to be buried in mud and "take the waters." Its very name comes from a drunken Samuel Brannan, a nineteenth-century journalist and gold rush millionaire who tried to equate the new town with Saratoga, New York: "We will make this town the Calistoga of Sarafornia!"

I came to learn that the rich clay that makes up the therapeutic mud of Calistoga's baths could have some culinary value. We take dried clay and create a cooking medium out of it, adding water and appropriate seasonings. Proteins, vegetables, even fruit emerge from the hardened clay, their natural flavors intact and enlivened by the dirt of Napa. From special dirt spring the grapes. The grapes bring forth the wine, and the wine brings the people. A chef follows and uses that dirt. . . .

PRESERVATION

An old wine cellar stands below one of the original buildings on the Meadowood property. Its existence is a secret to all but a few cooks and one engineer who was enlisted to assist in its maintenance. The shelves in the cellar are lined with a multitude of jars that make it look like a culinary apothecary and contain our *materia prima*: preserved manzanita blossoms, last year's fruit in various brines and syrups, *umeboshi* of wild local plums, fermented vegetables, sunflower flesh, and salted apple leaves. Our exercises in food preservation give us a chance to contain the abundance that the valley affords us while also building on and altering the original products. We don't attempt to freeze in time those ingredients that arrive sporadically and quickly. For us, preservation is not synonymous with stopping. Instead, sunflower flesh becomes less bitter after some time in light brine, and fermenting onions creates an altogether different product from the raw version. We make miso with the same acorns that the Wappo ground into meal along the Napa River hundreds of years ago. And we impart the gentle flavors of spice bush into vinegars and preserve the harvest of long-abandoned walnut orchards.

I sometimes imagine that if our root cellar were unearthed a thousand years from now, its contents would be an accurate marker of our time and place in the valley. The contents of the various jars, labeled in the handwriting of people long gone, would contain the artifacts of a chef's pursuits. Leaves and shoots, fruits and berries tell the story of my time here. *This is what we ate.* Even now, I can look at a jar from last year and remember when that item was preserved and stored away—like when a winemaker tastes an old vintage and reexperiences the emotions of the time during which it was bottled.

We are building more in that tiny room than a supply of food. We are preserving our collective memories of and associations with the place and the act of cooking. When we remove a jar and use its contents, writing on the menu something like "last year's peaches" or "preserved walnuts from our trees," we are sharing with diners an incredibly specific time, place, and feeling. I hope they see Napa from a new perspective, as they sit in the Napa of now and taste the Napa of times past. We can say to our guests, these are salted leaves from last fall. Remember that fall? Or, taste this green coriander from last winter. Oh, I think to myself, that was the winter my girl was born. Absent a farmhouse decorated with faded photographs of preceding generations, the root cellar is our way to hold on to memories and share them with our guests.

GIFTS OF PLACE

I always want to use the best products and local products. This is an obvious and fairly accepted tenet of modern cooking. There have been many conversations concerning which is of the greatest priority for a restaurant that strives for excellence. Is a consistent narrative exemplified by reliance on local more impactful, or is it better to procure and offer the best products regardless of their provenance?

In Napa Valley, I am blessed in not having to choose. There are purveyors and peddlers and craftspeople here who have carved out places for their passions among the tumult of grape growing and wine production. These are small-scale operations. Phillip Paine provides us with our squab and Peggy O'Kelly with our olive oil. Eric Alegria raises heritage breed rabbits on a small parcel that straddles a creek on Mount Veeder, and we harvest the products of the valley's bees, the comb and wax. There is a functioning grist mill in Calistoga that was first built in 1846. The Bale mill is where people would bring their wheat and corn to be milled while they socialized. Now it is restored with original fir and redwood and serving as a state park, and the grinding stones are turning again, which gives us ground rye and spelt and an understanding of what it means to separate the wheat from the chaff. We find ourselves in an agrarian Eden.

Things grow well here, benefiting from the same geological fortunes that allow the grape to flourish. Although the land is covered in vines now, this valley was once home to ranches and orchards and small family farms. Our purveyors are an extension of that not-so-distant history.

The benefit of working with these makers of our *materia prima* goes beyond the quality of the goods. In looking for a local chicken producer, I am also seeking the person who can share knowledge with us, who can instruct and inform us about chickens, about *élevage* and feed and breeds, the cost of corn and the role of ethanol, the dangers of coyotes, and the differences between farm and factory. We get more than great chicken. We become a little smarter and a bit better. Our guests will marvel at the chicken, we will delight in the new knowledge, and the farmer will find satisfaction knowing that the work is treated with the greatest respect. This is what this place gives us, and what we in turn can give to this place: economic as well as environmental sustainability. We buy what people raise, supporting at every turn the merchants of quality.

It would probably be more lucrative for these producers to grow grapes. In parts of the valley, an acre of growing land can fetch more than a quarter million dollars. By pursuing their paths as they do, our purveyors often choose the hardest way. Phillip gave up accounting in San Francisco to spend his days among low-slung buildings populated by families of pigeons. Peggy left a job in finance to oversee the area's best olive trees and the pressing of oil. Simply put, these people make the valley a better place. In an area crowded with monoculture, our purveyors represent something different and provide welcome texture. My life as a chef is better for their work.

Recently I was given a new walnut oil made by the daughter of a longtime valley farmer. She had grown up on this farm, left to pursue a career in Los Angeles, and then found her way back. She and her husband send their kids to the Montessori school. The oil is deep in color and flavor and more viscous and elegant than any I have seen. I look forward to playing with it and to visiting the farm with my cooks and learning a little bit more (piece by piece) about walnuts and trees, and about the valley's people and future.

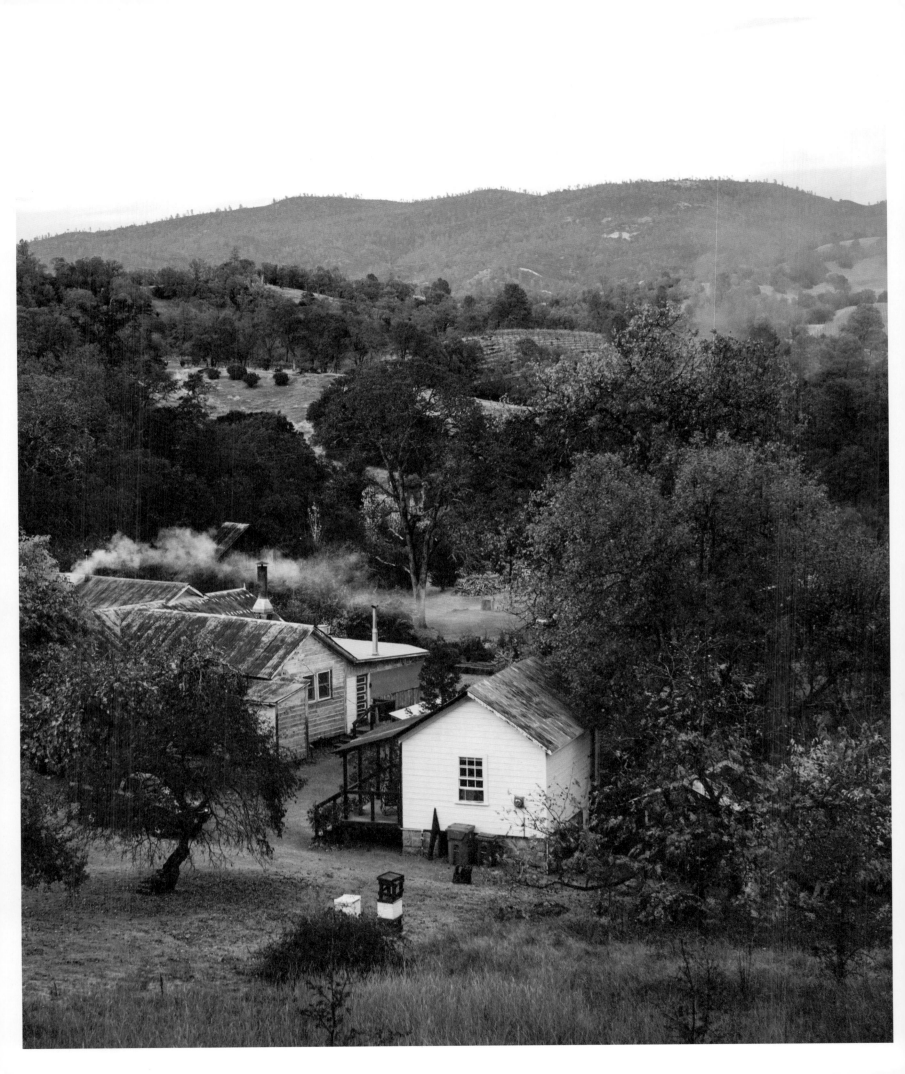

a new napa cuisine

Don't play what's there, play what's not there.
—MILES DAVIS

There was a time when Napa Valley was devoid of a singular or consistent architectural style. Driving its highways and back roads, you saw a preponderance of neo-Tuscan villas and some Mission Revival estates, with a little McMansion thrown into the mix. Over the last two decades, however, an architectural lexicon has evolved, led by architect Howard Backen and others. Consisting of wood and beams and agricultural references, this elegant style is a nod to the past created for today's sophisticated audience. In a similar way, wineries like Harlan Estate, Screaming Eagle, and others have produced wines—often adored and widely imitated—that have developed into the quintessential Napa Valley Cabernet. There is even, for better or worse, a wine-country design aesthetic, easily recognizable in catalogs and magazines, used to sell oven mitts and wooden bowls.

Our valley seems to be slowing down and defining itself through thoughtful curating and careful production. In truth, this place should probably have been spent by now, picked over by generations of people like me hoping to plant their flag. Herein lies the magic of the Napa Valley. People come here for the first time (or return after an absence) and see this place anew—as if they were the first to see it at all. The light playing through an overhang of oaks, fields of grape leaves turning autumnal colors after harvest, the valley provides these unparalleled moments that make all of us feel like we've discovered something entirely new. We are in California, true Californians, experiencing the motto imprinted on our state flag: Eureka! I have found it.

When I talk to other people my age in the valley, I recognize the same fervor that I feel. We believe as much in the magic of this place as in the ingenuity of our own ideas. Perhaps one couldn't exist without the other. We are all looking at the same valley, but we each see something new and fresh, wet with the dew of unimpeachable possibility. This place is ripe and fertile, and I see it! It is no longer a virginal landscape. Structure exists here, a history of predecessors and lessons to be learned from the mistakes and successes of the past. There is no shortage of others' flags dotting the landscape. The challenges of living in a region that's so desired are here, too: a cost of living that threatens young entrepreneurship and strict zoning that rightly protects the agrarian character of the place but limits potential commercial enterprises.

Although I have not been here that long and am thus blessed by the ignorance that fact brings, I have read about the battles of the 1980s and 1990s pitting development against ecological protection, vintners against the farm bureau, and old farmers against an influx of Silicon Valley wealth. Although I have my opinions about these issues, and the embers of these battles are still warm, these things are no more than the landscape that I have found—much like the collective history of a country and a world created the place into which we were all born.

Is this not the secret to America's success, a collective amnesia that allows us to build on what we find without the shackles that the past creates? Maybe this is the reason that regeneration happens here. We build our lives in the world that we find. The Napa that we have inherited, though different from the times before and the time that will follow, is still a place of stunning beauty and character.

This is the Napa that I hope my cuisine is based on and takes root in. A new Napa, not rediscovered but rather discovered anew. Admittedly, I don't have much to go on. There is no precedent here: no historical cuisine exists like that of Scandinavia or Oaxaca to drink from, to riff on, to emulate. How then can we hope to create something when there is so little to pull from, so little history to coax meaning from? Inspiration, sadly, is not enough.

To create something specific to this place, I must play the notes that aren't there.

And so I wrestle with ghosts: a barn structure crumbling in a field of tall grass, an abandoned walnut orchard, mortar rocks littering the riverbank. There is the sense that the definition or identity of this cuisine must be based on remembrances of things gone and must be assembled anew as if a poem written from memory. I hunt through the yellowed files of the historical society and listen raptly as longtime residents tell stories of Napa before the arrival of wine, want, and a branded way of life. They talk of the Silverado Trail, silent but for a passing car every few hours, and how there were prunes before grapes, farmers before vintners, and family plots before family crests. These ghosts need to be listened to; their voices the substratum of the Napa we find today, and of the work that springs from it.

In my effort to create a style of cooking that reflects this singular place, I will continue to work with the artists and craftspeople of the valley and harness their respective artistic and cultural perspectives. I will allow their artistic energies to bleed into my thinking and cooking. In quiet studios and among fiery kilns, I will try to allow clay and wood and food to become one thing. I will continue to look to the wilds of the valley, not as a nod to the waning foraging trend but as a tie to occurrences of the natural year and an inexorable bond to the past. The flow of a year: acorns falling, spice bushes flowering, the mustard taking over fields.

We will continue to engage in the agricultural pursuits, working under the same Napa sky that saw generations of farmers before us—and before the grapes and wine. We will tie ourselves to the land, and in so doing, to the valley's primary enterprise, gaining a better understanding of the nature of the seasons and the life of our crops. The community of the Napa Valley will remain a source of inspiration for our work, and hopefully the community will be a beneficiary of that work, too. To that end, I shall continue to seek out local producers of all sorts and shape the cooking around these products. We will try to serve the local charitable interests, continuing a tradition that has long existed in the Napa Valley.

Above all else, I will keep working and listening to the things around me. I will strive to see beyond the vineyard and allow the quiet to drown out the noise. In time, a new strain will be forged that is ours alone. Collective amnesia will be replaced by the shared voice of a new generation here, one that gives a foundation to our cooking and provides a voice that allows it to be shared. Here in this small American valley, I will strive to construct a perspective that is both personal and universal. I hope to keep holding the thread.

potatoes in beeswax

A block of beeswax from nearby hives appeared in the kitchen one day. We scratched our heads a bit and settled on melting the wax and cooking potatoes in it (see page 111). The potatoes took on the most incredible flavor—not sweet like honey but haunting and wholly unique. The dish needed some acidity and freshness, which the introduction of tiny sorrels and a sorrel vinegar provided. This dish speaks to the idea of simple, local, and fun in just a few bites.

SERVES 4

POTATO AND SORREL GRAVEL

510 grams | 18 ounces peeled and diced
   Yukon Gold potatoes, held in water
grapeseed oil, for deep-frying
100 grams | 4 cups French sorrel leaves,
   in medium-size pieces
100 grams | about 30 sheets bronze gelatin,
   bloomed in ice water and wrung gently
   of excess water
Maldon sea salt

BLOOD SORREL VINEGAR

30 grams | 1 3/4 cups blood sorrel leaves
300 grams | 1 1/4 cups white wine vinegar

BEESWAX POTATO PUREE

1.8 kilograms | 4 pounds beeswax
400 grams | 14 ounces Yukon Gold potatoes
200 grams | 3/4 cup heavy cream
200 grams | 3/4 cup crème fraîche
   (page 283)
10 grams | 1 1/2 teaspoons raw honey
kosher salt

POTATOES COOKED IN BEESWAX

800 grams | 1 3/4 pounds beeswax
4 | fingerling potatoes
kosher salt

8 | tiny French sorrel leaves
8 | tiny blood sorrel leaves
8 | silver shield sorrel leaves
8 | wild wood sorrel leaves
Twin Sisters olive oil
sel gris

FOR THE POTATO AND SORREL GRAVEL:

Drain the potatoes and place them in a food processor, add water just to cover, and pulse to break up the potatoes into small, uniform pieces about the size of a grain of rice. Drain the potatoes and rinse under cool running water for 5 minutes, then pat dry on paper towels.

Pour oil to a depth of 4 inches (10 centimeters) into a deep fryer or deep, heavy pot and heat to 315°F (155°C). Working in small batches, add the potatoes to the hot oil and fry for about 4 minutes, until light golden brown. Transfer to paper towels to drain. Arrange the fried potatoes on dehydrator trays and reserve in a dehydrator set at 125°F (52°C) for at least 2 hours.

Meanwhile, preheat the oven to 275°F (135°C). Bring a large pot of salted water to a boil. Add the sorrel leaves and blanch for 1 minute. Scoop the sorrel out of the water and put in a blender. Add the gelatin and pulse on medium speed to break up the sorrel and melt the gelatin, forming a puree. Transfer the puree (without straining) to a silicone baking mat and spread about 1/32 inch (1 millimeter) thick. Place the baking mat on a sheet pan and bake the puree for 15 minutes, until dry and crispy. Let cool on the pan for 30 minutes, then remove the sorrel sheet from the baking mat and break into pieces. Transfer the fried potatoes and sorrel to a food processor and pulse lightly until uniform. Season with Maldon salt and hold in an airtight container with silica gel packets at room temperature.

FOR THE BLOOD SORREL VINEGAR:

Combine the blood sorrel and vinegar in a vacuum bag and seal on high. Refrigerate for 12 hours. Strain through a very fine cloth filter, then transfer to a squeeze bottle and store in the refrigerator.

FOR THE BEESWAX POTATO PUREE:

Melt the beeswax in a deep, heavy pot over high heat. Add the potatoes, reduce the heat, and simmer for 5 minutes. Remove from the heat and place the pot in the refrigerator for 12 hours. Return the pot to medium heat, bring to a simmer, and cook the potatoes for 15 minutes. Remove the pot from the heat and the potatoes from the beeswax. Let cool slightly, then peel the potatoes and discard the skins. Pass the potatoes through a tamis into a bowl. Combine the cream and crème fraîche in a small saucepan over medium heat. Working in small batches, add the cream mixture to the potatoes, mixing gently with a rubber spatula. Do not overwork. Season with the honey and kosher salt, then strain through a chinois into a saucepan with a lid. Hold in a warm place (at least 130°F / 54°C).

FOR THE POTATOES COOKED IN BEESWAX:

Melt the beeswax in a small, heavy saucepan over high heat. Add the potatoes and simmer for 15 minutes. Remove the pan from the heat and remove the potatoes from the beeswax. Let cool slightly, then peel and discard the potato skins. Put the potatoes in a bowl, cover with plastic wrap, and hold warm.

TO SERVE:

Reheat the potato puree and place a small amount on each of 4 plates. Steam the fingerling potatoes in a basket steamer until warm. Place in a small bowl and season with the sorrel vinegar, oil, and sel gris. Cut into slices and lay them in a shingle pattern on top of the puree. Garnish with a light dusting of the potato and sorrel gravel. Finish with a few pieces of each sorrel variety.

champagne-fermented crudité

Here is a great way to start a meal, with a nod to both the West (Champagne to start) and the East (using the age-old nuka *pot). Spent Champagne lees are removed from the bottle, usually after several years, by employing the modern approach of freezing the neck of the bottle to solidify the lees, allowing for easy removal. We take these lees and add them to a traditional* nuka *pot of rice bran, dried bread, salt, and vegetables.*

FOR THE CHAMPAGNE NUKA:

Warm the Champagne and kosher salt in a saucepan over low heat to dissolve. Add the bread and stir continuously until a mash consistency forms. Mix the bran and vegetable peelings into the mash and pack into a ceramic container. Cover the container with a cloth towel and store in an area with an ambient temperature of 70°F (20°C). Every 24 to 36 hours, remove the nuka and agitate it to introduce more oxygen. After about 4 months have elapsed, the nuka will have the proper fermenting capabilities. Be sure to continue the aeration process to ensure beneficial microbial growth. If the nuka should ever rise in temperature on its own, add 3 percent more Champagne disgorgement and 5 percent more rice bran by weight to energize the bacteria and equalize the anaerobic process.

TO SERVE:

Bury the carrots, radishes, and turnips in the nuka and refrigerate for 12 hours. Rinse the vegetables in a bowl of room-temperature water just to remove the excess nuka and pat dry on paper towels.

SERVES 6

CHAMPAGNE NUKA

2 kilograms | 8 cups Champagne disgorgement (lees)

400 grams | 1 1/3 cups kosher salt

50 grams | 1/2 cup ground dried levain bread (page 288)

1.8 kilograms | 4 pounds toasted rice bran

100 grams | 1 cup carrot peelings

100 grams | 1 cup radish peelings

100 grams | 1 cup turnip peelings

12 | baby carrots with tops

12 | baby radishes with tops

12 | baby turnips with tops

lamb in clay black lime pistachio

We cook this lamb rack in a clay made from Calistoga ash, and then after showing the guest the entombed rack, we return with the lamb chop surrounded with what looks like shards and remnants of the cooked clay. This "clay" is actually a dried meringue made from pureed pistachios and dried lime.

SERVES 4

BLACK LIME STOCK
320 grams | 1 ⅓ cups water
60 grams | 2 ounces dried black lime

PISTACHIO CLAY
250 grams | about 2 cups pistachios
600 grams | 2 ½ cups water
320 grams | 1 cup plus 5 tablespoons black
 lime stock (recipe above)
80 grams | ¾ cup egg white powder
6.5 grams | about 2 sheets bronze gelatin,
 bloomed in ice water and wrung gently
 of excess water
80 grams | ⅓ cup sugar
27 grams | 2 tablespoons vegetable ash
 (page 289)
kosher salt

LAMB RACK PREPARATION
1 | lamb rack, 4-rib bone portion
750 grams | 3 ½ cups Calistoga clay
25 grams | 1 tablespoon kosher salt
19 grams | 3 tablespoons shabazi spice
30 grams | about 2 tablespoons extra virgin
 olive oil

Twin Sisters olive oil
Maldon sea salt

FOR THE BLACK LIME STOCK:

Prepare an ice bath. Combine the water and black lime in a small saucepan over high heat, heat to 140°F (60°C), cover, and simmer at that temperature for 1 hour. Strain the stock into a bowl, then nest the bowl in the ice bath to cool the stock. Store the stock in an airtight container in the refrigerator until ready to use.

FOR THE PISTACHIO CLAY:

Combine the pistachios and water in a saucepan over low heat, bring to a simmer, and simmer for 30 minutes to tenderize the pistachios. Meanwhile, prepare an ice bath. When the pistachios are ready, drain them, reserve the liquid, and transfer the nuts to a blender. Mix on high speed for about 30 seconds, until a smooth puree forms. Add cooking liquid as needed to get the right consistency. Strain the puree through a chinois into a bowl, then nest the bowl in the ice bath to cool the puree.

Combine 240 grams (1 cup) of the black lime stock and the egg white powder in the bowl of a stand mixer fitted with the whip attachment. Mix on low speed just to incorporate the egg whites into the liquid. Meanwhile, combine 40 grams (2 ½ tablespoons) of the stock with the gelatin in a small saucepan over low heat and heat just until the gelatin melts. Set the pan aside. Combine the remaining 40 grams (2 ½ tablespoons) of stock and the sugar in a second small saucepan and place over high heat to form a syrup. Do not agitate the pan too much or the sugar will crystallize. Increase the mixer speed to high and monitor the temperature of the syrup. Once it reaches 243°F (117°C), slowly pour the syrup into the whipping whites, being careful not to trap the sugar on the sides of the bowl. When all of the syrup has been added, carefully pour in the melted gelatin mixture and continue whipping to cool the now-formed meringue slightly. Turn off the mixer. Measure about 60 grams (¼ cup) of the pistachio puree and fold it and the vegetable ash into the meringue. Season the meringue with salt.

Spread the meringue on an acetate sheet in an even layer ½ inch (12 millimeters) thick. Transfer the sheet to a dehydrator tray and dehydrate the meringue at 135°F (57°C) for 14 hours, until dry and crispy. Break into small pieces and hold in the dehydrator at 135°F (57°C) until needed.

FOR THE LAMB:

Preheat the oven to 425°F (220°C). Trim and french the lamb rack. Season on all sides with kosher salt. Spray two sheets of parchment paper with nonstick cooking spray. Combine the clay, kosher salt, and shabazi spice in a food processor and mix for 2 to 3 minutes. With the processor running, slowly add the water until a dough forms. Transfer the dough to a clean work surface and knead to incorporate any unmoistened clay. Once the dough is dry yet still pliable, flatten it into a disk and place it on top of the coated side of a parchment sheet. Top with the second parchment sheet, coated side down, and feed through a dough sheeter set to a thickness of about ⅛ inch (3 millimeters).

Wrap the prepared lamb rack in the clay, leaving the bones exposed, and smooth the seams by applying a small amount of water with an offset spatula and pushing the exposed edges into the clay. Wrap the bones in aluminum foil. Bake for 15 to 20 minutes, until a thermometer inserted into the rack reads 125°F (52°C). Remove the rack from the oven and let it rest for 15 minutes. Crack the clay and remove the lamb. Let the lamb rest in a warm place until ready to serve.

continued

FOR THE EGGPLANT PUREE:

Combine the Twin Sisters oil and nigella seeds in a blender and mix on high speed for about 30 seconds, until liquefied. Strain through a very fine cloth filter into a bowl. Peel the eggplants and cut into 1-inch (2.5-centimeter) squares. Heat the extra virgin oil in a sauté pan over high heat. Add the eggplant and sauté for about 5 minutes, until beginning to soften. Add the lamb jus and continue cooking for 4 minutes longer, until the eggplant is completely glazed with the jus and the cooking liquid has reduced.

Transfer the eggplant to a blender and mix on high speed for 3 minutes, slowly adding about 30 grams (2 ¹/₂ tablespoons) of the nigella oil. Reserve the remaining oil for garnish. Strain the eggplant through a chinois into a bowl and season with salt. Hold warm until needed.

TO SERVE:

Heat a cast-iron pan over high and add the extra virgin oil. When the pan is hot, add the lamb rack and cook for about 20 seconds on each side, until lightly golden brown. Transfer the lamb to a wire rack and let rest for 5 minutes, then cut into individual chops. Brush with the Twin Sisters oil and season with Maldon salt.

Place a small dollop of the eggplant puree in the center of each of 4 plates. Set the lamb on the eggplant puree and arrange pistachio clay around each chop as garnish. Finish with a few dots of the reserved nigella oil and with the tiny purslane.

EGGPLANT PUREE

45 grams | 3 ¹/₂ tablespoons Twin Sisters olive oil

45 grams | ¹/₂ cup nigella seeds

600 grams | about 4 Japanese eggplants

30 grams | about 2 tablespoons extra virgin olive oil

50 grams | ¹/₄ cup roasted lamb jus (page 287)

kosher salt

12 | tiny purslane with roots intact

stages of the grape

These **mignardises** *are a showcase of the life stages of our grapes, from unripe juice to the oil of the seeds, the alcohol made from the must, and the flavors of Napa Valley Cabernet.*

SERVES 8 TO 10

VERJUS MERINGUE

300 grams | 1 ¼ cups white verjus

180 grams | ¾ cup water

9 grams | 2 ½ teaspoons citric acid

160 grams | ¾ cup sugar

15.3 grams | about 1 tablespoon
    Methocel F50

3.5 grams | ¾ teaspoon xanthan gum

GRAPESEED OIL JAM

8 grams | 2 teaspoons kosher salt

100 grams | ⅓ cup trimoline

100 grams | ⅓ cup liquid glucose

87 grams | about 5 egg yolks

500 grams | 2 ⅓ cups Chardonnay
    grapeseed oil

PORT REDUCTION

2 kilograms | about 8 cups ruby red port

10 grams | about 2 Bora Bora vanilla beans

100 grams | 3.5 ounces oak chips

20 grams | about 2 Ceylon cinnamon sticks

10 grams | about 6 Thai long peppers

CHOCOLATE MELTAWAY

460 grams | 2 cups heavy cream

90 grams | ¼ cup plus 1 tablespoon
    liquid glucose

90 grams | ¼ cup trimoline

480 grams | 17 ounces dark chocolate
    (64 percent cacao)

358 grams | 12 ounces milk chocolate
    (40 percent cacao)

120 grams | ½ cup unsalted butter

250 grams | about 1 cup port reduction
    (recipe above)

GRAPE MUST CRUMBLE

400 grams | 2 cups cocoa nibs

100 grams | ⅔ cup dried red grape must

chocolate meltaway (recipe above)

FOR THE VERJUS MERINGUE:

Combine the verjus, water, citric acid, and sugar in a blender and mix on high for about 3 minutes, until the sugar has dissolved. With the blender running, slowly incorporate the Methocel F50 and xanthan gum and mix for 1 minute, until completely incorporated. Transfer to a stand mixer fitted with the whip attachment and mix on medium speed until the meringue is firm and holds a peak. Line a dehydrator tray with an acetate sheet and spread the meringue on it in an even layer. Dehydrate at 100°F (38°C) for 12 hours, until dry. Break the meringue into roughly 30 (1 ½-inch/4-centimeter) squares and store in an airtight container with silica gel packets at room temperature.

FOR THE GRAPESEED OIL JAM:

Prepare an ice bath. Combine the salt, trimoline, and glucose in a saucepan over medium heat. Put the yolks in a food processor and begin mixing. When the sugars have reached 187°F (86°C), slowly add to the yolks in the processor. Continue to mix until the mixture begins to thicken, then slowly add the oil. When the oil has been incorporated, pour the jam into a heatproof bowl and nest the bowl in the ice bath to cool. Transfer to a squeeze bottle and reserve at room temperature.

FOR THE PORT REDUCTION:

Combine the port, vanilla, oak chips, cinnamon, and peppers in a small stockpot. Bring to a simmer over medium-high heat and cook for about 1 hour, reducing by three-fourths. Remove from the heat and strain through a chinois into an airtight container. Store in the refrigerator.

FOR THE CHOCOLATE MELTAWAY:

Line a quarter sheet pan with an acetate sheet. Combine the cream, glucose, and trimoline in a saucepan and bring to a boil over high heat. Meanwhile, put the dark chocolate and milk chocolate in a heatproof bowl. When the cream mixture begins to boil, remove from the heat and pour over the chocolate. Mix with an immersion blender to emulsify, then slowly add the butter and port reduction while continuing to mix. When the mixture is smooth, pour it onto the prepared sheet pan. Cover with plastic wrap and hold at room temperature for 24 hours, then cut into 1-inch (2.5-centimeter) squares.

FOR THE GRAPE MUST CRUMBLE:

Combine the cocoa nibs and grape must in a food processor and mix for 2 minutes, until a fine crumb forms. Dredge the chocolate meltaway squares in the crumble to coat evenly and store in an airtight container at around 70°F (21°C) until ready to serve.

FOR THE GRAPPA CORDIALS:

Combine the sugar and water in a small saucepan over high heat, stirring just to melt the sugar, to 246°F (119°C). Slowly pour the grappa into the hot syrup without stirring. Let cool to room temperature, then transfer to a squeeze bottle.

Using about half of the cornstarch, partially fill a quarter sheet pan, smoothing the surface with an offset spatula. Use a pen cap to create about 30 hollows in the cornstarch, spacing them about 1 inch (2.5 centimeters) apart. Fill the holes with the grappa syrup, then cover the entire surface with the remaining cornstarch. Place the pan in an area with a temperature of about 85°F (29°C) for 24 hours.

Using a tamis, carefully sift the candies from the cornstarch. Store the candies in an airtight container with silica gel packets at room temperature.

continued

FOR THE GRAPPA MARSHMALLOW:

Pour 100 grams (½ cup) of the water into a small saucepan and heat over low heat to 140°F (60°C). Add the chamomile and steep at 140°F (60°C) for 4 minutes, then strain through a very fine cloth filter, return to the pan, and return to high heat. Add the gelatin, 15 grams (1½ tablespoons) of the sugar, and 15 grams (1 tablespoon) of the water to the pan. Remove from the heat and stir to dissolve the sugar and gelatin.

Combine the remaining 375 grams (1¾ cups) of sugar and 180 grams (¾ cup) of water and the glucose in a saucepan over high heat and heat, stirring occasionally. Put the egg whites in the bowl of a stand mixer fitted with the whip attachment and begin whipping on medium speed. When the sugars have reached 115°F (46°C) and the egg whites have formed medium peaks, slowly stream the sugars into the whipping egg whites and follow with the chamomile mixture. Once both mixtures have been incorporated, whip for 2 minutes longer, until stiff peaks form. Spoon into a piping bag fitted with a small round tip.

Dust a half sheet pan with the dextrose. Using about half of the meringue, pipe small disks about the size of a dime onto the pan, spacing them about 1 inch (2.5 centimeters) apart. Place a grappa cordial in the center of each disk. Now pipe the remaining meringue onto the disks, covering the cordial and forming a "kiss" shape. Hold in the refrigerator until needed.

FOR THE GRAPE LEAF TUILE:

Prepare an ice bath. Fill a rondeau with water and bring to a boil over high heat. Add the grape leaves and blanch for 5 minutes, then scoop out and immediately immerse them in the ice bath until cold. Pat dry on paper towels. Combine the sugar and water in a saucepan and bring to a boil over high heat, stirring to dissolve the sugar. Turn down the heat to low, add the grape leaves, and simmer at about 160°F (71°C) for 1 hour. Drain the leaves and let cool to room temperature.

Preheat the oven to 325°F (165°C). Line a full sheet pan with a silicone baking mat. Transfer the grape leaves to a cutting board and cut into rectangles about 2 by 3 inches (5 by 7.5 centimeters). Lay a piece of plastic wrap on a work surface and arrange the rectangles in 3 rows of 10 on top of the wrap. Spray a copper pipe ½ inch (12 millimeters) in diameter and 10 inches (25 centimeters) long with nonstick cooking spray. Place the pipe on the lower half of a row of leaves. Starting from the bottom, tightly roll a row of the leaves around the pipe, using the plastic wrap to assist. Remove the plastic wrap from the pipe and put the pipe on the prepared sheet pan. Bake for 8 minutes, until the leaves feel tacky. Let cool slightly, then remove the leaves from the pipe and let cool completely. Repeat with the remaining rows. Store in an airtight container with silica gel packets at room temperature.

FOR THE WHITE CHOCOLATE CRÉMEUX:

Prepare an ice bath. Heat the cream in a saucepan over low heat to 120°F (49°C). Combine the chocolate and gellan base in a blender, add the warm cream, and mix on high speed for 3 minutes, until a smooth puree forms. Strain through a chinois into a bowl, then nest the bowl in the ice bath to cool the puree. Add the grapes and season with verjus. Spoon into a piping bag fitted with a small round tip and refrigerate until ready to use.

TO SERVE:

Fasten the branches of the grapevines together with twine. Arrange the grape leaves on the branches for holding the grape elements. Finish the verjus meringue by placing a few dots of the grapeseed oil jam on the underside of the meringues. Place the meringues, chocolates, and marshmallows on the branches. Pipe the crémeux into the grape leaf tuiles and place the tuiles on the branches.

GRAPPA CORDIALS

370 grams | 1¾ cups sugar
130 grams | ½ cup water
150 grams | ¾ cup chamomile grappa
500 grams | about 1 pound cornstarch
    (4 cups)

GRAPPA MARSHMALLOW

295 grams | 1¼ cups plus 1 tablespoon water
5 grams | about 1 tablespoon loose-leaf
    chamomile
15 grams | 6 sheets silver gelatin, bloomed in
    ice water and wrung gently
    of excess water
390 grams | 1¾ cups plus
    1½ tablespoons sugar
15 grams | 2 teaspoons liquid glucose
60 grams | about 2 egg whites
dextrose, for dredging
grappa cordials (recipe above)

GRAPE LEAF TUILE

35 | grape leaves
250 grams | 1¼ cups sugar
600 grams | 2½ cups water

WHITE CHOCOLATE CRÉMEUX

400 grams | 1⅔ cups cream
300 grams | 10.5 ounces white chocolate
    (35 percent)
300 grams | 10.5 ounces gellan base
    (page 285)
75 grams | about ¼ cup diced green grapes
white verjus

dried grapevine branches
fresh grape leaves

robiola bread and butter

We get honeycomb from hives found throughout the valley. For this dish, the comb, dark and wild, is served unadulterated with robiola cheese from Lombardy prepared two ways: made into a butter using the traditional method for making Mornay sauce and fashioned into a bread using a popular Brazilian technique in which tapioca starch provides the structure.

SERVES 4

ROBIOLA BUTTER

300 grams | 1 ¹/₃ cups cow's milk
    robiola cheese
400 grams | 1 ²/₃ cups whole milk
6 grams | 1 teaspoon kosher salt
300 grams | 10.5 ounces unsalted butter,
    at room temperature
20 grams | 1 ¹/₂ teaspoons Ultra-Tex 3

CHEESE BREAD

210 grams | about 7 ounces cow's milk
    robiola cheese
244 grams | 1 cup whole milk
10 grams | 1 ¹/₂ teaspoons kosher salt
108 grams | ¹/₂ cup Twin Sisters olive oil
300 grams | 2 ¹/₃ cups tapioca starch
100 grams | about 2 eggs

150 grams | 5.3 ounces honeycomb, broken
    into 4 pieces
12 | tiny curly endive leaves
12 | tiny dandelion leaves

FOR THE ROBIOLA BUTTER:

Prepare an ice bath. Put the robiola in a blender. Combine the milk and salt in a small saucepan and bring to a boil over medium-high heat. Pour the boiling milk into the blender and mix on high speed until the cheese has melted. With the blender still on high speed, slowly add the butter and then the Ultra-Tex and mix until the liquid thickens. Pour through a chinois into a bowl, then nest the bowl in the ice bath and stir to cool the mixture. Taste and adjust the seasoning if needed. Cover and refrigerate until serving.

FOR THE CHEESE BREAD:

Preheat the oven to 300°F (150°C). Line a half sheet pan with parchment paper. Put the robiola in a food processor and mix until smooth, stopping to scrape down the sides of the processor bowl as needed. Set aside. Combine the milk, salt, and olive oil in a saucepan and bring to a boil over high heat. Using a wooden spoon, quickly stir in the tapioca starch and then continue to stir rapidly to prevent scorching. When the mixture has thickened to the consistency of a paste, transfer it to the bowl of a stand mixer fitted with the paddle attachment. Mix on medium speed for about 5 minutes, until the dough starts to look shiny. Add the eggs, one at a time, mixing well after each addition until fully absorbed. Add the cheese in two batches, mixing after each addition until incorporated. Continue to mix for 2 to 3 minutes, until the dough is smooth and slightly sticky.

Spray a bench scraper and a work surface with nonstick cooking spray. Using the bench scraper, turn the dough out onto the work surface. Divide the dough into 35-gram (1.3-ounce) portions and shape each portion into a round. Arrange the rounds on the prepared sheet pan, spacing them about 2 inches (5 centimeters) apart. Bake for 30 to 35 minutes, until golden brown and half the weight of the beginning portion.

TO SERVE:

Form a quenelle of the robiola butter on each of 4 plates. Place a piece of the honeycomb next to the butter and finish with 2 pieces of bread, 3 endive leaves, and 3 dandelion leaves.

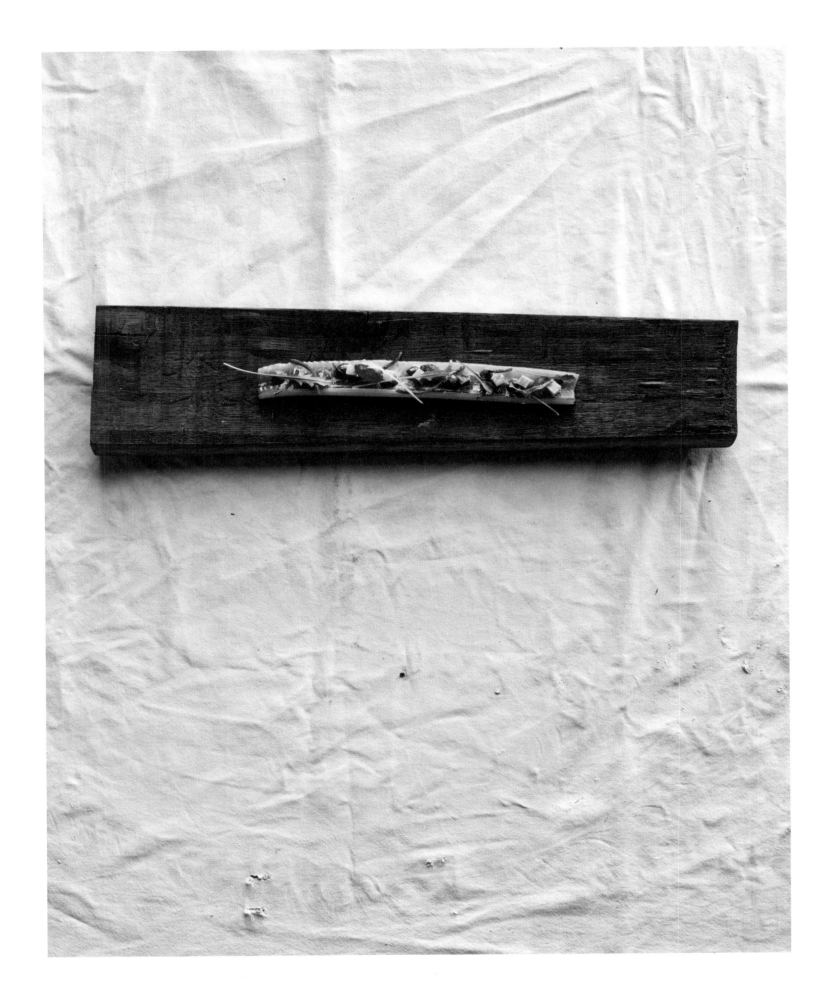

eel smoked over cabernet barrels
last year's grapes tongue

This dish began with a young cook-gardener who brought me an old Cabernet barrel and wondered what we might do with it. We played around with smoking eel over the barrel and found that the process imparted the wine flavor beautifully. We pair the eel with an equally fatty tongue and finish with other elements of the grape: barely dried raisins, a mustard made from the grape must of the previous year, and a vinegar made from the red wine itself.

WAGYU BEEF TONGUE

3.5 kilograms | about 3 $\frac{1}{2}$ quarts ice water
450 grams | 2 cups firmly packed
    brown sugar
450 grams | 1 $\frac{2}{3}$ cups kosher salt
4 grams | 2 teaspoons white peppercorns
7 grams | 2 teaspoons juniper berries
30 grams | about 5 cloves garlic
2 | bay leaves
10 grams | 2 tablespoons thyme leaves
36 grams | 2 tablespoons tinted curing mix #1
2 | Wagyu beef tongues
extra virgin grapeseed oil

FRESH RAISINS

10 | muscat grapes
300 grams | 1 $\frac{1}{4}$ cups Cabernet Sauvignon
75 grams | $\frac{1}{4}$ cup light corn syrup

SALTWATER EEL PREPARATION

1 | whole saltwater eel
1 kilogram | 3 $\frac{1}{3}$ cups kosher salt
500 grams | 2 $\frac{1}{4}$ cups firmly packed
    brown sugar
12 grams | 2 tablespoons ground dried red
    grape must
6 grams | 1 tablespoon five-spice powder
extra virgin grapeseed oil

FOR THE WAGYU BEEF TONGUE:

Pour 2.5 kilograms (about 10 cups) of the ice water into a large container. Heat the remaining 1 kilogram (about 4 cups) water in a saucepan over high heat. Add the brown sugar, salt, peppercorns, juniper, garlic, bay leaves, and thyme and heat, stirring, until the salt and sugar dissolve. Remove from the heat and pour into the container holding the ice water. Add the tinted curing mix and beef tongues, cover, and refrigerate for 5 days.

Remove the tongues from the brine and rinse under cool running water for 30 seconds. Put each tongue in a vacuum bag and seal on high. Cook the tongues in a hot-water bath at 155°F (68°C) for 24 hours. Remove the bags from the bath and immerse them in a large bowl of room-temperature water for 20 minutes, then transfer them to an ice bath for 3 hours.

Line a dehydrator tray with a silicone baking mat. Remove the tongues from the bags, reserving the liquid that was created during cooking, and peel away the skin. Using an electric slicer, thinly shave 1 tongue lengthwise into a fine julienne. Arrange the slices on the tray and dehydrate at 110°F (43°C) for 8 hours, until dry and crispy. Store in an airtight container at room temperature. Cut the remaining tongue into small dice, mix with a little grapeseed oil, and store in an airtight container in the refrigerator.

FOR THE FRESH RAISINS:

Peel the grapes. Line a dehydrator tray with a silicone baking mat and arrange the grapes on the mat. Dehydrate at 125°F (52°C) for 16 hours, until tacky and reduced to about half of their original size. Meanwhile, combine the red wine and corn syrup in a small saucepan over medium heat and cook for about 30 minutes, until reduced by about 80 percent. Let the syrup cool to room temperature, then immerse the dried grapes in the syrup and hold at room temperature until needed.

FOR THE SALTWATER EEL:

Remove the fillets from the eel by tracing around the perimeter of the fillets and inserting a knife into the tail of the eel. With the knife perpendicular to the body of the eel, slowly slice the fillets from the spine moving from the tail to the head. Be aware that many of the bones will be left behind and are thin enough to eat, but to ensure that the bones don't jeopardize the texture of the eel, score a crosshatch pattern on the skin side of each fillet to promote good texture and optimum smoke absorption. In a large bowl, combine the salt, sugar, grape must, and five-spice powder. Bury the eel fillets in the cure in a plastic container and refrigerate for 45 minutes. Rinse the fillets under running ice-cold water and pat dry on paper towels. Cut each fillet in half crosswise to yield 4 portions total.

Hot smoke (see page 287) the fillets at 135°F (57°C) for 30 minutes. Remove the fillets from the smoker, submerge in grapeseed oil, and let cool in the refrigerator until needed.

continued

FOR THE VIOLET MUSTARD:

Combine the grape must, port, malt vinegar, cinnamon, cloves, ginger, and mustard seeds in a small saucepan over low heat. Bring to a simmer and simmer for 2 hours, stirring occasionally, until the liquid is reduced by about half. Meanwhile, prepare an ice bath. When the must mixture is ready, transfer to a blender and mix on high speed for about 3 minutes, until a smooth puree forms. Strain the puree through a chinois into a bowl, then nest the bowl in the ice bath to cool the puree. Taste and adjust the seasoning with sugar and kosher salt if needed. Transfer the mustard to a squeeze bottle and reserve in the refrigerator.

FOR THE RED WINE VINAIGRETTE:

Combine the tongue cooking liquid, wine, and vinegar in a saucepan over low heat. Cook for about 20 minutes, until reduced by about half and slightly thickened. Meanwhile, prepare an ice bath. Strain the liquid through a chinois into a bowl, then nest the bowl in the ice bath to cool the vinaigrette. Transfer to a squeeze bottle.

TO SERVE:

Preheat a broiler to 600°F (316°C). Place the eel portions, skin side up, on a small metal tray and broil for 30 seconds. When the skin begins to blister, place each fillet on a rectangular plate. Garnish with a few pieces of diced tongue and dried tongue, the fresh raisins, and a few dots of the violet mustard. Finish with a few leaves of arugula and a small amount of vinaigrette on each fillet.

VIOLET MUSTARD

270 grams | 2 cups dried grape must

235 grams | 1 cup ruby red port

295 grams | 1 $\frac{1}{4}$ cups malt vinegar

6 grams | about 1 cinnamon stick

2 grams | about 8 whole cloves

2 grams | 1 teaspoon ground ginger

67 grams | $\frac{1}{2}$ cup yellow mustard seeds

sugar

kosher salt

RED WINE VINAIGRETTE

300 grams | 1 $\frac{1}{4}$ cups reserved tongue cooking liquid

100 grams | $\frac{1}{2}$ cup Cabernet Sauvignon

100 grams | $\frac{1}{2}$ cup red wine vinegar

12 | violet-streaked Sylvetta arugula leaves

coal-roasted sturgeon
fermented quince

Michael Passmore is a rancher-turned-sturgeon-farmer outside of Sacramento. He raises the finest sturgeon I have ever seen. We brine the sturgeon in salted water, wrap it in cabbage leaves, and then bury it in warm coals. This technique ensures that the uniquely clean flavor of the sturgeon shines. The fermented quince in this dish is a good example of our preservation efforts. In the fall, we are inundated with quinces from our trees, and this method is one way we coax complex flavor and texture from them.

SERVES 4

FERMENTING LIQUID

250 grams | 1 $^1/_4$ cups sugar

7 grams | 1 $^3/_4$ teaspoons active dry yeast

500 grams | 2 cups water (70°F/20°C)

FERMENTED QUINCE WEDGES

2 | quinces

250 grams | 1 $^1/_4$ cups sugar

1 kilogram | 4 $^1/_4$ cups fermenting liquid
   (recipe above)

STURGEON PREPARATION

450 grams | 1 pound sturgeon bullet, skinned
   and boned

1 kilogram | 4 $^1/_4$ cups ice water

200 grams | $^2/_3$ cup kosher salt

16 | large Savoy cabbage leaves

55 grams | $^1/_4$ cup extra virgin olive oil

kosher salt

WHIPPED PARSNIP

500 grams | 2 cups whole milk

250 grams | 1 cup water

500 grams | about 4 cups peeled and
   sliced parsnips

3.5 grams | 1 sheet bronze gelatin, bloomed
   in ice water and wrung gently of
   excess water

200 grams | $^3/_4$ cup heavy cream

kosher salt

FOR THE FERMENTING LIQUID:

Dissolve the sugar and yeast in the water in a bowl. Pour into a plastic container with a lid and hold in an area with an ambient temperature of 75°F (24°C) for 30 hours. The liquid is now ready to use as a fermentation medium.

FOR THE FERMENTED QUINCE WEDGES:

Peel the quinces. Combine the sugar and fermenting liquid in a plastic container with a lid, stir to dissolve the sugar, and immerse the quinces in the liquid. Hold in an area with an ambient temperature of 75°F (24°C) for 48 hours, until the quinces are fragrant and have become soft. Transfer the container to the refrigerator and store for at least 3 days before use. Before using, slice the quinces into wedges and hold in the fermenting liquid.

FOR THE STURGEON:

Trim the sturgeon bullet into a perfect rectangle. Pour 200 grams ($^3/_4$ cup) of the ice water into a small saucepan, bring to a boil over high heat, and dissolve the salt in the water. Pour the remaining 800 grams (3 $^1/_3$ cups) of ice water into a plastic container. Add the boiling water to the container with the ice water, then immerse the sturgeon for 40 minutes in the refrigerator to brine.

Meanwhile, prepare an ice bath. Bring a large pot of salted water (about 4 kilograms/4 quarts) to a boil. Add the cabbage leaves and blanch for 4 minutes, then scoop them out and immediately immerse in the ice bath for 1 minute. Transfer the leaves to paper towels to dry. On a cutting board, arrange the cabbage leaves in a sheet large enough to enclose the sturgeon. When the sturgeon has finished brining, pat the fish dry on paper towels and place in the center of the cabbage sheet. Wrap one side of the sheet around the sturgeon, then roll to the opposite side, covering the fish completely. Tie a few pieces of butcher's twine along the length of the packet to secure the cabbage in place. Reserve in the refrigerator.

FOR THE WHIPPED PARSNIP:

Combine the milk, water, and parsnips in a saucepan over high heat and bring to a boil. Turn down the heat to a simmer and simmer for about 12 minutes, until the parsnips are tender. Meanwhile, prepare an ice bath. When the parsnips are ready, drain them, removing as much of the liquid as possible (excess liquid will make the puree too loose). Put the parsnips in a blender and mix on high speed for 3 minutes, until a smooth puree forms. Strain the puree through a chinois into a bowl, add the gelatin, and let stand until the gelatin melts, then whisk to combine. Nest the bowl in the ice bath to cool the puree.

Whisk the cream in a bowl until stiff peaks form. Fold the chilled parsnip puree into the whipped cream and season with kosher salt. Cover and refrigerate until ready to use.

continued

FOR THE BONE MARROW VINAIGRETTE:

Line a plate with parchment paper. Immerse the marrowbones in room-temperature water for at least 30 minutes. Using a dowel similar in size to the marrow, push the dowel through the center of each marrowbone to extract the marrow in a single piece. Using a knife heated under very hot water and wiped dry, cut 8 crosswise slices, each about ¼ inch (6 millimeters) thick, from the whole marrow. Place the slices on the parchment paper, cover with another sheet of parchment paper, then wrap the plate in plastic wrap and store in the refrigerator until ready to use. Place the remaining marrow in a vacuum bag and seal on high. Cook the marrow trim in a steam oven set at 200°F (95°C) for 25 minutes. Pour the rendered marrow fat through a chinois into a bowl and discard the cooked marrow. Combine equal parts of the marrow fat and the fermenting liquid for the vinaigrette and reserve the remaining fat. Store in the refrigerator until needed.

FOR THE PRESSED BRUSSELS SPROUTS:

Preheat the oven to 300°F (150°C). Line a full baking sheet with parchment paper. Trim the leaves from the brussels sprouts and discard the cores and smaller leaves. Warm the reserved marrow fat just enough to melt it and brush the larger sprout leaves on both sides with the fat. Season lightly with salt. Arrange the leaves in a single layer on the prepared pan, spacing them about 1 inch (2.5 centimeters) apart. Lay a sheet of parchment paper over the sprout leaves and place another full baking sheet on top, pressing the leaves between the layers of parchment paper. Bake for about 25 minutes, checking periodically for doneness. The leaves should be golden brown and translucent. Transfer the leaves in a single layer to dehydrator trays lined with parchment paper and dehydrate at 125°F (52°C) for 12 hours, until completely dry and crispy.

FOR THE ASH BAKE:

Preheat the oven to 500°F (260°C). Combine the ash and salt in a large metal bowl and mix well. Put the ash and salt mixture in a deep metal pan and place in the oven 1 hour before you're ready to bake the sturgeon.

TO SERVE:

Bury the wrapped sturgeon in the ash bake and return the pan to the oven for 7 to 8 minutes, until the sturgeon is slightly firm but still undercooked. Unwrap the sturgeon and pat dry on paper towels. Heat the olive oil in a cast-iron pan over high heat until the oil begins to smoke. Gently place the sturgeon, skin side down, in the pan and roast for 4 minutes, until the exterior is a deep golden brown. Baste the top side of the sturgeon with the cooking oil for 30 seconds, then remove the sturgeon from the pan. Let the sturgeon rest for 4 minutes, then slice into 4 equal pieces. Warm the marrow slices in the oven for 5 seconds, just to soften. Spread a small amount of the whipped parsnip on each of 4 plates. Set a sturgeon piece on top of the puree and garnish with 2 pieces of the warmed marrow, the pressed brussels sprout leaves, and wedges of fermented quince. Finish with the bone marrow vinaigrette.

BONE MARROW VINAIGRETTE

1.8 kilograms | about 4 pounds marrowbones
100 grams | fermented quince liquid
   (page 249)
kosher salt

PRESSED BRUSSELS SPROUTS

8 | brussels sprouts
100 grams | ½ cup rendered marrow fat
   (recipe above)
kosher salt

ASH BAKE

1 kilogram | 2.3 pounds ash, from mesquite
   hardwood
1 kilogram | 2.3 pounds kosher salt

cockscomb prune truffle spelt

The famed Bale Grist Mill provides the spelt flour that we use as a base for this dish of cockscombs and truffles—a luxurious evocation of autumn. The gelatinous cockscombs in their jus are a nice counterpart to the earthy spelt porridge. Prunes, once a main agricultural product of the valley, play a prominent role.

FOR THE COCKSCOMB PREPARATION:

Cold smoke (see page 287) the cockscombs with hickory chips. Place a rondeau over medium heat and add the olive oil, carrots, onions, and celery. When the vegetables begin to turn golden brown, cook, stirring occasionally, for about 8 minutes, until tender. Add the smoked cockscombs to the pan and follow with the wine. Turn down the heat to medium-low and simmer for 4 minutes, until the wine is reduced by about half. Add the stock, thyme, savory, and chicken jus and braise at a temperature no higher than 170°F (77°C) for 1 hour, until the cockscombs are tender but still hold their shape. Transfer to a heatproof container and place in the refrigerator until the mixture cools to about 120°F (49°C).

Pick the cockscombs from the braising liquid and place in a separate container. Strain the liquid and discard the vegetables. Add a small amount of the liquid to the cockscombs to keep them moist and hold them in the refrigerator until needed. Place the remaining liquid in a saucepan over medium heat and cook down to a light jus; it should be viscous but not too reduced, 20 to 30 minutes. Strain through a chinois into a bowl and let cool in the refrigerator.

FOR THE SPELT PORRIDGE:

Add the spelt flour to a saucepan and toast over low heat for about 4 minutes, until the flour is fragrant. Whisk in the stock all at once. Bring the liquid to a boil, stirring constantly to avoid scorching. When the porridge is thick and smooth, slowly whisk in the butter and season with kosher salt. Hold in an airtight container in a warm place until needed.

FOR THE MIREPOIX:

Heat the Twin Sisters oil in a sauté pan over high heat, add the carrot and sauté lightly for 10 seconds, seasoning with kosher salt to avoid coloring. Add the onion and celery and continue cooking for an additional 20 seconds. Transfer to paper towels and dry slightly. Store in the refrigerator until needed.

FOR THE BLACK TRUFFLE FOAM:

Peel the truffle and reserve the peelings for garnish. Cut the trimmed truffle into a small dice. Combine the diced truffle with the milk and cream in a small saucepan, heat over low heat to 140°F (60°C), and hold at this temperature for 30 minutes. Remove from the heat and strain through a chinois into a metal container. Season with vinegar and salt, then hold warm until needed.

TO SERVE:

Place a small amount of porridge in each of 4 bowls. Reheat the cockscombs in the jus in which they were held, then place 3 cockscombs in each bowl of porridge. Garnish each bowl with a few piles of the mirepoix, some plum slices, black truffle peelings, and 4 pluches each of thyme and savory. Pour some of the jus from the cockscombs around the sides of the porridge. Put the end of an immersion blender in the black truffle foam, just beneath the surface. Mix on low speed to force the air bubbles to congregate in the corner of the container. Spoon a small amount of the foam onto each dish in various spots.

SERVES 4

COCKSCOMB PREPARATION

300 grams | 10.5 ounces fresh cockscombs
28 grams | 2 tablespoons extra virgin olive oil
75 grams | ²/₃ cup diced carrots
125 grams | ³/₄ cup diced yellow onions
50 grams | ¹/₂ cup diced celery
500 grams | about 2 cups dry red wine
700 grams | 3 cups chicken stock (page 283)
10 grams | 2 tablespoons thyme leaves
5 grams | 1 tablespoon winter savory leaves
100 grams | ¹/₃ cup dark chicken jus
   (page 284)
kosher salt

SPELT PORRIDGE

100 grams | ³/₄ cup spelt flour
400 grams | 1 ²/₃ cups chicken stock
   (page 283)
125 grams | ¹/₂ cup unsalted butter
kosher salt

MIREPOIX

40 grams | 3 tablespoons Twin Sisters
   olive oil
75 grams | ²/₃ cup carrot, in brunoise
kosher salt
75 grams | ²/₃ cup yellow onion, in brunoise
75 grams | ²/₃ cup celery, in brunoise

BLACK TRUFFLE FOAM

100 grams | 3.3 ounces Périgord black truffle
400 grams | 1 ²/₃ cups whole milk
100 grams | ¹/₂ cup heavy cream
sherry vinegar
kosher salt

4 | dried plums, sliced
16 | flowering thyme pluches
16 | winter savory pluches

rabbit pole beans meyer lemon

Heritage rabbit is on display here. It is cooked and presented in a jar, so its subtle flavor is unable to escape. Once removed and sliced, it is finished with Meyer lemon and olives and the tiniest pole beans from the garden.

SERVES 4

MEYER LEMON PUREE
7 | Meyer lemons, halved lengthwise
800 grams | 2 ³/₄ cups kosher salt
1 kilogram | 4 cups freshly squeezed
    lemon juice
100 grams | ¹/₂ cup extra virgin olive oil
kosher salt

GREEN OLIVE OIL
300 grams | 2 cups pitted Castelvetrano
    olives
600 grams | 2 ³/₄ cups extra virgin olive oil

RABBIT PREPARATION
2 kilograms | about 8 cups ice-cold water
75 grams | ¹/₄ cup kosher salt
30 grams | ¹/₂ cup lemon balm leaves
1 | whole rabbit, dressed

transglutaminase

FOR THE MEYER LEMON PUREE:
Rub the lemon halves with the kosher salt, then pack the lemons and salt into a large glass jar. Pour the lemon juice over the lemons, cover the jar, and hold in an area with an ambient temperature of 70°F (20°C) for at least 4 months, until the skins are tender and the astringency has subsided.

Prepare an ice bath. Remove the lemons from the jar, then cut away the pulp from the peel and discard the pulp. Place the peels in a blender and mix on high speed until smooth. With the blender running, slowly add the olive oil and continue to mix until a smooth puree forms. Strain through a chinois into a bowl, then nest the bowl in the ice bath to cool the puree. Transfer to a squeeze bottle and store in the refrigerator until ready to use.

FOR THE GREEN OLIVE OIL:
Wrap the olives in cheesecloth and press as much of the liquid from them as possible. Add the olives and olive oil to a blender and mix on high speed for 3 minutes, until a loose puree forms. Loosely drape a piece of cheesecloth over the opening of a container, then secure the cheesecloth in place with butcher's twine. Pour the olive puree into the cheesecloth and allow it to hang in the refrigerator for at least 24 hours. Remove and discard the cheesecloth and pulp. Transfer the olive oil to a squeeze bottle and hold at room temperature.

FOR THE RABBIT PREPARATION:
To make a brine, combine 500 grams (about 2 cups) of the water, the salt, and the lemon balm in a small saucepan and bring to a boil over high heat. Turn down the heat to medium and simmer for 3 minutes. Remove from the heat and combine with the remaining 1.5 kilograms (about 6 cups) water in a large container. Immerse the rabbit in the brine and refrigerate for 4 hours.

Remove the rabbit from the brine and pat dry on paper towels. Cut along the front and rear legs on both sides of the rabbit to remove the muscles. Working carefully, cut along the backbone and around the rib cage to remove the top loins. Turn the frame upside down and remove the tenderloins from underneath the saddle. Separate the bellies from the loins and remove any silver skin from the individual muscles. Reserve the tenderloins and bellies for making the mousse; store both in an airtight container in the refrigerator until needed. Cut the meat away from the leg portions and reserve the bones along with the frame and front legs in an airtight container in the refrigerator.

Wrap the loins tightly in plastic wrap to maintain a thin cylindrical shape. Knot the ends of the plastic wrap to keep the loins airtight. Prepare an ice bath. Bring a pot of water to a boil, add the wrapped loins, and blanch for 1 minute. Transfer the wrapped loins to the ice bath for 5 minutes. Place the leg meat between 2 pieces of plastic wrap and pound lightly with a butchery mallet ¹/₄ inch (6 millimeters) thick. Reserve the loins and legs in the refrigerator until needed.

continued

FOR THE RABBIT MOUSSE:

Put the rabbit bellies, tenderloins, and chicken breast in a food processor. With the processor running, slowly add the egg whites and cream, mixing until smooth. Stop the processor and scrape down the sides of the bowl. Add the sodium phosphate and mix for 1 minute, until the mousse is light and airy. Season with kosher salt and pass through a tamis, easing it through with a bench scraper. Reserve in an airtight container in the refrigerator.

TO ASSEMBLE THE RABBIT:

Lay a piece of plastic wrap on a flat surface. Lay the pounded meat from one leg, skin side down, on top of the plastic wrap. Using a fine-mesh strainer, dust the exposed surface of the leg lightly with transglutaminase. Using an offset spatula, spread half of the rabbit mousse in a thin layer on top of the prepared leg. Dust the mousse with a thin layer of transglutaminase. Unwrap the blanched loins and pat dry on paper towels. Place a loin in the center of the mousse. Roll the leg in a roulade around the loin, securing it with plastic wrap. Repeat with the other leg, loin, and the remaining mousse. Knot the ends of the plastic firmly on either side of the roulade. Hold both of the roulades in the refrigerator for 12 hours.

FOR THE RABBIT BROTH DUMPLINGS:

Combine the reserved rabbit frame and bones, carrot, onion, celery, and water in a pressure cooker and cook on high pressure for 45 minutes. Meanwhile, prepare an ice bath. When the broth is ready, strain through a very fine cloth filter into a saucepan, place over high heat, and cook until reduced by one-third. Remove from the heat and nest the pan in the ice bath to cool. Set aside half of the broth.

Prepare an ice bath. To make the dumplings, weigh the remaining broth and calculate 8 percent of the weight. Pour the broth into a saucepan. Weigh the calculated amount in kuzu root starch and whisk it into the broth. Place over low heat and bring to a boil while stirring constantly. Boil for 30 seconds, until thickened. Remove from the heat and nest the pan in the ice bath to cool to about 120°F (49°C).

Prepare a bowl of ice-cold water. Spoon the mixture into a piping bag fitted with a ¹/₂-inch (12-millimeter) plain tip. Pipe small dumplings into the water and hold for at least 2 minutes. Remove the dumplings from the ice water and hold in a small portion of the reserved broth. Rewarm to 130°F (54°C) and use within 2 hours.

TO SERVE:

Place the wrapped roulades in a steam oven set at 200°F (95°C) for 10 minutes. Remove from the steam oven, then remove the plastic wrap and place the roulades in a heatproof jar. Pour the reserved rabbit broth into the jar just to cover the roulades and add the pole beans and dumplings. Secure a lid on the jar, place the jar in the steam oven set at 200°F (95°C), and cook for 10 minutes.

Remove the rabbit from the jar and cut 2 slices from each roulade. Place a few dots of the Meyer lemon puree and the green olive oil in the center of each of 4 plates. Place one slice of the rabbit on each plate. Garnish with the dumplings, pole beans, bean flowers, and lemon balm leaves.

RABBIT MOUSSE
reserved rabbit bellies, diced
reserved tenderloins, diced
200 grams | 7 ounces boneless, skinless chicken breast, diced
20 grams | 4 teaspoons egg whites
125 grams | ¹/₂ cup heavy cream
2 grams | 1 teaspoon sodium phosphate
kosher salt

RABBIT BROTH DUMPLINGS
reserved rabbit bones
100 grams | about 1 carrot, peeled and diced
100 grams | about 1 small yellow onion, diced
60 grams | about 1 celery stalk, diced
4 kilograms | 4 quarts water
kosher salt
kuzu root starch

24 | mixed pole beans
24 | pole bean flowers
lemon balm leaves

kohlrabi mustard rye

When I tell chef friends of mine that a grist mill stands just a stone's throw from my home and kitchen, they are incredulous. The miller, in the traditional miller's garb of the nineteenth century, grinds, among other things, a fantastic rye flour. We feature it in this porridge, served with smashed kohlrabi that has been glazed in its own cooking juices and with pickled mustard seeds.

SERVES 4

SMOKED KOHLRABI GLAZE
500 grams | 4 ²/₃ cups peeled and diced kohlrabi, with leaves reserved
3 kilograms | about 3 quarts water
kuzu root starch
kosher salt
sherry vinegar

BRAISED KOHLRABI
150 grams | 5.3 ounces peeled kohlrabi, with leaves reserved
kosher salt

PICKLED MUSTARD SEEDS
62 grams | ¹/₃ cup yellow mustard seeds
125 grams | ¹/₂ cup white wine vinegar
62 grams | ¹/₃ cup water
kosher salt

BRAISED KOHLRABI LEAVES
reserved kohlrabi leaves
20 grams | 1 ¹/₂ tablespoons extra virgin olive oil
50 grams | ¹/₄ cup water
kosher salt

PICKLED KOHLRABI
200 grams | 1 ³/₄ cups kohlrabi, in brunoise
250 grams | 1 cup white wine vinegar
150 grams | ²/₃ cup water
kosher salt

FOR THE SMOKED KOHLRABI GLAZE:
Cold smoke (see page 287) the kohlrabi pieces for 1 hour. Just before they are ready, pour the water into a saucepan and begin to heat slowly. Transfer the kohlrabi pieces to the saucepan, cover, and bring the water to a simmer. Turn down the heat to 140°F (60°C) and hold for 1 ¹/₂ hours. Strain the liquid through a very fine cloth filter into a bowl, discarding the kohlrabi, and let cool slightly. Weigh the liquid and calculate 5 percent of the weight. Weigh the calculated amount in kuzu root starch and whisk it into the liquid. Place over high heat and bring to a boil while stirring constantly. Boil for 3 minutes, until the glaze evenly coats the back of a spoon. Strain through a chinois into a clean saucepan, then season with salt and vinegar, cover, and keep in a warm place.

FOR THE BRAISED KOHLRABI:
Cut the kohlrabi into sections about 1 inch (2.5 centimeters) thick. Put them into a bowl and season on all sides with kosher salt. Transfer to vacuum bags, keeping like pieces together, and seal on high. Put the kohlrabi into a steam oven set at 200°F (95°C) for 25 minutes for larger pieces and 15 to 20 minutes for smaller end pieces. The pieces are ready when they collapse easily from moderate pressure. Just before the kohlrabi is ready, prepare an ice bath. Remove the bags from the steam oven and immerse them in the ice bath for 2 hours, then remove the kohlrabi from the bags. Break into ¹/₂-inch (12-millimeter) jagged shapes and store in an airtight container in the refrigerator.

FOR THE PICKLED MUSTARD SEEDS:
Combine the mustard seeds, vinegar, and water in a small saucepan and bring to a boil over high heat. Turn down the heat to a simmer and cook for about 1 hour, until the seeds have absorbed all of the liquid. Season to taste with kosher salt and transfer to a metal container. Let cool in the refrigerator.

FOR THE BRAISED KOHLRABI LEAVES:
Line a sheet pan with parchment paper. Rinse the reserved kohlrabi leaves in cold water and run through a salad spinner to remove the excess liquid. Heat the extra virgin oil in a large rondeau just until it begins to smoke. Add the leaves and water, cover immediately, and cook for 15 seconds. Uncover and stir the leaves to wilt them evenly. Transfer the leaves to the prepared sheet pan and let cool completely in the refrigerator. Very finely mince the leaves, season with kosher salt, and reserve in the refrigerator.

FOR THE PICKLED KOHLRABI:
Put the kohlrabi in a heatproof container. Combine the vinegar and water in a small saucepan and bring to a boil. Remove from the heat and pour over the kohlrabi. Hold at about 190°F (88°C) for 10 minutes. Season with kosher salt and store in the refrigerator.

continued

FOR THE PUMPERNICKEL RYE PORRIDGE:

Combine the rye flour and water in a shallow saucepan over medium heat and bring to a simmer while whisking constantly. As the mixture begins to thicken, turn down the heat to low and continue to whisk the porridge. When the porridge has thickened but is still pourable (10 to 12 minutes), incorporate the butter and season with kosher salt, then remove from the heat. As it sits it will continue to thicken; add a little water as needed to maintain the correct consistency.

TO SERVE:

Pour a small amount of the porridge into the bottom of each of 4 flat-bottomed bowls. Arrange about 5 pieces of braised kohlrabi in each bowl. In a small saucepan, heat the glaze and add a small amount of the braised kohlrabi leaves, dispersing them evenly throughout the glaze. Repeat with the mustard seeds, dispersing them until the glaze is evenly studded. Spoon the glaze into the bowls to cover the kohlrabi; leave the porridge exposed. Place a few piles of the pickled kohlrabi in each bowl, and garnish each serving with a few dots of mustard oil and some mustard flowers and kale leaves.

PUMPERNICKEL RYE PORRIDGE

50 grams | $^1/_3$ cup pumpernickel rye flour
300 grams | 1 $^1/_4$ cups water
22.5 grams | 1 $^1/_2$ tablespoons unsalted butter
kosher salt

mustard oil
wild mustard flowers
tiny red Russian kale

a few root cellar favorites

Here are a few treasures that showcase the bounty of our gardens and the wilds. The Pluots can be used in many dishes, both sweet and savory (see Époisses last year's Pluots, page 141). The umeboshi makes a great salty and tart counterpoint to a fattier dish like yogurt black sesame shiso (page 113). The cilantro capers provide an amazing way to utilize the green coriander buds that are plentiful once the cilantro has finished flowering, and the salted apple leaves make a great wrapper for cheese (see goat cheese salted apple leaf oats, page 271).

preserved pluots

MAKES 1 GALLON (3.7 LITERS)

6 | Pluots, halved and pitted
2 grams | ½ teaspoon ascorbic acid
800 grams | 4 cups sugar
800 grams | 3 ⅓ cups water

Put the Pluots in a sterilized 1-gallon (3.7-liter) jar and sprinkle with the ascorbic acid. Combine the sugar and water in a saucepan over high heat and bring to a boil, stirring to dissolve the sugar. Meanwhile, bring a deep pot of water to a boil. Remove the syrup from the heat and pour over the fruit. Fasten a lid on the jar without tightening it, then immerse the jar in the boiling water for 10 minutes. Remove the jar from the water and tighten the lid. Store the jar in an area with an ambient temperature of 65°F (18°C) for at least 1 year before eating.

umeboshi

MAKES 2 QUARTS (2 LITERS)

900 grams | about 2 pounds wild plums
150 grams | ½ cup kosher salt

Rinse the plums in warm water to remove any residue. Place in a bowl, add the salt, and mix well. Tightly pack the salted plums in an airtight container. Hold the container in an area with an ambient temperature of about 65°F (18°C) for 1 week.

Remove the plums from the container, reserving the liquid. Arrange evenly on a linen cloth. Allow to air-dry in direct sunlight for at least 3 days. Place the plums in 2 (1-quart/1-liter) sterilized jars and add enough of the reserved plum liquid just to cover. Fasten lids on the jars and store in an area with an ambient temperature of about 65°F (18°C) for at least 3 months before eating.

cilantro capers

MAKES 1.5 QUARTS (1.5 LITERS)

600 grams | about 1.3 pounds green
   coriander buds
200 grams | ⅔ cup kosher salt, plus more
   for curing
400 grams | 1 ⅔ cups water

Pack the coriander buds in the salt in a covered container and cure in the refrigerator for 3 days. Rinse under cold running water and place in 3 sterilized pint (500 milliliter) jars. Combine the measured amount of salt and the water in a saucepan and bring to a boil over high heat, stirring to dissolve the salt. Remove from the heat and pour over the coriander buds. Fasten the lids on the jars and store the jars in an area with an ambient temperature of about 65°F (18°C) for at least 2 months before eating.

salted apple leaves

MAKES 1 GALLON (3.7 LITERS)

100 | large apple leaves
2 kilograms | about 8 cups water
200 grams | ⅔ cup kosher salt

Bring a large pot of water to a boil over high heat. Add the apple leaves and blanch for about 20 minutes. Scoop out the leaves and discard the water. Combine the measured amount of water, salt, and leaves in a stockpot and bring to a boil over high heat. Turn down the heat and simmer at about 180°F (82°C) for 1 hour. Remove from the heat and let the leaves cool in the liquid. Transfer the leaves with the liquid to a sterilized 1-gallon (3.7-liter) jar. Fasten a lid on the jar and store the jar for up to 1 year in an area with an ambient temperature of about 65°F (18°C). Wait at least 24 hours before using.

swordfish caponata

Swordfish, caught locally with harpoons, is a fish that plays nicely with these elements of caponata: young, tender grape leaves, pickled tiny shoots, and dried grapes from the previous year's harvest.

SERVES 4

EGGPLANT CONFIT

1 | globe eggplant, 425 grams (15 ounces)
300 grams | 1 cup kosher salt, plus more
    for seasoning
20 grams | about 3 cloves garlic
300 grams | 1 1/3 cups extra virgin olive oil
10 grams | leaves from about 2 thyme sprigs

SWORDFISH PREPARATION

800 grams | 2 3/4 cups kosher salt
20 grams | 1 1/4 cups fresh grape leaves
240 grams | 8.5 ounces swordfish loin
100 grams | 1/2 cup extra virgin olive oil

CRISPY ARTICHOKES

20 grams | 1 1/2 tablespoons ascorbic acid
2 kilograms | about 8 cups water
8 | baby artichokes
20 grams | 1 1/2 tablespoons extra virgin
    olive oil
40 grams | 1/3 cup carrot, in 1-inch
    (2.5-centimeter) pieces
40 grams | 1/3 cup celery, in 1-inch
    (2.5-centimeter) pieces
60 grams | 1/3 cup yellow onion, in 1-inch
    (2.5-centimeter) pieces
kosher salt
750 grams | about 3 cups dry white wine
500 grams | about 2 cups freshly squeezed
    lemon juice
rice bran oil, for deep-frying

FOR THE EGGPLANT CONFIT:

Cut the eggplant in half and score the flesh with a paring knife. Cover the eggplant with the salt and let cure for 1 hour. Preheat the oven to 300°F (150°C). Rinse the eggplant halves under cold water and pat dry on paper towels. Place the halves, cut side down, in a baking pan. Crush the garlic and place in the pan along with the olive oil and thyme. Cover the pan with aluminum foil and bake for 1 hour, until very tender.

Remove the eggplant from the pan and scrape the flesh from the skin, discarding the skin. Loosely drape a piece of cheesecloth over the opening of a container, then secure the cheesecloth in place with butcher's twine. Put the eggplant pulp in the cheesecloth and let stand for 1 hour to remove excess liquid. Mince the pulp with a knife to a fine puree and season with kosher salt.

FOR THE SWORDFISH PREPARATION:

Combine the kosher salt and grape leaves in a food processor and mix until pulverized. Bury the swordfish in the salt mixture in a plastic container and let cure for 45 minutes in the refrigerator. Rinse in a bowl of ice water and pat dry on paper towels. Cut the loin into 4 equal pieces, put the pieces and the oil in a vacuum bag, and seal on high. Cook the swordfish in a hot-water bath at 138°F (59°C) for 20 minutes. Meanwhile, prepare an ice bath. When the swordfish is ready, immerse the bag in the ice bath for 1 hour, then store on ice in the refrigerator.

FOR THE CRISPY ARTICHOKES:

In a bowl, dissolve the ascorbic acid in 1 kilogram (4 cups) of the water. Working with 1 artichoke at a time, use a paring knife to remove and discard the green leaves by peeling them away from the artichoke, exposing the white leaves underneath. Remove the tips of the white leaves and, using a vegetable peeler, peel away the green skin from the stem. Immediately submerge the artichoke in the acidulated water. Repeat with the remaining artichokes.

Heat the olive oil in a rondeau over high heat. Add the carrot, celery, and onion and sweat for about 5 minutes, until translucent. As the vegetables cook, season with kosher salt to inhibit caramelization. Drain the artichokes, add them to the pan, and then add the wine and cook for 20 minutes, until the wine is reduced by half. Add the lemon juice and the remaining 1 kilogram (4 cups) water and bring the liquid to a simmer. Cook the artichokes for about 20 minutes, until tender when pierced with a knife tip. Remove the pan from the heat and cool the artichokes in their cooking liquid in the refrigerator.

Pour the oil to a depth of 4 inches (10 centimeters) into a deep fryer or deep, heavy pot and heat to 300°F (150°C). While the oil is heating, remove the artichokes from the cooking liquid and pat dry on paper towels. Working in batches, add the artichokes to the hot oil and fry, keeping just the leaves submerged, for 3 minutes, until the leaves are crispy but the heart and stem are still soft. Transfer to paper towels to drain and season with kosher salt. Keep warm until ready to serve.

continued

FOR THE PRESERVED GRAPE SHOOTS AND LEAVES:

Combine the water, kosher salt, and ascorbic acid in a small saucepan and bring to a boil over high heat. Add the shoots and leaves, turn down the heat to a simmer, and cook at 160°F (71°C) for 40 minutes. Remove the pan from the heat and let the leaves and shoots cool in the cooking liquid. Refrigerate until ready to use.

FOR THE PINE NUT CLUSTERS:

Preheat the oven to 300°F (150°C). Line a sheet pan with a silicone baking mat. Spread the pine nuts on the prepared pan and toast in the oven for 10 minutes, until golden brown. Transfer to a bowl, add the grape leaves, brown rice syrup, and kosher salt to the warm nuts, and toss to coat evenly. Return the pine nuts to the sheet pan and bake for 5 minutes longer, until the nuts are dry. Let cool on the pan on a wire rack, then break into small clusters. Store the clusters in an airtight container with silica gel packets at room temperature.

TO SERVE:

Line a dehydrator tray with parchment paper. Peel the grapes, arrange them on the prepared tray, and dehydrate at 95°F (35°C) for 3 hours. Place the bag of swordfish portions in a hot-water bath at 138°F (59°C) for 10 minutes to reheat. Remove the portions from the bag and pat dry on paper towels. Heat the olive oil in a cast-iron pan over high heat, add the swordfish portions, and shallow fry for about 8 minutes, until golden brown on all sides. Let rest on paper towels for 2 minutes. Add the Padrón peppers to the same hot oil and fry for 30 to 40 seconds, until golden brown. Transfer to paper towels. Season the swordfish and peppers with Maldon salt.

Place the swordfish portions on each of 4 plates and garnish each plate with a quenelle of eggplant confit. Place 2 crispy artichokes, 4 fried Padrón peppers, 4 dried grapes, 2 preserved grape leaves, and 6 preserved grape shoots on each plate. Finish with 4 pluches of thyme and 2 pluches of savory.

PRESERVED GRAPE SHOOTS AND LEAVES

1 kilogram | 4 $^1/_2$ cups water
100 grams | $^1/_3$ cup kosher salt
10 grams | 2 $^1/_4$ teaspoons ascorbic acid
24 | young grape shoots
8 | young grape leaves

PINE NUT CLUSTERS

150 grams | 1 cup pine nuts
20 grams | $^2/_3$ ounce grape leaves, dehydrated at 125°F (52°C) for 10 hours
25 grams | scant 1 $^1/_2$ tablespoons brown rice syrup
kosher salt

16 | green grapes
100 grams | $^1/_2$ cup extra virgin olive oil
12 | Padrón peppers
Maldon sea salt
16 | flowering thyme pluches
8 | summer savory pluches

pork seaweed tomatillo oyster

Lee Hudson is a grape grower, vintner, horticulturalist, and friend who began his vineyards at the southern tip of the valley in the early 1980s. I have been fortunate to walk and drive his enormous property with him and hear the stories of its past as a cattle ranch and, later, as the first area to be planted with phylloxera-resistant rootstock at a time when the vineyards of Europe were being decimated by the pest. Lee makes great Chardonnay and raises with care legendary pigs that have long been treasured by chefs and charcutiers throughout the Bay Area. We take the pork, cure it, and wrap it in seaweed from Mendocino. We then slowly hot smoke (see page 287) it over native oak and serve it with acidic tomatillos and a jus finished with oyster.

SERVES 8

PORK SHOULDER PREPARATION

1 | Hudson Ranch bone-in pork shoulder,
    about 1.5 kilograms (3.3 pounds)
300 grams | 1 ⅓ cups firmly packed
    brown sugar
300 grams | 1 cup kosher salt
5 grams | 2 tablespoons thyme leaves
15 grams | 2 tablespoons garlic
    cloves, minced
20 grams | ¼ cup grated lemon zest
5 grams | 1 tablespoon smoked sweet
    Spanish paprika
200 grams | about 7 ounces Mendocino
    wakame, soaked in water for 24 hours
150 grams | ¾ cup pork lard

OYSTER JUS

20 grams | 1 ½ tablespoons extra virgin
    olive oil
reserved shoulder bones (recipe above)
240 grams | 8 ounces carrots, diced
240 grams | 8 ounces celery, diced
300 grams | 10.5 ounces yellow
    onions, diced
9 liters | about 8.5 quarts chicken stock
    (page 283)
200 grams | 7 ounces fresh oyster shells
100 grams | 3.5 ounces fresh oysters

FOR THE PORK SHOULDER PREPARATION:

Bone the pork shoulder and reserve the bones for making the jus. Cut the meat into 3 roughly equal pieces, each with a rectangular shape. Combine the sugar, salt, thyme, garlic, lemon zest, and Spanish paprika in a bowl and mix well. Add the pork pieces to the bowl and coat heavily with the sugar mixture. Cure in the refrigerator for 10 hours.

Rinse the pork pieces under ice-cold running water and pat dry on paper towels. Pat the wakame dry on paper towels, then, on a clean work surface, arrange some of the wakame pieces in a sheet, overlapping them slightly in a shingle pattern and making the sheet long and wide enough to enclose a piece of the pork. Place a piece of pork on the sheet and wrap the seaweed around it, covering it completely and pressing lightly to seal the ends and the long seam. Repeat to make 2 more wakame sheets and wrap the remaining 2 pork pieces. Using oak chips, hot smoke (see page 287) the pork at 160°F (71°C) for 8 hours. Remove from the smoker and transfer the wakame-wrapped pork to three separate vacuum bags. Add 50 grams (¼ cup) of the pork lard to each bag and seal on high. Immerse the bag in an ice bath for 2 hours, then hold the bag in the refrigerator until ready to use.

FOR THE OYSTER JUS:

Heat the olive oil in a large stockpot over high heat. Add the bones and roast on all sides until evenly golden brown. Remove the bones from the pot. Add the carrots, celery, and onions and caramelize the vegetables for about 8 minutes, until soft and golden brown. Return the bones to the pot, add the stock, and bring to a boil. Turn down the heat to a simmer and simmer for 8 hours, skimming the surface occasionally to remove any fat and solid protein.

Remove from the heat and strain through a chinois into a clean pot. Add the oyster shells, return to high heat, and cook until reduced by about 80 percent, a rich amber color, and slightly thickened, about 6 hours. Meanwhile, cold smoke (see page 287) the oysters for 30 minutes. When the jus is at the correct consistency, add the smoked oysters and steep off the heat for 1 hour. Strain the jus through a very fine cloth filter into a container and let cool in the refrigerator.

continued

FOR THE GRAIN BREAD DUMPLINGS:

Cut the bread into small pieces and place in a metal bowl. In a separate bowl, whisk together the cream and eggs until blended. Add the egg mixture to the bread and mix with a spoon to break up the bread slightly. Let stand at room temperature for about 1 hour, until the bread has absorbed all of the liquid. Season lightly with salt.

Lay a piece of plastic wrap on a work surface and place a marble-sized dollop of the dumpling batter in the center. Use the plastic wrap to shape the dumpling into a sphere, then wrap the ends of the plastic wrap around the dumpling tightly to seal it. Repeat this process to create 24 dumplings. Arrange the wrapped dumplings in a perforated hotel pan and place in a steam oven set at 200°F (95°C) for 15 minutes. Meanwhile, prepare an ice bath. When the dumplings are ready, transfer them to the ice bath and let cool for 20 minutes. Unwrap the dumplings and hold in an airtight container in the refrigerator until ready to serve.

FOR THE TOMATILLO JAM:

Combine the tomatillos and onions in a bowl. Heat a small rondeau over high heat and add the olive oil. When the oil is hot, add the tomatillos and onions and sauté for about 5 minutes, until the vegetables begin to caramelize heavily. Add the coriander, bay, and honey and continue to caramelize for about 6 minutes longer. When the honey becomes dark and fragrant, deglaze the pan with the vinegar and then allow the vinegar to evaporate. Season with salt and remove and discard the bay leaves. Transfer to a metal pan and let cool in the refrigerator for 2 hours. Transfer the cooled jam to a cutting board, cut into fine mince, and store in an airtight container in the refrigerator until needed.

FOR THE MENDOCINO SEAWEEDS:

Place the sea whip, kombu, nori, and bladder wrack in separate containers and add water to cover to each container. Let stand for 1 hour, until slightly softened. Remove from the water and pat dry on paper towels. Cut any large pieces into pieces no larger than 3 inches (7.5 centimeters) square. Put the seaweeds in a bowl, dress with the mustard oil, and hold at room temperature.

TO SERVE:

Reheat the pork in a hot-water bath at 138°F (59°C) for 15 minutes. Meanwhile, bring a saucepan of salted water to a boil over high heat, add the dumplings, and blanch for 1 minute, then drain. Heat a small amount of the oyster jus and season it with salt and mustard oil. Remove the wakame-wrapped pork pieces from the bags and slice 8 pieces from the most marbled portion. Place a pork slice on each of 8 plates. Garnish each plate with 3 dumplings, dots of tomatillo jam, and a few pieces of each type of seaweed. Finish with the warmed jus and the oyster leaf sprouts.

GRAIN BREAD DUMPLINGS

300 grams | 10.5 ounces dark rye bread
75 grams | 1/3 cup heavy cream
200 grams | 3/4 cup eggs
kosher salt

TOMATILLO JAM

450 grams | 1 pound tomatillos, husked
   and quartered
200 grams | 1 1/4 cups diced white onions
54 grams | 1/4 cup extra virgin olive oil
2 grams | 1/2 teaspoon ground coriander
3 | bay leaves
100 grams | 1/3 cup raw honey
30 grams | 2 tablespoons sherry vinegar
kosher salt

MENDOCINO SEAWEEDS

100 grams | 3.5 ounces dried sea whip fronds
100 grams | 3.5 ounces dried kombu
100 grams | 3.5 ounces dried nori
100 grams | 3.5 ounces dried bladder wrack
20 grams | 1 1/2 tablespoons mustard oil

kosher salt
mustard oil
12 | tiny oyster leaf sprouts

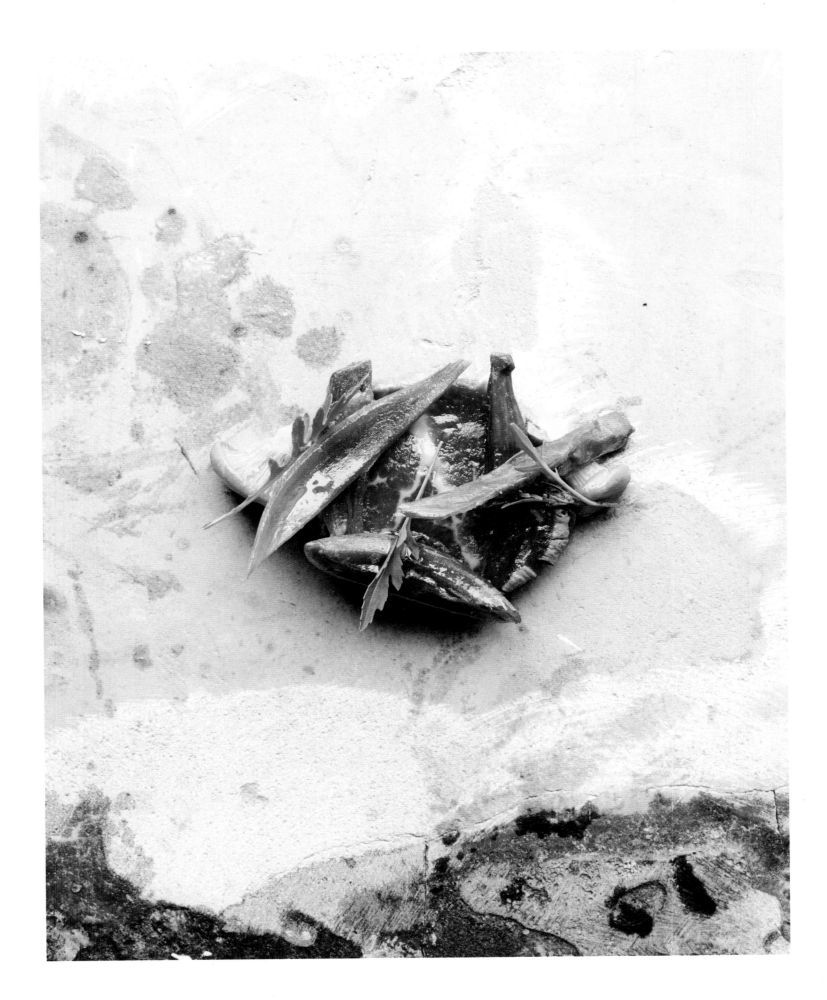

black shallot beef chanterelle

Here, the slow caramelization used for preparing Korean black garlic (a technique in which garlic is placed in a terra cotta pot and left in direct sunlight for three to four months) is applied to the shallot surplus from the garden. The resulting flavor is both complex and familiar, recalling the base of all the bouillons and broths tasted in the past. The black shallots, which are paired with aged beef tenderloin that has been poached in its own fat and with tiny chanterelles, are a good expression of our food preservation efforts: our garden surplus invariably inspires new and exciting flavors and techniques.

SERVES 4

BLACK SHALLOTS
4 | shallots, unpeeled

AGED BEEF TENDERLOIN
500 grams | about 1 pound beef tenderloin

3 kilograms | about 6.5 pounds rendered
    beef fat (page 286)
kosher salt
black pepper

BEEF JUS
2.2 kilograms | about 5 pounds beef oxtails,
    cut into 3-inch (7.5-centimeter) pieces
reserved beef trim (recipe above)
40 grams | 3 tablespoons extra virgin olive oil
900 grams | 2 pounds diced yellow onions
    (about 3 large onions)
220 grams | scant 8 ounces diced carrots
    (about 2 carrots)
220 grams | scant 8 ounces diced celery
    (about 2 stalks)
100 grams | about 1 cup diced leek tops
3 | bay leaves
12.5 kilograms | about 12 1/2 quarts water
kosher salt

CHANTERELLE STOCK
100 grams | 3.5 ounces dried chanterelles
200 grams | 3/4 cup dry white wine
600 grams | 2 1/2 cups water
kosher salt

8 | tiny fresh Saskatchewan chanterelles
Twin Sisters olive oil
24 | tiny arugula leaves
Maldon sea salt
mustard oil

FOR THE BLACK SHALLOTS:
Place the shallots in dry plastic containers with lids and dehydrate for 1 month at 150°F (66°C). Peel the skin from the shallots. Cut each shallot in half lengthwise and remove a few outer petals, to reveal the thinner core. Hold in an airtight container in the refrigerator.

FOR THE AGED BEEF TENDERLOIN:
Place the tenderloin, uncovered, in a sanitary refrigerated area and leave to age for 2 to 3 weeks. Trim off the fat and connective tissue and discard. Cut into a perfect cylinder, reserving the trim. Refrigerate until serving.

FOR THE BEEF JUS:
Preheat the oven to 500°F (260°C). Place the oxtails and beef trim on a rack in a roasting pan and roast for 25 minutes, until dark golden brown. Let cool to room temperature.

Pour the oil into a large stockpot and place over high heat. Add the onions, carrots, celery, leek tops, and bay leaves and caramelize the vegetables, stirring occasionally, for about 10 minutes, until soft and golden brown. Add the cooled oxtails and water to the vegetables and bring to a boil over high heat. Turn down the heat to a simmer and cook, uncovered, at 180°F (82°C) for about 10 hours, until the stock has a rich flavor and aroma. As the stock simmers, occasionally skim the fat and solid protein that forms on the surface. Strain the stock through a chinois into a rondeau set over low heat. Cook the stock until reduced by about 80 percent to a thickened jus that coats the back of a spoon, about 5 hours.

Prepare an ice bath. Strain the jus through a very fine cloth filter into a metal container, then nest the container in the ice bath to cool the jus. To season, heat the desired amount of jus in a saucepan and season with kosher salt.

FOR THE CHANTERELLE STOCK:
Combine the chanterelles, wine, and water in a saucepan and bring to a boil over high heat. Turn down the heat to low and gently simmer, uncovered, for 2 hours. Strain through a very fine cloth filter into a bowl nested in an ice bath.

TO SERVE:
To finish the tenderloin, heat the beef fat in a deep metal pan to 130°F (54°C) and hold at that temperature. Season the tenderloin with kosher salt and pepper. Prepare a fire in a wood-burning oven with a hot plate centered in the oven. When the fire is at about 600°F (315°C), roast the tenderloin on the hot plate, turning as needed, for about 30 seconds on each side. Place the beef in the fat to rest for at least 35 minutes, then remove from the fat and slice into 4 rounds.

Place a beef round on each plate. Heat the black shallots and fresh chanterelles in a small amount of the chanterelle stock, then season with olive oil. Use to garnish both the beef and the plate. Dress the purslane with mustard oil and Maldon salt and scatter the leaves over the beef. Finish with a small amount of the beef jus.

goat cheese salted apple leaf oats

We gather the young apple leaves from the trees in the garden at the Napa Valley Reserve and jar them in a salt brine, mimicking the traditional Japanese sakura, *or salted cherry leaves. We then wrap the salted leaves around disks of fresh goat's milk cheese. The resulting flavor is complex, with the apple flavor from the leaves imparted in a discernible yet ephemeral way. We serve the cheese with oat butter, bitter greens, and a scattering of dried apples.*

SERVES 6

GOAT'S MILK CHEESE PREPARATION
50 | apple leaves
1 kilogram | 4 ¹/₂ cups water
100 grams | ¹/₃ cup kosher salt
510 grams | 1 pound, 2 ounces fresh goat's
    milk cheese

DRIED APPLES
4 grams | 1 teaspoon ascorbic acid
4.5 kilograms | about 4 ¹/₂ quarts water
2 | Gala apples
1 kilogram | 4 ¹/₂ cups firmly packed
    brown sugar

OAT BUTTER
440 grams | 2 cups firmly packed
    brown sugar
12 grams | 2 teaspoons kosher salt
120 grams | 2 cups steel-cut oats
160 grams | 1 ¹/₄ cups all-purpose flour
450 grams | 1 pound unsalted butter,
    at room temperature

FOR THE GOAT'S MILK CHEESE PREPARATION:

Soak the apple leaves in cold water for 5 minutes. Combine the water and salt in a stockpot and bring to a boil over high heat. Add the leaves, turn down the heat to a simmer, and cook for about 45 minutes, until slightly tender. Remove from the heat and let cool in the brine to room temperature. Transfer the leaves and brine to a plastic container and refrigerate for 24 hours before using. For long preservation, pack the leaves in glass jars, add the brine to cover, cap tightly, and store in a cool, dark place.

Shape the cheese into a small wheel about 4 inches (10 centimeters) in diameter. Remove about 15 apple leaves from the brine, pat dry with paper towels, and arrange in a star pattern on a work surface, with the stems pointing away from the center of the star. Dip the cheese wheel in some of the apple leaf brine for 3 minutes. Place the cheese wheel in the center of the leaf star pattern. Cut off the stems of the leaves, then wrap the exposed portion of the leaves around the cheese wheel, covering the cheese completely and securing the ends by lightly pressing them into the cheese. Place on a wire rack and refrigerate for at least 1 week before serving.

FOR THE DRIED APPLES:

In a large bowl, dissolve the ascorbic acid in 4 kilograms (4 quarts) of the water. Peel the apples, cut into medium dice, and immerse in the acidulated water to avoid oxidation. Combine the sugar and the remaining 500 grams (about 2 cups) of water in a shallow saucepan and warm over low heat just until the sugar melts, then transfer to a pressure cooker. Drain the apples, add to the pressure cooker, and cook on low pressure for 15 minutes. Let the apples cool in the liquid to room temperature. Line a dehydrator tray with a silicone baking mat. Drain the apple pieces from the syrup and arrange on the mat-lined tray in a single layer. Dehydrate for 16 hours at 100°F (38°C), until dry on the outside and chewy on the inside. Store in an airtight container in a cool, dry area until needed.

FOR THE OAT BUTTER:

Preheat the oven to 325°F (165°C). Combine the sugar, salt, oats, flour, and butter in the bowl of a stand mixer fitted with the paddle attachment and mix on low speed for about 3 minutes, just until the butter is fully incorporated into the dry ingredients. Press the mixture into a 12 ¹/₂ by 7-inch (31.5 by 18-centimeter) baking pan and bake for about 15 minutes, until golden brown. Let cool to room temperature.

Transfer the cooled oat mixture to a food processor and mix for 4 minutes, until a smooth paste forms. Store in an airtight container at room temperature.

continued

FOR THE MARINATED ENDIVE:

Prepare an ice bath. Heat a sauté pan over medium-high heat. When the pan is hot, add the brown sugar and stir aggressively to avoid burning. Once the sugar has liquefied, after about 15 seconds, add the vinegars. When the sugar has dissolved and is well mixed with the vinegars, strain the mixture through a chinois into a heatpoof bowl, then nest the bowl in the ice bath to cool the liquid.

Cut the endive bulbs in half lengthwise and arrange in a vacuum bag. Pour the vinegar mixture over the endives and seal the bag on high. Refrigerate for at least 2 hours. Open the bag, remove the endives, and drain the vinegar mixture into a shallow bowl. Cut the endives into diagonal squares, removing the core. Submerge the pieces in the vinegar mixture.

TO SERVE:

Place a few dots of the oat butter on a plate. Scatter some dried apple pieces next to the oat butter and arrange some marinated endive pieces around the other components. Garnish with the Treviso and curly endive leaves. Set the cheese wheel next to the composition, with the leaves slightly opened, exposing the cheese.

MARINATED ENDIVE

200 grams | 1 cup firmly packed brown sugar
400 grams | 1 ²/₃ cups aged apple cider vinegar
200 grams | ³/₄ cup Champagne vinegar
2 | Belgian endive bulbs

24 | tiny Treviso leaves
24 | tiny curly endive leaves

chocolate chestnuts longan

We created this dish with chestnuts grown in the valley. Using chestnut-shaped silicone molds, we create faux chestnuts that sit atop a roasted chocolate crumble with the texture of a brownie crust.

SERVES 6

ROASTED MILK CHOCOLATE

1 kilogram | about 2 pounds, 3 ounces milk chocolate pistoles (40 percent cacao)

LONGAN JAM

500 grams | 2 ¼ cups longan pulp
200 grams | 1 cup sugar
40 grams | 3 tablespoons pectin NH

CHESTNUT MOLDS

775 grams | 3 ¼ cups silicone A
775 grams | 3 ¼ cups silicone B
24 | chestnuts in the shell

CHESTNUT PREPARATION

850 grams | 4 cups chestnut paste
30 grams | ⅓ cup cocoa powder
100 grams | ½ cup sugar
450 grams | 1 ⅔ cups plus ¼ cup water
30 grams | 12 sheets silver gelatin, bloomed in ice water and wrung gently of excess water
300 grams | 1 ⅓ cups cocoa butter
440 grams | 1 ⅓ cups roasted milk chocolate (recipe above)
5 grams | 1 ½ sheets bronze gelatin, bloomed in ice water and wrung gently of excess water
100 grams | ¾ cup dextrose
50 grams | 2 tablespoons liquid glucose
675 grams | 2 ¾ cups heavy cream
3.5 grams | 1 teaspoon powdered agar

FOR THE ROASTED MILK CHOCOLATE:

Preheat the oven to 280°F (140°C). Arrange the chocolate pieces in an even layer in a baking pan. Roast for 1 hour, until the chocolate darkens slightly and has a very strong roasted odor. Let cool at room temperature for at least 30 minutes before using.

FOR THE LONGAN JAM:

Put the longan pulp in a blender and mix on high speed for about 30 seconds, until liquefied. Transfer to a saucepan and warm over low heat. Stir together the sugar and pectin in a small bowl. Add to the warm longan pulp, whisk to disperse the pectin mixture evenly, and increase the heat to high. Bring the mixture to a boil, and cook for 15 seconds, until the jam begins to thicken, then transfer to a heat-proof container and let cool in the refrigerator. Transfer the jam to a squeeze bottle and keep in the refrigerator until ready to use.

FOR THE CHESTNUT MOLDS:

Place the silicone A and silicone B in a disposable pail and stir with a wooden stick to combine. Using a strong, instant-bond glue, secure the chestnuts onto a sheet of acetate, spacing them about 1 inch (2.5 centimeters) apart. Place a sturdy metal frame around the edge of the acetate sheet, surrounding the chestnuts. Pour the silicone mixture in a thin ribbon (to avoid air bubbles) into the frame, submerging the chestnuts completely. Let stand for 6 hours, until set. Lift off the frame with the 24 chestnut molds and discard the chestnuts.

FOR THE CHESTNUT PREPARATION:

Combine the chestnut paste, cocoa powder, sugar, and 400 grams (1 ⅔ cups) of the water in a blender and mix on low speed for 15 seconds, until well incorporated. Meanwhile, melt the silver gelatin in a small saucepan. Remove from the heat, add to the blender, and increase the speed to high. Once the puree is smooth, slowly add the cocoa butter to emulsify. Strain through a chinois into a bowl, then transfer to a squeeze bottle. While the mixture is still warm, fill the chestnut molds and tap out the excess, creating a shell in each mold. Freeze for at least 30 minutes to freeze the shells completely.

Put the roasted chocolate in a blender. Combine the bronze gelatin, 50 grams (¼ cup) of water, dextrose, glucose, and cream in a small saucepan over low heat and stir to melt the gelatin. Using a whisk, disperse the agar into the liquid, increase the heat to high, and bring to a full boil. Remove from the heat, pour over the chocolate in the blender, and mix on high speed for 30 seconds to emulsify. Strain through a chinois into a bowl and let cool to just warm (about 120°F/49°C). Transfer to a squeeze bottle and fill the shell-lined molds. Return the molds to the freezer for at least 2 hours, until fully frozen.

continued

FOR THE DEHYDRATED CHOCOLATE:

Melt the chocolate in the top of a double boiler over gently simmering water. Meanwhile, in a stand mixer fitted with the whip attachment, mix the egg whites on medium speed until soft peaks form. Slowly add the sugar and continue mixing until medium peaks form. Combine the melted chocolate and egg yolks in a blender and mix on high speed until a smooth puree forms. Transfer to a bowl and gently fold the egg whites into the chocolate just until combined. Line a dehydrator tray with an acetate sheet. Transfer the chocolate mixture to the acetate and spread in an even layer $^{1}/_{4}$ inch (6 millimeters) thick. Dehydrate at 140°F (60°C) for at least 12 hours, until dry and crispy.

Break up the dehydrated chocolate, put in a food processor, and mix until a coarse powder forms. Store in an airtight container with silica gel packets at room temperature.

FOR THE CARAMELIZED CHESTNUT PUREE:

Prepare an ice bath. Heat a saucepan over medium-high heat. Add the sugar all at once and stir constantly to prevent scorching. Once the sugar begins to turn amber, add the butter and continue stirring. Once the butter has melted, add the chestnut paste and stir to incorporate. Boil for 1 minute, until very fragrant. Transfer to a blender and mix on high speed until a smooth puree forms. Strain through a chinois into a bowl, then nest the bowl in the ice bath to cool the puree. Transfer to a squeeze bottle and hold at room temperature.

FOR THE SWEETENED BUTTERMILK:

Prepare an ice bath. Combine the buttermilk, sugar, and gellan base in a blender. Mix on medium speed for 2 minutes, until smooth. Do not mix longer or you risk overheating the mixture. Strain though a chinois into a bowl, then nest the bowl in the ice bath and stir to cool the puree. Season with kosher salt and transfer to a squeeze bottle.

TO SERVE:

Unmold the frozen chestnuts, transfer to an airtight container, and thaw for 1 hour before serving. Dip the chestnuts in the ground dehydrated chocolate and arrange 4 chestnuts on each of 6 plates, varying the size and shape of the nuts on each plate. Place a few dots of the longan jam, chestnut puree, and sweetened buttermilk in the center of each plate. Place a pair of longan halves on each plate and scatter some of the dehydrated chocolate around the chestnuts as a garnish. Finish with a grating of raw chestnut over each serving.

DEHYDRATED CHOCOLATE

240 grams | 1 $^{3}/_{4}$ cups roasted milk
  chocolate (page 273)
300 grams | 1 $^{1}/_{4}$ cups egg whites
80 grams | $^{1}/_{3}$ cup sugar
80 grams | $^{1}/_{3}$ cup egg yolks

CARAMELIZED CHESTNUT PUREE

200 grams | 1 cup sugar
150 grams | $^{2}/_{3}$ cup unsalted butter
280 grams | 1 $^{1}/_{3}$ cups chestnut paste

SWEETENED BUTTERMILK

400 grams | 1 $^{3}/_{4}$ cups buttermilk (page 284)
50 grams | $^{1}/_{4}$ cup sugar
200 grams | 7 ounces gellan base (page 285)
kosher salt

6 | fresh longans, shelled and halved
peeled raw chestnut

silverado strawberry tableau

During the warm months, strawberry stands line the Silverado Trail, the well-known artery that runs north to south through the valley. This tableau was created with these Silverado strawberries in mind and features the fermented flavor of nuka and also faux strawberries made using homemade silicone molds.

SERVES 8

NUKA MILK

100 grams | 1/2 cup oatmeal stout nuka (page 285)
2 kilograms | 8 cups whole milk

STRAWBERRY MOLDS

775 grams | 3 1/4 cups silicone A
775 grams | 3 1/4 cups silicone B
16 | unripe strawberries

WHITE CHOCOLATE GLAZE

300 grams | 2 cups unripe strawberries
400 grams | 4 2/3 cups oatmeal stout nuka (page 285)
80 grams | 1/3 cup water
200 grams | 1 1/2 cups chopped white chocolate (35 percent cacao)
100 grams | 1/2 cup sugar
220 grams | 1 cup nuka milk (recipe above)
100 grams | 1/2 cup heavy cream
24 grams | 12 sheets gold gelatin, bloomed in ice water and wrung gently of excess water

FERMENTED STRAWBERRY PUREE

500 grams | 3 1/4 cups Silverado Trail strawberries, hulled
1 kilogram | 4 cups oatmeal stout nuka (page 285)

STRAWBERRY SORBET

800 grams | 3 1/2 cups strawberry puree
200 grams | 3/4 cup fermented strawberry puree (recipe above)
150 grams | 1/2 cup trimoline
75 grams | 1/3 cup sugar
9 grams | 2 teaspoons sorbet stabilizer
200 grams | 3/4 cup water
5 grams | 1 teaspoon citric acid

FOR THE NUKA MILK:

Combine the nuka and half of the milk in a blender and mix on low speed until smooth. Strain through a chinois into a bowl and add the remaining milk. Hold at room temperature for later use.

FOR THE STRAWBERRY MOLDS:

Place the silicone A and silicone B in a disposable pail and stir with a wooden stick to combine. Using a strong, instant-bond glue, secure the strawberries, stem side down, onto a sheet of acetate, spacing them about 1 inch (2.5 centimeters) apart. Place a sturdy metal frame around the edge of the acetate sheet, surrounding the strawberries. Pour the silicone mixture in a thin ribbon (to avoid air bubbles) into the frame, submerging the strawberries completely. Let stand for 6 hours, until set. Lift off the frame with the 24 strawberry molds and discard the strawberries.

FOR THE WHITE CHOCOLATE GLAZE:

Bury the unripe strawberries in the nuka in a plastic container and refrigerate for 12 hours. Rinse the nuka from the strawberries under cool running water, transfer to a blender, add the water, and mix on high speed for 2 minutes, until smooth. Strain through a chinois into a heatproof bowl. Place the bowl over a saucepan of gently simmering water and add the chocolate, sugar, nuka milk, cream, and gelatin. Heat, stirring, for about 2 minutes, until evenly melted, forming a glaze. Remove the chocolate glaze from the heat and pour through a chinois into a sauce gun or a funnel. Fill the strawberry molds with the glaze and let stand for 2 minutes. Flip the molds upside down to remove any excess glaze, then place in the freezer for 20 minutes. Scrape the excess glaze from the exterior of each mold, then apply a second coat of glaze, following the same steps. Store the molds in the freezer.

FOR THE FERMENTED STRAWBERRY PUREE:

Bury the strawberries in the nuka in a plastic container and refrigerate for 12 hours. Rinse the berries under cool running water, pat dry, and transfer to a blender. Mix on high speed for about 3 minutes, until smooth. Strain through a chinois into a bowl and hold for later use.

FOR THE STRAWBERRY SORBET:

Combine both strawberry purees in a heatproof bowl and set aside. Combine the trimoline, half of the sugar, and the water in a small saucepan over low heat and bring to a simmer. Meanwhile, stir together the remaining sugar and the sorbet stabilizer in a small bowl. When the trimoline mixture begins to simmer, whisk in the sorbet stabilizer mixture and increase the heat to high. Bring to a boil and boil for 1 minute, then remove from the heat and pour through a chinois into the puree mixture. Whisk until well mixed, then stir in the citric acid.

Pour into an ice cream machine and run a cycle for about 4 minutes, until the sorbet is dense but not terribly stiff. Spoon into a piping bag fitted with a small round tip. Fill the chocolate-coated strawberry molds with the sorbet, cleaning off the surface of the mold to ensure the strawberries have a flat side. Place the completed strawberries in the freezer for at least 4 hours.

continued

FOR THE STRAWBERRY CAKE:

Preheat the oven to 325°F (165°C). Spray a quarter sheet pan with nonstick cooking spray. Combine the flour, sugar, baking soda, and salt in a food processor and mix briefly to blend. Combine the nuka milk, strawberry puree, and egg in a bowl and stir to mix well. Add the nuka milk mixture to the food processor and pulse, adding the butter at the same time, until the batter is smooth. Pour the batter into the prepared sheet pan and bake for 15 to 20 minutes, until the cake is golden brown and springs back when lightly touched with a finger. Let cool in the pan on a wire rack for 2 hours.

Place a wire rack on a half sheet pan. Invert the cake onto a cutting board, then turn it top side up. Cut the cake into 8 equal squares. Slice off the top of each square with a bread knife to expose the inside texture of the cake, then arrange the squares on the wire rack. Combine the chocolate, cocoa butter, and titanium dioxide in a double boiler over gently simmering water and heat, stirring occasionally, to 120°F (49°C). Strain the chocolate through a chinois and transfer to a chocolate sprayer. Spray the cakes with the chocolate twice and store in the refrigerator.

FOR THE STRAWBERRY GEL:

Combine the strawberries and gellan base in a blender and mix on high speed for 2 minutes, until smooth. Strain through a chinois into a bowl, then transfer to a squeeze bottle and store in the refrigerator.

FOR THE DEHYDRATED MILK FOAM:

Line a dehydrator tray with a silicone baking mat. Stir together the nuka milk and glucose in a shallow saucepan, place over medium-high heat, and heat to 180°F (82°C). Remove from the heat and froth the milk with an immersion blender. Using a slotted spoon, lift off the top layer of the foam and place it on the mat-lined tray. Dehydrate at 120°F (49°C) for at least 6 hours, until light and crispy.

FOR THE AERATED WHITE CHOCOLATE:

Combine the chocolate and cocoa butter in a double boiler over gently simmering water and heat, stirring occasionally to melt fully, to 140°F (60°C). Transfer to a siphon canister and charge with 3 nitrous oxide cartridges. Discharge the chocolate into a vacuum storage box, compress on high, and immediately transfer the box to the freezer for about 3 hours, until the chocolate has fully solidified. The aerated white chocolate can be stored in its vacuum storage box at room temperature for up to 1 month.

Release the pressure from the box and break the white chocolate into small pieces. Put the freeze-dried strawberries in a spice grinder and pulverize them. Dust a fine layer of strawberry powder over the white chocolate pieces. Store in an airtight container in cool, dry area.

FOR THE CRYSTALLIZED STRAWBERRY LEAVES:

Line a dehydrator tray with a silicone baking mat. Warm the gelatin in a shallow pan over low heat until melted. Remove from the heat, add the egg whites, and whisk to incorporate. Using a brush, paint a thin layer of the gelatin mixture on both sides of a strawberry leaf, dip the leaf into the coarse sugar to coat evenly, and place on the prepared dehydrator tray. When all of the leaves are coated, dehydrate at 125°F (52°C) for at least 2 hours, until completely dry.

STRAWBERRY CAKE

150 grams | 1 1/4 cups all-purpose flour
225 grams | 1 cup plus 1 tablespoon sugar
4 grams | 1 teaspoon baking soda
3 grams | 1/2 teaspoon kosher salt
150 grams | 2/3 cup nuka milk (page 277)
250 grams | 1 cup fresh strawberry puree
50 grams | about 1 egg
50 grams | 1/4 cup unsalted butter, melted
400 grams | 14 ounces chopped white
    chocolate (35 percent cacao)
200 grams | 7 ounces cocoa butter
1.5 grams | scant 1/2 teaspoon titanium
    dioxide

STRAWBERRY GEL

300 grams | 2 cups Silverado Trail
    strawberries, hulled
300 grams | 10.5 ounces gellan base
    (page 285)

DEHYDRATED MILK FOAM

360 grams | 1 1/2 cups nuka milk (page 277)
170 grams | 1/2 cup liquid glucose

AERATED WHITE CHOCOLATE

900 grams | 4 cups chopped white
    chocolate (35 percent cacao)
100 grams | 1/2 cup cocoa butter
20 grams | 1/4 cup freeze-dried strawberries

CRYSTALLIZED STRAWBERRY LEAVES

6 grams | 3 sheets gold gelatin,
    bloomed in ice water and wrung
    gently of excess water
120 grams | 1/2 cup egg whites
8 | strawberry leaves
100 grams | 1/2 cup coarse granulated sugar

NUKA MILK GEL

200 grams | ³/₄ cup nuka milk (page 277)
400 grams | 14.1 ounces gellan base
(page 285)
kosher salt

8 | Silverado Trail strawberries
8 | strawberry flowers

FOR THE NUKA MILK GEL:

Combine the nuka milk and gellan base in a blender and mix on high speed for 2 minutes, until smooth. Strain through a chinois into a bowl, then transfer to a squeeze bottle.

TO SERVE:

Preheat the oven to 325°F (165°C). Place a rack on a sheet pan, and arrange the Silverado Trail strawberries on the rack. Roast for 8 minutes, just until they begin to soften. Let cool for 30 minutes at room temperature. Lay a square of the white chocolate-sprayed cake on each of 8 flat plates. Garnish each plate with a few dots of the strawberry gel and the nuka milk gel. Arrange 2 frozen "strawberries" and 1 roasted strawberry on top. Finish with the dehydrated milk foam, aerated white chocolate, crystallized leaves, and strawberry flowers.

TECHNIQUES

butter stock

MAKES ABOUT 3 KILOGRAMS
(3 QUARTS)

3 kilograms | about 3 quarts water
1.8 kilograms | 4 pounds unsalted butter
kosher salt

Combine the water and butter in a large pot over high heat and bring to a boil. Remove from the heat and let cool to 120°F (49°C), then hold at this temperature for 3 hours. Pour the entire contents of the pot into a container with a lid, cover, and refrigerate for up to 3 days, or store in a vacuum bag sealed on high in the freezer for up to 1 month. Just before using, strain the stock through a chinois and discard the solids. Season with salt, then strain the stock through a very fine cloth filter.

carrot puree

MAKES ABOUT 1.5 KILOGRAMS (6 1/2 CUPS)

10 | large carrots, peeled
kosher salt

Juice half of the carrots. Slice the remaining carrots into rounds about 1/8 inch (3 millimeters) thick. Combine the carrot juice and sliced carrots in a large saucepan and bring to a boil over high heat. Turn down the heat to a simmer and cook for about 20 minutes, until the carrot slices are very tender. Drain the carrots and discard the liquid.

Loosely drape a piece of cheesecloth over the opening of a container, then secure the cheesecloth in place with butcher's twine. Transfer the carrots to the cheesecloth and let stand for 5 minutes to remove any remaining liquid. Meanwhile, prepare an ice bath. When the carrots have finished draining, discard the liquid and transfer the carrots to a blender. Mix on high speed for about 3 minutes, until a smooth puree forms. Strain the puree through a chinois into a bowl, then nest the bowl in the ice bath and stir to cool the puree. Season with salt and refrigerate in an airtight container for up to 2 days.

crème fraîche

MAKES ABOUT 200 GRAMS (3/4 CUP)

250 grams | 1 cup heavy cream
60 grams | 1/4 cup buttermilk (page 284)

Combine the cream and buttermilk in a plastic container and whisk to mix well. Cover loosely with plastic wrap and incubate the mixture in an area with an ambient temperature of 90°F to 105°F (32°C to 41°C) for 48 hours. Then, refrigerate the container for 2 hours.

Loosely drape a piece of cheesecloth over the opening of a second plastic container and secure the cheesecloth in place with butcher's twine. Pour the crème fraîche into the cheesecloth, cover the container tightly with plastic wrap, and return to the refrigerator for 24 hours or longer, depending on the desired thickness. Store in an airtight container in the refrigerator for up to 1 month.

rendered squab fat

MAKES ABOUT 500 GRAMS (2 CUPS)

600 grams | 21 ounces squab skin and wings
200 grams | 3/4 cup water

Combine the squab skin and wings with the water in a saucepan and place over low heat to render the skin. When the skin begins to turn golden brown, remove from the heat and let steep for 2 hours. Strain the rendered fat through a chinois into a vacuum bag and seal on high. Discard the solids and cool the fat in the refrigerator for up to 2 weeks.

chicken stock

MAKES ABOUT 10 KILOGRAMS (10.5 QUARTS)

3.5 kilograms | about 7.5 pounds chicken frames
10 kilograms | about 10.5 quarts water
400 grams | 13 ounces carrots, peeled and cut
    into 2-inch (5-centimeter) pieces
400 grams | 13 ounces celery stalks, cut into
    2-inch (5-centimeter) pieces
500 grams | 1.1 pounds yellow onions, cut into
    2-inch (5-centimeter) pieces

Combine the chicken frames and water in a large stockpot and bring to a boil over high heat. Turn down the heat to a simmer and skim off any fat and solid protein from the surface. Add the carrots, celery, and onions, remove from the heat, and let steep for 5 hours, skimming the surface occasionally as the fat and protein continue to rise to the surface. Strain the stock through a very fine cloth filter into a metal container, then nest the container in an ice bath to cool completely. Transfer to an airtight container and refrigerate for up to 4 days, or freeze 1 quart (1 liter) at a time in vacuum bags sealed on high then laid flat on a metal tray for up to 1 month.

cultured butter and buttermilk

Pour the cream into a rondeau, place over low heat, and heat slowly, stirring occasionally, to 180°F (82°C). Hold the cream at this temperature for 30 minutes. Remove from the heat and let cool naturally to 110°F (43°C). Add the yogurt to the cream, whisk to combine, and pour into a plastic container with a lid. Hold in an area with an ambient temperature of 105°F (41°C) for 14 hours. Refrigerate the cultured cream until fully chilled, about 3 hours.

Pour the chilled cream into a stand mixer fitted with the whip attachment and mix on medium speed for about 5 minutes, until butter begins to form and release buttermilk. Meanwhile, prepare a bowl of ice water. Drain the butter, reserving the butter and the buttermilk separately. Store the buttermilk in an airtight container in the refrigerator for up to 2 weeks.

Submerge the butter in the ice water, putting pressure on the butter to release excess buttermilk. Change the ice water and submerge the butter in the fresh water the same way. Repeat this process until the ice water remains clear. Press the butter into cheesecloth and allow to air-dry in the refrigerator for at least 6 hours or up to 24 hours. Place the butter in a vacuum bag and seal on high. Store for up to 1 month in the refrigerator.

To serve, put the butter in a stand mixer fitted with the whip attachment and mix on high speed for 3 minutes, until aerated. Season with Maldon salt. Store in an airtight container for up to 2 days.

MAKES ABOUT 900 GRAMS (2 POUNDS) OF BUTTER AND 1.1 KILOGRAMS (4 ¹/₂ CUPS) OF BUTTERMILK

2 kilograms | about 8 cups heavy cream
70 grams | ¹/₄ cup plain full-fat Greek-style yogurt
Maldon sea salt

cultured yogurt

Pour the milk into a stockpot, place over low heat, and heat slowly, stirring occasionally, to 180°F (82°C). Hold the milk at this temperature for 1 hour. Remove from the heat and let cool naturally to 110°F (43°C). Add the yogurt to the cream, whisk to combine, and pour into a plastic container with a lid. Hold in an area with an ambient temperature of 105°F (41°C) for 24 hours. Refrigerate the cultured milk for 12 hours.

Line a perforated hotel pan with cheesecloth and set it over a deeper hotel pan. Pour the cultured milk into the cheesecloth, then cover the pan tightly with plastic wrap. Refrigerate for at least 3 days, until a very thick yogurt has formed. Scoop the finished yogurt from the cheesecloth into a vacuum bag and seal on high. Discard the whey. Store the sealed bag of yogurt in the refrigerator for up to 8 days.

MAKES ABOUT 3 KILOGRAMS (3 QUARTS)

5 kilograms | about 5 quarts whole milk
375 grams | 1 ¹/₂ cups plain full-fat Greek-style yogurt

dark chicken jus

Preheat the oven to 500°F (260°C). Place racks in roasting pans and arrange the chicken frames on the racks. Roast for 25 minutes, until dark golden brown. Let cool to room temperature.

Heat the olive oil in a large stockpot over high heat. Add the carrots, celery, onions, leek tops, and bay leaves and caramelize the vegetables for about 15 minutes, until soft and golden brown. Add the chicken frames and stock and bring to a boil. Turn down the heat to a simmer and simmer for 2 hours at 180°F (82°C), skimming the surface occasionally to remove any fat and solid protein.

Remove from the heat and strain through a very fine cloth filter into a clean pot. Return to low heat and cook for 5 to 6 hours, until reduced by about 80 percent and slightly thickened with a rich amber color. Strain through a very fine cloth filter into a metal container, season with salt and vinegar, then nest in an ice bath to cool completely. Transfer to an airtight container and refrigerate for up to 4 days, or freeze in a vacuum bag sealed on high for up to 1 month.

MAKES ABOUT 500 GRAMS (2 CUPS)

2.2 kilograms | about 5 pounds chicken frames
50 grams | 2 tablespoons extra virgin olive oil
400 grams | 13 ounces carrots, peeled and cut into 2-inch (5-centimeter) pieces
400 grams | 13 ounces celery stalks, cut into 2-inch (5-centimeter) pieces
500 grams | 1.5 pounds yellow onions, cut into 2-inch (5-centimeter) pieces
200 grams | 7 ounces green leek tops
3 | bay leaves
10 kilograms | 10.5 quarts chicken stock (page 283)
kosher salt
sherry vinegar

2 kilograms | about 8 cups water
30 grams | 2 tablespoons low acyl gellan gum
15 grams | 1 tablespoon calcium lactate
    gluconate

gellan base

Pour the water into a blender. Turn the blender on low speed and mix until a vortex forms. Slowly add the gellan gum, then continue to mix for 1 minute. Pour into a saucepan and bring to a boil over high heat, whisking occasionally to promote even heat dispersion. Boil the liquid for 20 seconds, then remove from the heat and slowly incorporate the calcium lactate gluconate, mixing until fully dissolved. Pour the liquid into a wide metal pan and let cool in the refrigerator for at least 2 hours. Cut the gellan base into small squares (about $1/2$ inch/12 millimeters) and store in an airtight container in the refrigerator for up to 1 week.

MAKES ABOUT 400 GRAMS (14 OUNCES)

500 grams | 1 pound Mangalitsa fatback,
    skin removed
70 grams | $1/4$ cup kosher salt
34 grams | $2 1/2$ tablespoons brown sugar
9 grams | $1 1/2$ teaspoons tinted curing mix #2
6 grams | 1 teaspoon minced garlic
5 grams | 1 tablespoon black peppercorns,
    ground
3 grams | 1 teaspoon ground fennel seeds
3 grams | 1 teaspoon crushed juniper berries
2 grams | 1 teaspoon ground star anise
2 grams | 2 tablespoons thyme leaves
3 | bay leaves, crushed

mangalitsa lardo

Trim the fatback into an even square (about 7 inches/18 centimeters). To make the curing mixture, combine the kosher salt, brown sugar, curing mix, garlic, peppercorns, fennel seeds, juniper berries, star anise, thyme, and bay leaves in a bowl and mix well. Apply the cure mixture to the fatback, making sure that all surfaces are covered with the cure. Place in a stainless-steel container and top with a weight of at least 2.3 kilograms (5 pounds). Cover and refrigerate for 12 days, rotating the fatback every 3 days to ensure even curing.

Rinse the fatback well under cold running water. Pat dry with paper towels and pierce a hole toward the top of the fatback. Insert a piece of butcher's twine through the hole and hang the fatback in an area with an ambient temperature of 45°F to 55°F (7°C to 13°C) for at least 3 months, checking periodically for any mold or blemishes. If any should occur, mix together a solution of 6 parts water and 1 part distilled white vinegar and apply it lightly with a pastry brush to any mold or blemishes. When the 3 months have elapsed, place the lardo in a vacuum bag and seal on high. Freeze for up to 6 months.

MAKES ABOUT 4.4 KILOGRAMS (4.8 QUARTS)

400 grams | $1 1/3$ cups kosher salt
2 kilograms | about 8 cups oatmeal stout
50 grams | $1/2$ cup ground dried levain bread
    (page 288)
1.8 kilograms | 4 pounds toasted rice bran
100 grams | 1 cup sliced strawberries

oatmeal stout nuka

Warm the salt and oatmeal stout in a saucepan over low heat, stirring occasionally, until the salt dissolves. Add the bread and stir continuously until the liquid forms a mash consistency. Mix the bran and sliced strawberries into the mash and pack into a ceramic container without a lid. Cover with a cloth towel and store in an area with an ambient temperature of 70°F (21°C). Every 24 to 36 hours, remove the nuka from the container, agitate it to introduce more oxygen, and then return it to the container. After about 4 months have elapsed, the nuka will smell sour and yeasty, be moist but still crumbly, and have the proper fermenting capabilities. Be sure to continue the aeration process to ensure beneficial microbial growth. If the nuka should ever rise in temperature on its own, add 3 percent more stout and 5 percent more toasted rice bran by weight to energize the bacteria and equalize the anaerobic process. Properly tended, the nuka will last indefinitely.

MAKES ABOUT 6 KILOGRAMS (6 QUARTS)

2.4 kilograms | about 5 pounds white fish
    bones (such as snapper, cod, or halibut)
7 kilograms | about 7 quarts water
120 grams | $3/4$ cup sliced leeks
120 grams | $3/4$ cup diced celery
200 grams | $1 1/4$ cups sliced shallots
5 grams | 2 tablespoons thyme leaves
10 grams | $1/4$ cup flat-leaf parsley leaves

fish fumet

Combine the fish bones, water, leeks, celery, and shallots in a pressure cooker and cook on high pressure for 30 minutes. Prepare an ice bath. Strain the stock through a very fine cloth filter into a metal bowl, add the thyme and parsley leaves, then nest the bowl in the ice bath to cool the stock. Skim the surface of any fat, then strain the herbs from the stock. Store in an airtight container in the refrigerator for up to 3 days, or freeze 1 quart (1 liter) at a time in vacuum bags sealed on high then laid flat on a metal tray for up to 1 month.

rendered beef fat

Process the beef suet through a meat grinder fitted with a large die. Transfer the ground suet to a stockpot and add water just to cover. Bring the mixture to a boil over high heat and, mixing with a spatula occasionally, boil for about 1 hour, until the water has evaporated completely and the fat has begun to caramelize slightly. Meanwhile, prepare an ice bath. Strain the rendered fat through a very fine cloth filter into a metal bowl and discard the solids. Nest the bowl in the ice bath to cool the fat, then transfer the fat to vacuum bags and seal on high. Store the fat in the refrigerator for up to 2 weeks or in the freezer for up to 6 months.

1.4 kilograms | 3 pounds chilled beef suet

tomato water

Transfer the tomatoes to a blender in batches and mix on medium speed for 30 seconds, until liquefied. Line a perforated hotel pan with 2 layers of cheesecloth and set it over a deeper hotel pan. Pour the liquefied tomatoes into the cheesecloth, then cover the pan tightly with plastic wrap. Refrigerate for 2 days, until the tomatoes drain through the cheesecloth, leaving clear tomato water in the bottom pan. Discard the pulp. Store the tomato water in an airtight container in the refrigerator for up to 1 week, or freeze 1 liter (1 quart) at a time in vacuum bags sealed on high then laid flat on a metal tray for up to 2 months.

MAKES ABOUT 3 LITERS (3 QUARTS)

4.2 kilograms | about 10 pounds tomatoes, cored and halved

shiro dashi

Combine the kombu, bonito flakes, water, and hondashi in a stockpot over low heat and heat to 160°F (71°C). Hold at this temperature for 1 hour, then prepare an ice bath. Strain the broth through a chinois into a metal bowl, then nest the bowl in the ice bath to cool the broth. Add soy sauce to taste. Transfer to an airtight container and refrigerate for up to 1 week, or place in a vacuum bag and seal on high, then freeze for up to 1 month.

MAKES ABOUT 3 KILOGRAMS (3 QUARTS)

100 grams | 3.5 ounces dried kombu
60 grams | 2 cups bonito flakes
3.3 kilograms | 3 $^{1}/_{2}$ quarts water
6 grams | 1 tablespoon hondashi
white soy sauce

roasted duck jus

Preheat the oven to 500°F (260°C). Place racks in roasting pans and arrange the duck frames on the racks. Roast for 25 minutes, until dark golden brown. Let cool to room temperature.

Pour the olive oil into a large stockpot and place over high heat. Add the carrots, celery, onions, leek tops, and bay leaves and caramelize the vegetables for about 15 minutes, until soft and golden brown. Add the duck frames and stock and bring to a boil. Turn down the heat to a simmer and simmer for 2 hours at 180°F (82°C), skimming the surface occasionally to remove any fat and solid protein.

Remove from the heat and strain through a very fine cloth filter into a clean pot. Return to low heat and cook for about 5 hours, until reduced by about 80 percent and slightly thickened with a rich amber color. Prepare an ice bath. Strain the jus through a very fine cloth filter into a metal container, season with salt and vinegar, then nest in the ice bath to cool completely. Transfer to an airtight container and refrigerate for up to 1 week, or freeze in a vacuum bag sealed on high for up to 1 month.

MAKES ABOUT 500 GRAMS (2 CUPS)

2.2 kilograms | about 5 pounds duck frames
50 grams | 2 tablespoons extra virgin olive oil
400 grams | 13 ounces carrots, peeled and cut into 2-inch (5-centimeter) pieces
400 grams | 13 ounces celery stalks, cut into 2-inch (5-centimeter) pieces
500 grams | 1.5 pounds yellow onions, cut into 2-inch (5-centimeter) pieces
200 grams | 7 ounces green leek tops
3 | bay leaves
10 kilograms | 10.5 quarts chicken stock (page 283)
kosher salt
sherry vinegar

foie gras cure

Combine the salt, sugar, curing mix, and five-spice powder in a bowl and mix well. Use 40 grams (2 $^{1}/_{4}$ tablespoons) of the curing mix for every 1.5 kilograms (3.3 pounds) of foie gras.

MAKES ABOUT 570 GRAMS (1.3 POUNDS)

500 grams | 1 $^{3}/_{4}$ cups kosher salt
50 grams | $^{1}/_{4}$ cup sugar
15 grams | about 1 tablespoon tinted curing mix #1
5 grams | about 1 tablespoon five-spice powder

4.5 kilograms | about 10 pounds lamb bones
50 grams | 2 tablespoons extra virgin olive oil
800 grams | 1.8 pounds carrots, peeled and
    cut into 2-inch (5-centimeter) pieces
800 grams | 1.8 pounds celery stalks, cut
    into 2-inch (5-centimeter) pieces
1.1 kilograms | 2.5 pounds yellow onions, cut
    into 2-inch (5-centimeter) pieces
200 grams | 7 ounces green leek tops
3 | bay leaves
22 liters | about 23 quarts veal stock
kosher salt

MAKES 350 GRAMS | 1 ½ CUPS

450 grams | 1 pound Bing cherries,
    stemmed and pitted
sugar
kosher salt

roasted lamb jus

Preheat the oven to 500°F (260°C). Place racks in roasting pans and arrange the lamb bones on the racks. Roast for 25 minutes, until dark golden brown. Let cool to room temperature.

Pour the olive oil into a large stockpot and place over high heat. Add the carrots, celery, onions, leek tops, and bay leaves and caramelize the vegetables for about 15 minutes, until soft and golden brown. Add the lamb bones and stock and bring to a boil. Turn down the heat to a simmer and simmer for 2 hours at 180°F (82°C), skimming the surface occasionally to remove any fat and solid protein.

Remove from the heat and strain through a very fine cloth filter into a clean pot. Return to low heat and cook for 5 to 6 hours, until reduced by about 80 percent and slightly thickened with a rich amber color. Prepare an ice bath. Strain the jus through a very fine cloth filter into a metal container, season with salt, then nest in the ice bath to cool completely. Transfer to an airtight container and refrigerate for up to 1 week, or freeze 500 grams (2 cups) at a time in vacuum bags sealed on high for up to 1 month.

bing cherry puree

Place the cherries in a blender and mix on high for 2 minutes, until the puree is very smooth. Strain through a chinois into a bowl, then nest the bowl in the ice bath to cool the mixture. Season with sugar and salt to taste. Transfer to a sealed container and store in the refrigerator for up to a week.

smoking techniques

COLD SMOKING:

Unless otherwise noted, use fruitwood chips (such as apple wood or fig wood). Line a deep hotel pan with aluminum foil, lay a large handful of wood chips (about 2 cups) in the center, and ignite with a kitchen torch. Allow the wood chips to burn for a few minutes. Place a perforated hotel pan over the smoldering chips and arrange a single layer of ice cubes in the perforated pan. Arrange the ingredients to be smoked on top of the ice, avoiding stacking to ensure maximum contact with the smoke. When the smoke begins to permeate through the ice and ingredients, cover the pan tightly with plastic wrap. Hold at room temperature for the time indicated in the recipe. When the time has elapsed, remove the ingredients from the smoker and use as directed. Allow the wood chips to cool completely before discarding.

HOT SMOKING:

As with cold smoking, fruitwood chips are used unless otherwise noted. Line a deep hotel pan with aluminum foil, lay a large handful of wood chips (about 2 cups) in the center, ignite with a kitchen torch, and place the pan directly on a heat source, such as a burner on a stove top or a French cooktop. As the wood chips begin to burn, immediately place a perforated hotel pan over the smoldering chips. Arrange the ingredients to be smoked in the pan, avoiding stacking to ensure maximum contact with the smoke. Insert a thermometer near or in the food (depending on the application) to monitor the temperature. Quickly cover the pan with aluminum foil, wrapping tightly to trap as much smoke as possible. Smoke for the time indicated in the recipe. When the time has elapsed, remove the smoker from the heat source, then remove the ingredients from the smoker and use as directed. Allow the wood chips to cool completely before discarding.

levain bread

FOR THE SPONGE:

Combine the flour, water, and yeast in the bowl of a stand mixer fitted with the dough hook. Mix on medium speed for 6 to 8 minutes, until the dough is elastic. Transfer to a plastic container with a lid and place it in a proof box set at 70°F (21°C) for 14 hours.

FOR THE LIQUID LEVAIN:

Combine the flour, water, and yeast into the bowl of a stand mixer fitted with the paddle attachment. Mix on medium speed for 3 minutes, until well combined. Transfer the dough to a vessel with a lid and place it in a proof box set at 90°F (32°C) for 50 minutes. Remove the dough from the proof box and refrigerate until needed, or for up to 36 hours.

FOR THE LEVAIN BREAD:

In the bowl of a stand mixer, combine the water and yeast and let stand for 10 minutes, until the yeast is frothy. Add the flour, salt, malt, sponge, and liquid levain, fit the mixer with the dough hook, and mix on medium speed for 10 to 15 minutes, until the dough is elastic. Check the temperature; it should be between 73°F and 76°F (23°C and 24°C). Transfer the dough to a plastic container and leave to rise at room temperature for 2 hours. After 1 hour, fold the dough onto itself twice, starting from the bottom and pulling up toward the center, then starting from the top and pulling the top portion down toward the center. Allow the dough to rest at room temperature for 1 hour more. Transfer the dough to a work surface, gently punch it down, then divide the dough into 350-gram (12-ounce) pieces and shape into loose rounds. Lay a sheet of plastic wrap over the surface of the dough to prevent a skin from forming on the dough and let rest for 25 to 30 minutes.

Spray a full sheet pan with nonstick cooking spray. Working with 1 dough portion at a time, shape the cylinders into baguettes by rolling the dough into a rectangle about 10 by 6 inches (25 by 15 centimeters). Fold the top third of the cylinder down to the center, then fold the bottom third up so it slightly overlaps and creates an oval. Fold the long end of the dough to the opposing side of the dough and gently seal the seam by firmly punching it down. Starting from the middle of the dough piece and using both hands, press lightly on the dough and roll it back and forth to stretch it into a long cylinder. Transfer to the prepared pan and spray the surface of the dough with nonstick cooking spray. When all 3 baguettes are formed, transfer to a proof box set at 90°F (32°C) for 45 minutes.

Preheat the oven to 450°F (230°C). Season the tops of the baguettes with Maldon salt and bake for 15 to 20 minutes, until golden brown. Remove from the oven and cool on racks at room temperature. For long-term storage, wrap the cooled baguettes in plastic wrap and freeze for up to 6 months. Thaw the baguettes at room temperature before using.

MAKES 3 (300-GRAM/10.5-OUNCE) BAGUETTES

SPONGE
630 grams | 5 cups all-purpose flour
140 grams | $^2/_3$ cup water
1 gram | $^1/_4$ teaspoon active dry yeast

LIQUID LEVAIN
800 grams | 5 $^3/_4$ cups bread flour
800 grams | 3 $^1/_3$ cups water
1 gram | $^1/_4$ teaspoon active dry yeast

LEVAIN BREAD
260 grams | 1 cup water
1.5 grams | $^1/_2$ teaspoon active dry yeast
435 grams | 3 $^1/_2$ cups all-purpose flour
13 grams | $^3/_4$ tablespoon kosher salt
3 grams | $^2/_3$ teaspoon bread malt
295 grams | 10 $^1/_3$ ounces sponge
   (recipe above)
65 grams | 2 $^1/_3$ ounces liquid levain
   (recipe above)
Maldon sea salt

veal stock

Preheat the oven to 500°F (260°C). Place the oxtails and veal neck bones on roasting racks and roast for 25 minutes, until they are a dark golden brown. Cool to room temperature.

Pour the olive oil in a large stockpot and place over high heat. Add the onions, carrots, celery, leek tops, and bay leaves. Caramelize the vegetables until soft and golden brown, about 15 minutes. Add the oxtails, neck bones, and water, then bring to a boil over high heat. Reduce the heat to low and simmer for 10 hours at 180°F (82°C), occasionally skimming the fat and solid protein that forms at the surface of the stock.

Prepare an ice bath. Strain the stock through a very fine cloth filter into a metal bowl, then nest the bowl in the ice bath to cool. Store the stock in an airtight container the refrigerator for up to 1 week or transfer to vacuum bags, seal on high, and store in freeze for up to 1 month.

MAKES 10 LITERS (ABOUT 2 $^1/_2$ GALLONS)

2.2 kilograms | about 5 pounds beef oxtails, cut into 3-inch (7.5-centimeter) pieces
6.8 kilograms | about 15 pounds veal neck bones
40 grams | 3 tablespoons extra-virgin olive oil
900 grams | about 3 onions, diced
220 grams | about 2 carrots, diced
220 grams | about 2 celery stalks, diced
100 grams | 3 $^1/_2$ ounces leek tops, diced
3 | bay leaves
12 liters | about 3 gallons water
kosher salt

10 liters | 2 ½ gallons veal stock (page 288)

veal jus

In a large rondeau over medium-high heat, bring the stock to a simmer. Reduce for about 6 hours, skimming the surface to remove the solids that accumulate around the edges. Toward the end of the reducing time, prepare an ice bath.

Once the liquid has reduced by about 80 percent, has darkened significantly, and has become slightly thick, strain the jus through a chinois. Strain once more through a very fine cloth filter into several small containers and nestle these in the ice bath. Once the jus is cool and solid, store it in the refrigerator in sealed containers for up to a week. If freezing, place it in vacuum bags and seal on high, then store in the freezer for up to a month.

MAKES 24 (32-GRAM/1.1-OUNCE) ROLLS

325 grams | 3 ¼ cups bread flour
215 grams | 2 cups pumpernickel rye flour
18 grams | ¼ cup cocoa powder
240 grams | 1 cup water
110 grams | ½ cup cold brewed coffee
60 grams | ¼ cup liquid levain (page 288)
13 grams | 2 teaspoons kosher salt
2.5 grams | 1 teaspoon active dry yeast
65 grams | ¼ cup molasses
24 grams | 2 tablespoons sugar
92 grams | ½ cup lard, chilled
27 grams | 2 tablespoons unsalted butter,
    cut into pieces and at room temperature
6 grams | 1 tablespoon caraway seeds

equal parts egg and water, for egg wash

pumpernickel rye bread

In the bowl of a stand mixer fitted with the dough hook, combine the bread flour, pumpernickel rye flour, cocoa powder, water, coffee, and liquid levain and mix for 3 minutes at low speed. Add the salt, yeast, molasses, and sugar and mix for 10 more minutes. Slowly add the lard and butter and mix to fully incorporate into the dough. Continue mixing on medium speed until the dough is elastic, about 10 minutes. To test the elasticity of the dough, take a small amount of dough and pull it into a square shape; it should become thin enough to see light through the center, while not tearing. Transfer to a plastic container with a lid and place in a proof box set at 90°F (32°C) for 2 hours. After 1 hour, fold the dough onto itself twice, starting from the bottom and pulling up toward the center, then starting from the top and pulling the top portion down toward the center.

Line 3 half sheet pans with parchment paper. Turn the dough out onto a lightly floured surface and divide into 32-gram (1.1-ounce) pieces. Shape these into approximate rounds and let rest for 15 minutes covered with plastic wrap to prevent a skin from forming on the dough. Shape the dough into perfect rounds and place on the lined half sheet pans. Transfer to a proof box set at 90°F (32°C) for 1 hour. Preheat the oven to 400°F (200°C). Brush each round with egg wash and bake for 20 minutes. Cool slightly before serving. Store the bread in a plastic bag at room temperature for up to 2 days, or freeze in an airtight container for up to 1 month.

MAKES ABOUT 100 GRAMS | 1 CUP

800 grams | 1 ¾ pounds turnips
450 grams | 1 pound leeks, roots trimmed

vegetable ash

Preheat the oven to 500°F (260°C). Slice the turnips into 1/8-inch-thick rounds and slice the whole leeks lengthwise into quarters. Arrange the vegetables in a single layer in a large roasting pan and roast for 2 hours. Make sure that the oven is well ventilated as the vegetables will smoke as they begin to blacken. Once the vegetables have completely charred, remove from the oven and allow to come to room temperature. Transfer to a blender and mix on medium speed to create a fine powder. Store the vegetable ash in sealed containers in a cool dry area for up to 6 months.

ACKNOWLEDGMENTS

I have done nothing alone, and I'm not sure that I would even want to. Everything I have accomplished to this point in my career, including this book, has been created in concert with scores of friends and partners. In fact, writing this book has helped clarify for me that I don't collaborate because it enables the cooking. Instead, I cook because it allows for collaboration. The food, without the relationships and experiences that it creates, is of no value.

The dishes shared here are created and served at The Restaurant at Meadowood with help from the restaurant team. Many thanks must go to my sous chefs throughout my career who have always had unwavering belief in my vision: Michaela, Dettmer, Kim, Dan, Ben, Kat, John, Poncho, and Oliver. This book belongs in part to all of you and to all the young cooks who have trusted me with their valuable time and their finite energies. You keep me grounded, young(ish), and honest. It is an honor to work for all of you. I would also like to recognize the work of the service staff of The Restaurant at Meadowood, helmed by Nathaniel Dorn, all of whom share the work of the kitchen with grace and dedication. I hope we all continue to go great distances together.

Bill Harlan, owner of Meadowood and proprietor of Harlan Estates and BOND, has been instrumental in helping shape my thinking about excellence and perseverance. The same can be said about the chefs for whom I've had the honor to work, specifically Trey Foshee, Christian Morisset, and Daniel Humm. I am standing on your shoulders and on those of countless luminaries who preceded my time in the kitchen. I am honored to share a craft with the numerous great chefs whose books I have read and whose menus I have studied. I hope one day to be considered among you.

My wife, Martina, deserves thanks for tolerating me while I was writing this book (and for all of the projects that preceded it and will follow it). She is patient and thoughtful and protective of the family during those moments when I am carelessly engrossed in work. She is more exemplary as Daisy's mother and my wife than I could ever be as a chef. Thanks also to my little Daisy, for making me want to be a better man and dada.

The Kostow boys, Robby and Mike, and their growing families deserve thanks for still inviting me to things even though my schedule for the last decade has prohibited me from playing as active a part in everyone's lives as I hoped to. Gratitude as well to my father, who has never shied away from a good meal or a good book (both of which have led me here), and my mother, who continues to be an advocate for good and lost causes such as myself.

Photographers Jen and Taylor poured themselves into this book. If the final product is well received, it will be in great part due to their willingness always to try one more shot or take one more trip to Richard's. It is worth mentioning that they somehow found time during the shooting of this book to get engaged. This is one thing for which I will take all the credit.

Thanks also must go to Heidi Brown, who helped keep this project on track, and to the incredible Sarah and Luise, whose design work has helped to create something singular and substantial out of my often questionable ideas.

I am appreciative of the folks at Ten Speed Press, who took a chance on this book when others did not, and who have provided guidance in a nearly imperceptibly careful way. They allowed the book to be mine, but ensured it would be better than I knew it could be.

I would be remiss not to thank the community of the Napa Valley, which has embraced me and my family and that continues to provide a great impetus for doing good work. I hope this book represents you well.

INDEX

RECIPE INDEX